Embedded Systems Architecture

Explore architectural concepts, pragmatic design patterns, and best practices to produce robust systems

Daniele Lacamera

BIRMINGHAM - MUMBAI

Embedded Systems Architecture

Commissioning Editor: Richa Tripathi
Acquisition Editor: Shriram Shekhar
Content Development Editor: Zeeyan Pinheiro
Technical Editor: Romy Dias
Copy Editor: Safis Editing
Project Coordinator: Vaidehi Sawant
Proofreader: Safis Editing
Indexer: Mariammal Chettiyar
Graphics: Jason Monteiro
Production Coordinator: Aparna Bhagat

First published: May 2018

Production reference: 1280518

Published by Packt Publishing Ltd.
Livery Place
35 Livery Street
Birmingham
B3 2PB, UK.

ISBN 978-1-78883-250-2

www.packtpub.com

mapt.io

Mapt is an online digital library that gives you full access to over 5,000 books and videos, as well as industry leading tools to help you plan your personal development and advance your career. For more information, please visit our website.

Why subscribe?

- Spend less time learning and more time coding with practical eBooks and Videos from over 4,000 industry professionals

- Improve your learning with Skill Plans built especially for you

- Get a free eBook or video every month

- Mapt is fully searchable

- Copy and paste, print, and bookmark content

PacktPub.com

Did you know that Packt offers eBook versions of every book published, with PDF and ePub files available? You can upgrade to the eBook version at www.PacktPub.com and as a print book customer, you are entitled to a discount on the eBook copy. Get in touch with us at service@packtpub.com for more details.

At www.PacktPub.com, you can also read a collection of free technical articles, sign up for a range of free newsletters, and receive exclusive discounts and offers on Packt books and eBooks.

Contributors

About the author

Daniele Lacamera is a software technologist and researcher with vast experience in software design and development on embedded systems for different industries, currently working as freelance software developer and trainer. He is a worldwide expert in TCP/IP and transport protocol design and optimization, with more than 20 academic publications on the topic. He supports free software by contributing to several projects, including the Linux kernel, and his involvement within a number of communities and organizations that promote the use of free and open source software in the IoT.

I would like to express my gratitude to Alessandro Rubini for the patience and accuracy he has put in the technical review of this book.

About the reviewer

Alessandro Rubini discovered free software during his PhD, so despite being an electronic engineer, he spent 20 years writing device drivers for a free operating system, and even wrote *Linux Device Drivers* about this art. He has been teaching *Real Time Systems* as contract professor in Pavia. He's a member of FSFE and a number of other freedom-oriented associations. Currently, he's mostly designing PCBs for peripheral devices and writing firmware for the microcontrollers he places in there.

Packt is searching for authors like you

If you're interested in becoming an author for Packt, please visit `authors.packtpub.com` and apply today. We have worked with thousands of developers and tech professionals, just like you, to help them share their insight with the global tech community. You can make a general application, apply for a specific hot topic that we are recruiting an author for, or submit your own idea.

Table of Contents

Preface

Embedded systems have become increasingly popular in the last two decades, thanks to the technological progress made by microelectronics manufacturers and designers, aimed at increasing the computing power and decreasing the size of microprocessors' and peripherals' logic.

Designing, implementing, and integrating the software components for these systems requires a direct approach to the hardware functionalities in most cases, where tasks are implemented in a single thread and there is no operating system to provide abstractions to access CPU features and external peripherals. For this reason, embedded development is considered a domain on its own in the universe of software development, where the developer's approach and workflow need to be adapted accordingly.

This book briefly explains the hardware architecture of a typical embedded system, introduces tools and methodologies to get started with development of a target architecture, and then guides the readers through the interaction with system features and peripheral interaction. Some areas, such as energy efficiency and connectivity, are addressed in more detail to give a closer view of the techniques used to design low-power and connected systems. Further on, a more complex design, incorporating a (simplified) real-time operating system, is built from the bottom up, starting from the implementation of single system components. Finally, an overview of valid existing open source operating systems designed for embedded devices is provided, including considerations about their internal implementation and indications about their ideal fields of application.

The discussion is often focused on specific security and safety mechanisms, by suggesting specific technologies aimed at improving the robustness of the system against programming errors in the application code, or even malicious attempts to compromise its integrity.

Who this book is for

Most of the content of this book has been addressed to software developers and designers with experience in different fields, who are willing to learn about embedded systems.

Beginners and less experienced embedded programmers can extend their knowledge in specific areas of development.

More experienced embedded software engineers might be inspired by the discussion points raised in the book, particularly about safety, secure connectivity, and energy efficiency for the next generations of embedded systems.

What this book covers

Chapter 1, *Embedded Systems – A Pragmatic Approach*, is an introduction to microcontroller-based embedded systems.

Chapter 2, *Work Environment and Workflow Optimization*, describes the tools used and the development workflow.

Chapter 3, *Architectural Patterns*, is about strategies and development methodologies for collaborative development and testing.

Chapter 4, *The Boot-Up Procedure*, analyzes the boot phase of an embedded system, boot stages, and bootloaders.

Chapter 5, *Memory Management*, suggests optimal strategies for memory management.

Chapter 6, *General-Purpose Peripherals*, describes access to GPIO pins and other generic integrated peripherals.

Chapter 7, *Local Bus Interfaces*, guides the reader through the integration of serial bus controllers (UART, SPI, I²C).

Chapter 8, *Low-Power Optimizations*, explores the available techniques of reducing power consumption on energy-efficient systems.

Chapter 9, *Distributed Systems and IoT Architecture*, introduces the available protocols and interfaces required to build distributed and connected systems.

Chapter 10, *Parallel Tasks and Scheduling*, explains the infrastructure of a multi-tasking operating system through the implementation of a real-time task scheduler.

Chapter 11, *Embedded Operating Systems*, is an overview of the available open source operating systems for the embedded world, focusing on the safety and security mechanisms implemented.

To get the most out of this book

- It is expected that the reader is proficient in the C language and understands how computer systems work
- A GNU/Linux development machine is required to apply the concepts explained
- Going through the example code provided is sometimes necessary to fully understand the mechanisms implemented
- The reader is encouraged to modify, improve, and reuse the examples provided, applying the methodologies suggested

Download the example code files

You can download the example code files for this book from your account at www.packtpub.com. If you purchased this book elsewhere, you can visit www.packtpub.com/support and register to have the files emailed directly to you.

You can download the code files by following these steps:

1. Log in or register at www.packtpub.com.
2. Select the **SUPPORT** tab.
3. Click on **Code Downloads & Errata**.
4. Enter the name of the book in the **Search** box and follow the onscreen instructions.

Once the file is downloaded, please make sure that you unzip or extract the folder using the latest version of:

- WinRAR/7-Zip for Windows
- Zipeg/iZip/UnRarX for Mac
- 7-Zip/PeaZip for Linux

The code bundle for the book is also hosted on GitHub at `https://github.com/PacktPublishing/Embedded-Systems-Architecture`. In case there's an update to the code, it will be updated on the existing GitHub repository.

We also have other code bundles from our rich catalog of books and videos available at `https://github.com/PacktPublishing/`. Check them out!

Download the color images

We also provide a PDF file that has color images of the screenshots/diagrams used in this book. You can download it here: `https://www.packtpub.com/sites/default/files/downloads/EmbeddedSystemsArchitecture_ColorImages.pdf`.

Conventions used

There are a number of text conventions used throughout this book.

`code_in_text`: Indicates code words in text, folder names, filenames, file extensions, pathnames, user input, and interaction with the command console. Here is an example: "Compile the source file, `hello.c`, to produce the executable."

A block of code is set as follows:

```
#include <stdio.h>
int main(void) {
    printf("Hello, world!");
    return 0;
}
```

When we wish to draw your attention to a particular part of a code block, the relevant lines or items are set in bold:

```
CFLAGS=-Wall

hello.o: hello.c
    gcc -c -o $(@) $(^) $(CFLAGS)
```

Any command-line input or output is written as follows:

```
$ gcc -c -o hello.o hello.c
$ make clean
```

Commands for the debugger console are written as follows:

```
> add-symbol-file app.elf 0x1000
> bt full
```

Bold: Indicates a new term, an important word, or words that you see onscreen.

Get in touch

Feedback from our readers is always welcome.

General feedback: Email `feedback@packtpub.com` and mention the book title in the subject of your message. If you have questions about any aspect of this book, please email us at `questions@packtpub.com`.

Errata: Although we have taken every care to ensure the accuracy of our content, mistakes do happen. If you have found a mistake in this book, we would be grateful if you would report this to us. Please visit `www.packtpub.com/submit-errata`, selecting your book, clicking on the Errata Submission Form link, and entering the details.

Piracy: If you come across any illegal copies of our works in any form on the Internet, we would be grateful if you would provide us with the location address or website name. Please contact us at `copyright@packtpub.com` with a link to the material.

If you are interested in becoming an author: If there is a topic that you have expertise in and you are interested in either writing or contributing to a book, please visit `authors.packtpub.com`.

Reviews

Please leave a review. Once you have read and used this book, why not leave a review on the site that you purchased it from? Potential readers can then see and use your unbiased opinion to make purchase decisions, we at Packt can understand what you think about our products, and our authors can see your feedback on their book. Thank you!

For more information about Packt, please visit `packtpub.com`.

Embedded Systems – A Pragmatic Approach

1

Designing and writing software for embedded systems poses a different set of challenges than traditional high-level software development. This chapter gives an overview of these challenges and introduces the basic components and the platform that will be used as a reference in this book.

In this chapter, we will discuss the following topics:

- Domain definition
- RAM
- Flash memory
- Interfaces and peripherals
- Connected systems
- The reference platform

Domain definition

Embedded systems are computing devices performing specific, dedicated tasks with no direct or continued user interaction. Due to the variety of markets and technologies, these objects have different shapes and sizes, but often all have a small size and a limited amount of resources.

In this book, the concepts and the building blocks of embedded systems are analyzed through the development of the software components that interact with its resources and peripherals. The first step is to define the scope for the validity of the techniques and the architectural patterns explained here, within the broader definition of embedded systems.

Embedded Linux systems

One part of the embedded market relies on devices with enough power and resources to run a variant of the GNU/Linux operating system. These systems, often referred to as **embedded Linux**, are outside the scope of this book, as their development includes different strategies of design and integration of the components. A typical hardware platform that is capable of running a system based on the Linux kernel is equipped with a reasonably large amount of RAM, up to a few gigabytes, and sufficient storage space on board to store all the software components provided in the GNU/Linux distribution. Additionally, for Linux memory management to provide separate virtual address spaces to each process on the system, the hardware must be equipped with a **memory management unit (MMU)**, a hardware component that assists the OS in translating physical addresses to virtual addresses, and vice versa, at runtime.

This class of devices presents different characteristics that are often overkill for building tailored solutions, which can use a much simpler design and reduce the production costs of the single units. Hardware manufacturers and chip designers have researched new techniques to improve the performance of microcontroller-based systems, providing, in the past decade, a new generation of platforms that would cut hardware costs, firmware complexity, size, and power consumption to provide a set of features that are most interesting for the embedded market.

Due to their specifications, in some real-life scenarios, embedded systems must be able to execute a series of tasks within a short, measurable, and predictable amount of time. These kinds of systems are called **real-time systems**, and differ from the approach of multi-task computing used in desktops, servers, and mobile phones. Real-time processing is a goal that is extremely hard, if not impossible, to reach on embedded Linux platforms. The Linux kernel is not designed for hard real-time processing, and even if patches are available to modify the kernel scheduler to help meet these requirements, the results are not comparable to bare-metal, constrained systems that are designed with this purpose in mind.

Some other application domains, such as battery-powered and energy-harvesting devices, can benefit from the low power consumption capabilities of smaller embedded devices and the energy efficiency of the wireless communication technologies often integrated in embedded connected devices. The higher amount of resources and the increased hardware complexity of Linux-based systems often does not scale down enough on energy levels, or requires much more effort to meet similar figures in power consumption.

The type of microcontroller-based systems that we'll analyze in this book are 32-bit systems, capable of running software in a single-threaded, bare-metal application as well as integrating minimalist real-time operating systems, which are very popular in the industrial manufacturing of embedded systems that we use on a daily basis to accomplish specific tasks, and are becoming more and more adopted to define more generic, multiple-purpose development platforms.

Low-end 8-bit microcontrollers

In the past, 8-bit microcontrollers have dominated the embedded market. The simplicity of their design allows us to write small applications that can accomplish a set of pre-defined tasks, but are too simple and usually equipped with way too few resources to implement an embedded system, especially since 32-bit microcontrollers have evolved to cover all the use cases for these devices within the same range of price, size, and power consumption.

8-bit microcontrollers nowadays are mostly relegated to the market of educational platform kits, aimed at introducing hobbyists and newcomers to the basics of software development on electronic devices. 8-bit platforms are not covered in this book, because they lack the characteristics that allow advanced system programming, multithreading, and advanced features developed to build professional embedded systems.

In the context of this book, the term **embedded systems** is used to indicate a class of systems running on microcontroller-based hardware architecture, offering constrained resources but allowing to build real-time systems, through features provided by the hardware architecture to implement system programming.

Hardware architecture

The architecture of an embedded system is centered around its microcontroller, also sometimes referred to as the **microcontroller unit** (**MCU**), typically a single integrated circuit containing the processor, RAM, flash memory, serial receivers and transmitters, and other core components. The market offers many different choices among architectures, vendors, price range, features, and integrated resources. These are typically designed to be inexpensive, low-resource, low-energy consuming, self-contained systems on a single integrated circuit, which is the reason why they are often referred to as **System-on-Chip** (**SoC**).

Due to the variety of processors, memories, and interfaces that can be integrated, there is no actual reference architecture for microcontrollers. Nevertheless, some architectural elements are common across a wide range of models and brands, and even across different processor architectures.

Some microcontrollers are dedicated to specific applications and exposing a particular set of interfaces to communicate to peripherals and to the outside world. Others are focused on providing solutions with reduced hardware costs, or with very limited energy consumption. Nevertheless, the following set of components is hardcoded into almost every microcontroller:

- Microprocessor
- RAM
- Flash memory
- Serial transceivers

Additionally, more and more devices are capable of accessing a network, to communicate with other devices and gateways. Some microcontrollers may provide either well-established standards, such as Ethernet or Wi-Fi interfaces, or specific protocols specifically designed to meet the constraints of embedded systems, such as Sub-GHz radio interfaces or **Controller Area Network** (**CAN**) bus, being partially or fully implemented within the IC.

All the components must share a bus line with the processor, which is responsible for coordinating the logic. The RAM, flash memory, and control registers of the transceivers are all mapped in the same physical address space:

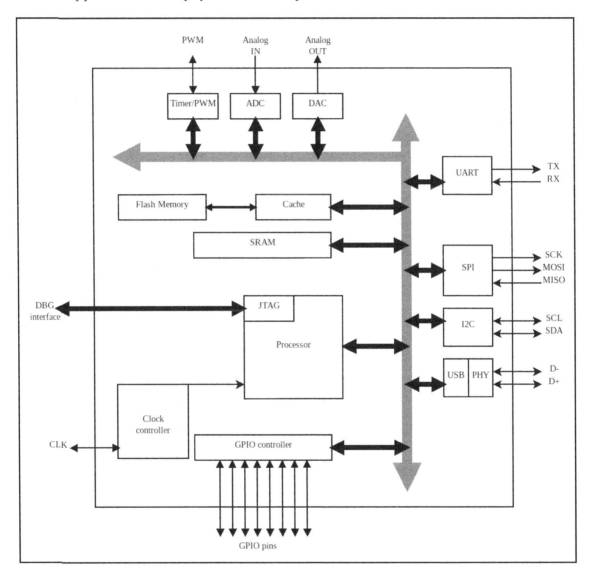

A simplified block diagram of the components inside a generic microcontroller

The addresses where the RAM and flash are mapped to depend on the specific model, and are usually provided in the datasheet. A microcontroller is able to run code in its own native machine language, a sequence of instructions conveyed into a binary file that is specific for the architecture it is running on. By default, compilers provide a generic executable file as the output of the compilation and assembly operations, which needs to be converted into the format that is executable for the target.

The processor is designed to execute the instructions stored, in its own specific binary format directly from RAM as well as from its internal flash memory, usually mapped starting from position zero in memory, or from another well-known address specified in the microcontroller manual. The CPU can fetch and execute code from RAM faster, but the final firmware is stored in the flash memory, which is usually bigger than the RAM on almost all microcontrollers, and permits it to retain the data across power cycles and reboots.

Compiling a software operating environment for an embedded microcontroller and loading it onto the flash memory requires a host machine, which is a specific set of hardware and software tools. Some knowledge about the target device's characteristics is also needed to instruct the compiler to organize the symbols within the executable image. For many valid reasons, C is the most popular language in embedded software, although not the only available option. Higher-level languages, such as Rust and C++, can produce embedded code when combined with a specific embedded runtime, or even in some cases by entirely removing the runtime support from the language. This book will focus entirely on C code, because it abstracts less than any other high-level language, thus making easier to describe the behavior of the underlying hardware while looking at the code.

All modern embedded systems platforms also have at least one mechanism (such as JTAG) for debugging purposes, and to upload the software to the flash. When the debug interface is accessed from the host machine, a debugger can interact with the breakpoint unit in the processor, interrupting and resuming the execution, and can also read and write from any address in memory.

A significant part of embedded programming is the communication with the peripherals, using the interfaces that the MCU exposes. Embedded software development requires basic knowledge of electronics, the ability to understand schematics and datasheets, and confidence with the measurement tools, such as logic analyzers or oscilloscopes.

Understanding the challenge

Approaching embedded development means keeping the focus on the specifications as well as the hardware restrictions at all times. Embedded software development is a constant challenge to focus on the most efficient way to perform a set of specific tasks, but keeping in strong consideration the limited resources available. There are a number of compromises to deal with, which are uncommon in other environments. Here are some examples:

- There might be not enough space in the flash to implement a new feature
- There might not be enough RAM to store complex structures or make copies of large data buffers
- The processor might be not fast enough to accomplish all the required calculations and data processing in due time
- Battery-powered and resources-harvesting devices might require lower energy consumption to meet lifetime expectations

Moreover, PC and mobile operating systems make large use of the MMU, a component of the processor that allows runtime translations between physical and virtual addresses. The MMU is a necessary abstraction to implement address space separation among the tasks, and between the tasks and the kernel itself. Embedded microcontrollers do not have an MMU, and usually lack the amount of non-volatile memory required to store kernel, applications, and libraries. For this reason, embedded systems are often running in a single task, with a main loop performing all the data processing and communication in a specific order. Some devices can run embedded operating systems, which are far less complex than their PC counterparts.

Application developers often see the underlying system as a commodity, while embedded development often means that the entire system has to be implemented from scratch, from the boot procedure up to the application logic. In an embedded environment, the various software components are more closely related to each other, because of the lack of more complex abstractions, such as memory separations between the processes and the operating system kernel. A developer approaching embedded systems for the first time might find testing and debugging on some of the systems a bit more intricate than just running the software and reading out the results. This becomes especially true on those systems that have been designed with little or no human interaction interfaces.

A successful approach requires a healthy workflow, which includes well-defined test cases, a list of key performance indicators coming from the analysis of the specifications to identify possibilities of trade-offs, a number of tools and procedures at hand to perform all the needed measurements, and a well-established and efficient prototyping phase.

In this context, security deserves some special consideration. As usual, when writing code at the system level, it is wise to keep in mind the system-wide consequences of possible faults. Most embedded application code run with extended privileges on the hardware, and a single task misbehaving can affect the stability and the integrity of the entire firmware. As we will see, some platforms offer specific memory-protection mechanisms and built-in privilege separation, which are useful for building fail-safe systems even in the absence of a full operating system based on separating process address spaces.

Multithreading

One of the advantages of using microcontrollers designed to build embedded systems is the possibility to run logically separated tasks within separate execution units by time-sharing the resources.

The most popular type of design for embedded software is based on a single loop-based sequential execution model, where modules and components are connected to each other exposing callback interfaces. However, modern microcontrollers offer features and core logic characteristics that can be used by system developers to build a multi-tasking environment to run logically separated applications.

These features are particularly handy in the approach to more complex real-time systems, and interesting to understand the possibilities of the implementation of safety models based on process isolation and memory segmentation.

RAM

"640 KB of memory ought to be enough for everyone"

– Bill Gates (founder and former director of Microsoft)

This famous statement has been cited many times in the past three decades to underline the progress in technology and the outstanding achievements of the PC industry. While it may sound like a joke for many software engineers out there, it is still in these figures that embedded programming has to be thought about, more than 30 years after MS-DOS was initially released.

Although most embedded systems are capable of breaking that limit today, especially due to the availability of external DRAM interfaces, the simplest devices that can be programmed in C may have as little as 4 KB of RAM available to implement the entire system logic. Obviously this has to be taken into account when approaching the design of an embedded system, by estimating the amount of memory potentially needed for all the operations that the system has to perform, and the buffers that may be used at any time to communicate with peripherals and nearby devices.

The memory model at the system level is simpler than that of PCs and mobile devices. Memory access is typically done at the physical level, so all the pointers in your code are telling you the physical location of the data they are pointing to. In modern computers, the operating system is responsible for translating physical addresses to a virtual representation of the running tasks. The advantage of the physical-only memory access on those systems that do not have an MMU is the reduced complexity of having to deal with address translations while coding and debugging. On the other hand, some of the features implemented by any modern OS, such as process swapping and dynamically resizing address spaces through memory relocation, become cumbersome and sometimes impossible.

Handling memory is particularly important in embedded systems. Programmers who are used to writing application code expect a certain level of protection to be provided by the underlying OS. In fact, a virtual address space does not allow memory areas to overlap, and the OS can easily detect unauthorized memory accesses and segmentation violations, it then promptly terminates the process and avoids having the whole system compromised. On embedded systems, especially when writing bare-metal code, the boundaries of each address pool must be checked manually. Accidentally modifying a few bits in the wrong memory, or even accessing a different area of memory, may result in a fatal, irrevocable error. The entire system may hang, or, in the worst case, become unpredictable. A safe approach is required when handling memory in embedded systems, in particular when dealing with life-critical devices. Identifying memory errors too late in the development process is complex and often requires more resources than forcing yourself to write safe code and protecting the system from a programmer's mistakes.

Proper memory-handling techniques are explained in `Chapter 5`, *General Purpose Peripherals*.

Flash memory

In a server or a personal computer, the executable applications and libraries reside in storage devices. At the beginning of the execution, they are accessed, transformed, possibly uncompressed, and stored in RAM before the execution starts.

The firmware of an embedded device is in general one single binary file containing all the software components, which can be transferred to the internal flash memory of the MCU. Since the flash memory is directly mapped to a fixed address in the memory space, the processor is capable of sequentially fetching and executing single instructions from it with no intermediate steps. This mechanism is called **execute in place** (**XIP**). All non-modifiable sections on the firmware don't need to be loaded in memory, and are accessible through direct addressing in the memory space. This includes not only the executable instructions, but also all the variables that are marked as constant by the compiler. On the other hand, supporting XIP requires a few extra steps in the preparation of the firmware image to be stored in flash, and the linker needs to be instructed about the different memory-mapped areas on the target.

The internal flash memory mapped in the address space of the microcontroller is not accessible for writing. Altering the content of the internal flash can be done only by using a block-based access, due to the hardware characteristics of flash memory devices. Before changing the value of a single byte in flash memory, in fact, the whole block containing it must be erased and rewritten. The mechanism offered by most manufacturers to access block-based flash memory for writing is known as **In-Application Programming** (**IAP**). Some filesystem implementations take care of abstracting write operations on a block-based flash device, by creating a temporary copy of the block where the write operation is performed.

During the selection of the components for a microcontroller-based solution, it is vital to properly match the size of the flash memory to the space required by the firmware. The flash is in fact often one of the most expensive components in the MCU, so for a deployment on a large scale, choosing an MCU with a smaller flash could be more cost-effective. Developing software with code size in mind is not very usual nowadays within other domains, but it may be required when trying to fit multiple features in such little storage. Finally, compiler optimizations may exist on specific architectures to reduce code size when building the firmware and linking its components.

Additional non-volatile memories that reside outside of the MCU silicon can typically be accessed using specific interfaces, such as Serial Peripheral Interface. External flash memories use different technologies than the internal flash, which is designed to be fast and execute code in place. While being generally more dense and less expensive, external flash memories do not allow direct memory mapping in the physical address space, which makes them not suitable for storing firmware images, as it would be impossible to execute the code fetching the instructions sequentially, unless a mechanism is used to load the executable symbols in RAM, because read access on these kinds of devices is performed one block at a time. On the other hand, write access may be faster when compared to IAP, making these kinds of non-volatile memory devices ideal for storing data retrieved at runtime in some designs.

Interfaces and peripherals

In order to communicate with peripherals and other microcontrollers, a number of *de facto* standards are well established in the embedded world. Some of the external pins of the microcontroller can be programmed to carry out communication with external peripherals using specific protocols. A few of the common interfaces available on most architectures are:

- Asynchronous UART-based serial communication
- **Serial Peripheral Interface (SPI) bus**
- **Inter-integrated circuit (I^2C) bus**
- **Universal Serial Bus (USB)**

Asynchronous UART-based serial communication

Asynchronous communication is provided by the **Universal Asynchronous Receiver-Transmitter (UART)**. These kind of interfaces, commonly simply known as *serial ports*, are called asynchronous because they do not need to share a clock signal to synchronize the sender and the receiver, but rather work on pre-defined clock rates that can be aligned while the communication is ongoing. Microcontrollers may contain multiple UARTs that can be attached to a specific set of pins upon request. Asynchronous communication is provided by UART as a full-duplex channel, through two independent wires, connecting the RX pin of each endpoint to the TX pin on the opposite side.

To properly understand each other, the systems at the two endpoints must set up the UART using the same parameters. This includes the framing of the bytes on the wire, and the frame rate. All of these parameters have to be known in advance by both endpoints in order to correctly establish a communication channel. Despite being simpler than the other types of serial communication, UART-based serial communication is still widely used in electronic devices, particularly as an interface toward modems and GPS receivers. Furthermore, using TTL-to-USB serial converters, it is easy to connect a UART to a console on the host machine, which is often handy for providing log messages.

SPI

A different approach is SPI. Introduced in the late 1980s, this technology aimed to replace asynchronous serial communication towards peripherals, by introducing a number of improvements:

- Serial clock line to synchronize the endpoints
- Master-slave protocol
- One-to-many communication over the same three-wire bus

The master device, usually the microcontroller, shares the bus with one or more slaves. To trigger the communication, a separate **slave select** (**SS**) signal is used to address each slave connected to the bus. The bus uses two independent signals for data transfer, one per direction, and a shared clock line that synchronizes the two ends of the communication. Due to the clock line being generated by the master, the data transfer is more reliable, making it possible to achieve higher bitrates than ordinary UART. One of the keys for the continued success of SPI over multiple generations of microcontrollers is the low complexity required for the design of slaves, which can be as simple as a single shift register. SPI is commonly used in sensor devices, LCD displays, flash memory controllers, and network interfaces.

I²C

I²C is slightly more complex, and that is because it is designed with a different purpose in mind: interconnecting multiple microcontrollers, as well as multiple slave devices, on the same two-wire bus. The two signals are **serial clock** (**SCL**) and **serial data** (**SDA**). Unlike SPI or UART, the bus is half-duplex, as the two directions of the flow share the same signal. Thanks to a 7-bit slave-addressing mechanism incorporated in the protocol, it does not require additional signals dedicated to the selection of the slaves. Multiple masters are allowed on the same line, given that all the masters in the system follow the arbitration logic in the case of bus contention.

USB

The USB protocol, originally designed to replace UART and include many protocols in the same hardware connector, is very popular in personal computers, portable devices, and a huge number of peripherals.

This protocol works in host-device mode, with one side of communication, the device, exposing services that can be used by the controller, on the host side. USB transceivers present in many microcontrollers can work in both modes. By implementing the upper layer of the USB standards, different types of devices can be emulated by the microcontroller, such as serial ports, storage devices, and point-to-point Ethernet interfaces, creating microcontroller-based USB devices that can be connected to a host system.

If the transceiver supports host mode, the embedded system can act as a USB host and devices can be connected to it. In this case, the system should implement device drivers and applications to access the functionality provided by the device.

When both modes are implemented on the same USB controller, the transceiver works in **on-the-go** (**OTG**) mode, and the selection and configuration of the desired mode can be done at runtime.

Connected systems

An increasing number of embedded devices designed for different markets are now capable of network communication with their peers in the surrounding area, or with gateways routing their traffic to a broader network or to the internet. The term **Internet of Things (IoT)** has been used to describe the networks where those embedded devices are able to communicate using internet protocols. This means that IoT devices can be addressed within the network in the same way as more complex systems, such as PCs or mobile devices, and most importantly, use the transport layer protocols typical of internet communications to exchange data. TCP/IP is a suite of protocols standardized by the IETF, and it is the fabric of the infrastructure for the internet and other self-contained, local area networks. The **Internet Protocol (IP)** provides network connectivity, but on the condition that the underlying link provides packet-based communication and mechanisms to control and regulate access to the physical media. Fortunately, there are many network interfaces that meet these requirements. Alternative protocol families, which are not compatible with TCP/IP, are still in use in several distributed embedded systems, but a clear advantage of using the TCP/IP standard on the target is that, in the case of communication with non-embedded systems, there is no need for a translation mechanism to route the frames outside the scope of the LAN.

Besides the types of links that are widely used in non-embedded systems, such as Ethernet or wireless LAN, embedded systems can benefit from a wide choice of technologies that are specifically designed for the requirements introduced by IoT. New standards have been researched and put into effect to provide efficient communication for constrained devices, defining communication models to cope with specific resource usage limits and energy efficiency requirements.

Recently, new link technologies have been developed in the direction of lower bitrates and power consumption for wide-area network communication. These protocols are designed to provide narrow-band, long-range communication. The frame is too small to fit IP packets, so these technologies are mostly employed to transmit small payloads, such as periodic sensor data, or device configuration parameters if a bidirectional channel is available, and they require some form of gateway to translate the communication to travel across the internet.

The interaction with the cloud services, however, requires, in most cases, to connect all the nodes in the network, and to implement the same technologies used by the servers and the IT infrastructure directly in the host. Enabling TCP/IP communication on an embedded device is not always straightforward. Even though there are several open source implementations available, system TCP/IP code is complex, big in size, and often has memory requirements that may be difficult to meet.

The same observation applies for the **Secure Socket Layer (SSL) / Transport Layer Security (TLS)** library. Choosing the right microcontroller for the task is again crucial, and if the system has to be connected to the internet and support secure socket communication, then the flash and RAM requirements have to be updated in the design phase to ensure integration with third-party libraries.

Designing distributed embedded systems, especially those that are based on wireless link technologies, adds a set of interesting challenges. Some of these challenges are related to:

- Selection of the correct technologies and protocols
- Limitations on bitrate, packet size, and media access
- Availability of the nodes
- Single points of failure in the topology
- Configuration of the routes
- Authentication of the hosts involved
- Confidentiality of the communication over the media
- Impact of buffering on network speed, latency, and RAM usage
- Complexity of the implementation of the protocol stacks

Chapter 9, *Parallel Tasks and Scheduling*, analyzes some of the link-layer technologies implemented in embedded systems to provide remote communication, integrating TCP/IP communication to the design of distributed systems integrated in IoT services.

The reference platform

The preferred design strategy for embedded CPU cores is **reduced instruction set computer (RISC)**. Among all the RISC CPU architectures, a number of reference designs are used as guidelines by silicon manufacturers to produce the core logic to integrate into the microcontroller. Each reference design differs from the others in a number of characteristics of the CPU implementation. Each reference design includes one or more families of microprocessors integrated in embedded systems, sharing the following characteristics:

- Word size used for registers and addresses (8-bit, 16-bit, 32-bit, or 64-bit)
- Instruction set
- Register configurations
- Endianness

- Extended CPU features (interrupt controller, FPU, MMU)
- Caching strategies
- Pipeline design

Choosing a reference platform for your embedded system depends on your project needs. Smaller, less feature-rich processors are generally more suited to low energy consumption, have a smaller MCU packaging, and are less expensive. Higher-end systems, on the other hand, come with a bigger set of resources and some of them have dedicated hardware to cope with challenging calculations (such as a floating point unit, or an **Advanced Encryption Standard** (**AES**) hardware module to offload symmetric encryption operations). 8-bit and 16-bit core designs are slowly giving way to 32-bit architectures, but some successful designs remain relatively popular in some niche markets and among hobbyists.

ARM reference design

ARM is the most ubiquitous reference design supplier in the embedded market, with more than 10 billion ARM-based microcontrollers produced for embedded applications. One of the most interesting core designs in the embedded industry is the ARM Cortex-M family, which includes a range of models scaling from cost-effective and energy-efficient, to high-performance cores specifically designed for multimedia microcontrollers. Despite ranging among three different instruction sets (ARMv6, ARMv7 and ARMv8), all Cortex-M CPUs share the same programming interface, which improves portability across microcontrollers in the same families.

Most of the examples in this book will be based on this family of CPUs. Though most of the concepts expressed will be applicable to other core designs as well, picking a reference platform now opens the door to a more complete analysis of the interactions with the underlying hardware. In particular, some of the examples in this book use specific assembly instructions from the ARMv7 instruction set, which is implemented in some Cortex-M CPU cores.

The Cortex-M microprocessor

The main characteristic of the 32-bit cores in the Cortex-M family are:

- 16 generic-purpose CPU registers
- Thumb 16-bit only instructions for code density optimizations
- Built-in **Nested Vector Interrupt Controller** (**NVIC**) with 8 to 16 priority levels

- ARMv6 (M0, M0+) or ARMv7 (M3, M4, M7) architecture
- Optional 8-region **memory protection unit (MPU)**

The total memory address space is 4 GB. The beginning of the internal RAM is typically mapped at the fixed address of `0x20000000`. The mapping of the internal flash, as well as the other peripherals, depends on the silicon manufacturer. However, the highest 512 MB (`0xE0000000` to `0xFFFFFFFF`) addresses are reserved for the **System Control Block (SCB)**, which groups together several configuration parameters and diagnostics that can be accessed by the software at any time to directly interact with the core.

Synchronous communication with peripherals and other hardware components can be triggered through interrupt lines. The processor can receive and recognize a number of different digital input signals and react to them promptly, interrupting the execution of the software and temporarily jumping to a specific location in the memory. Cortex-M supports up to 240 interrupt lines on the high-end cores of the family. The interrupt vector, located at the beginning of the software image in flash, contains the addresses of the interrupt routines that will automatically execute on specific events. Thanks to the NVIC, interrupt lines can be assigned priorities, so that when a higher-priority interrupt occurs while the routine for a lower interrupt is executed, the current interrupt routine is temporarily suspended to allow the higher-priority interrupt line to be serviced. This ensures minimal interrupt latency for these signal lines, which are somewhat critical for the system to execute as fast as possible.

At any time, the software on the target can run in two privilege modes: unprivileged or privileged. The CPU has built-in support for privilege separation between system and application software, even providing two different registers for the two separate stack pointers. We will examine in more detail how to properly implement privilege separation, and how to enforce memory separation when running untrusted code on the target.

A Cortex-M core is present in many microcontrollers, from different silicon vendors. Software tools are similar for all the platforms, but each MCU has a different configuration to take into account. Convergence libraries are available to hide manufacturer-specific details and improve portability across different models and brands. Manufacturers provide reference kits and all the documentation required to get started, which are intended to be used for evaluation during the design phase, and may also be useful for developing prototypes at a later stage. Some of these evaluation boards are equipped with sensors, multimedia electronics, or other peripherals that extend the functionality of the microcontroller.

Summary

Approaching embedded software requires, before anything else, a good understanding of the hardware platform and its components. Through the description of the architecture of modern microcontrollers, this chapter pointed out some of the peculiarities of embedded devices, and how developers should efficiently rethink their approach to meeting requirements and solving problems, while at the same time taking into account the features and the limits of the target platform. In the next chapter, we'll analyze the tools and procedures typically used in embedded development, how to organize the workflow, and how to effectively prevent, locate, and fix bugs.

Work Environment and Workflow Optimization

2

The first step toward a successful software project is choosing the right tools. Embedded development requires a set of hardware and software instruments that make the developer's life easier, and may significantly improve productivity and cut down the total development time. This chapter is meant to provide a description of the tools, and give advice on how to use them, to improve the workflow. The first section gives an overview of the workflow in native C programming, and gradually reveals the changes necessary to translate the model to an embedded development environment. Then, the GCC toolchain, a set of development tools to build the embedded application, is introduced through the analysis of its components. Finally, in the last two sections, strategies of interaction with the target are proposed, to provide mechanisms for the debug and validation of the embedded software running on the platform.

The topics covered in this chapter are:

- Workflow overview
- The GCC toolchain
- Interaction with the target
- Validation

Workflow overview

Writing software in C, as well as in every compiled language, requires the code to be transformed to an executable format for a specific target to run it. C is portable across different architectures and execution environments. Programmers rely on a set of tools to compile, link, execute, and debug software to a specific target.

Building the firmware image of an embedded system relies on a similar set of tools, which can produce firmware images for specific targets, called a **toolchain**. This section gives an overview of the common sets of tools required to write software in C and produce programs that are directly executable on the machine that compiled them. The workflow must then be extended and adapted to integrate the toolchain components, and produce executable code for the target platform.

C compiler

The C compiler is a tool responsible for translating source code into machine code, which can be interpreted by a specific CPU. Each compiler can produce machine code for one environment only, as it translates the functions into machine-specific instructions, and it is configured to use the address model and the register layout of one specific architecture. The native compiler included in most GNU/Linux distributions is the **GNU Compiler Collection**, commonly known as **GCC**. The GCC is a free software compiler system, distributed under the GNU general public license since 1987, and since then it has been successfully used to build UNIX-like systems. The GCC included in the system can compile C code into applications and libraries capable of running on the same architecture as the one of the machine running the compiler.

The GCC compiler takes source code files as input, with the .c extension, and produces object files, with .o extensions, containing the functions and the initial values of the variables, translated from the input source code into machine instructions. The compiler can be configured to perform additional optimization steps at the end of the compilation, which are specific for the target platform, and insert debug data to facilitate debugging at a later stage. A minimalist command line used to compile a source file into an object using the host compiler only requires the −c option, instructing the GCC program to compile the sources into an object of the same name:

```
$ gcc -c hello.c
```

This statement will try to compile the C source contained in the hello.c file and transform it into machine-specific code, that is stored in the newly created hello.o file.

Compiling code for a specific target platform requires a set of tools designed for that purpose. Architecture-specific compilers exist, which provide compilers creating machine instructions for a specific target, different from the building machine. The process of generating code for a different target is called **cross-compilation**. The cross-compiler runs on a development machine, the host, to produce machine-specific code that can execute on the target. In the next section, a GCC-based toolchain is introduced with the purpose of creating the firmware for an embedded target. The syntax and the characteristics of the GCC compiler are described there.

The first step for building a program made of separate modules is to compile all the sources into object files, so that the components needed by the system are grouped and organized together in the final step, consisting of linking together all the required symbols and arranging the memory areas to prepare the final executable, which is done by another dedicated component in the toolchain.

Linker

The linker is a tool that can compose an executable program, resolving all the dependencies among the symbols used by the modules, represented by the collection of object files provided as input. The executable that is produced by the linker is an ELF executable. **ELF** stands for **Executable and Linkable Format**, and it is the default standard format for programs, objects, and shared libraries, and even GDB core dumps on many Unix and Unix-like systems. The format has been designed to store programs on disks and other media supports, so the host operating system is able to execute it by loading the instructions in RAM, and allocating the space for the program data. ELF files are divided into sections, each corresponding to specific areas in memory needed by the program to execute. The ELF file starts with a header, containing the pointer to the various sections within the file itself, containing the program's code and data. The sections necessary to describe an executable program provided by ELF, conventionally starting with a ., are:

- `.text`: Containing the code of the program, accessed in read-only. It contains the executable instructions of the program. The functions compiled into object files are arranged by the linker into this section, and the program always executes instructions within this memory area.
- `.rodata`: Containing the value of constants that cannot be altered at runtime. It is used by the compiler as the default section to store constants, and is used as a hint to the system executing the ELF that the section can be mapped in a read-only area in memory, because it is not allowed to modify the stored values at runtime.

- `.data`: Containing the values of all the initialized variables of the program, accessible in the read/write mode at runtime. It is a section that contains all the variables, static or global, that have been initialized in the code. Before executing, this area is generally remapped to a writable location in RAM, and the content of the ELF is automatically copied during the initialization of the program, at runtime, before executing the main function.

- `.bss`: A section reserved for uninitialized data, accessible in the read/write mode at runtime. It derives its name from an ancient assembly instruction of an old microcode written for IBM 704 in the 1950s. It was originally an acronym for **Block Started by Symbol (BSS)**, used to reserve a fixed amount of uninitialized memory. In the ELF context, it contains all the uninitialized global and static symbols, which must be accessible in the read-write mode at runtime. Because there is no value assigned, the ELF file only describes the section in the header, but does not provide any content for it. The initialization code should ensure that all the variables in this section are set to zero before the execution of the `main()` function.

When building native software on the host machine, much of the complexity of the linking step is hidden, but the linker is actually configured by default to arrange the compiled symbols into specific sections, which can be later used by the operating system to assign the corresponding section in the process' virtual address space when executing the program. It is possible to create a working executable for the host machine by simply invoking `gcc`, this time without the `-c` option, providing the list of the object files that must be linked together to produce the ELF file. The `-o` option is used to specify the output file name, which otherwise would default to `a.out`:

```
$ gcc -o helloworld hello.o world.o
```

This command will try to build the `helloworld` file, which is an ELF executable for the host system, using the symbols previously compiled into the two objects.

In an embedded system, things change a bit, as booting a bare-metal application implies that the sections must be mapped to physical areas in memory at linking time. To instruct the linker to associate the sections to well-known physical addresses, a custom linker script file must be provided, describing the memory layout of the executable bare-metal application, and providing additional custom sections that may be required by the target system. A more detailed explanation of the linking step is provided later in this chapter.

Build automation

In order to automate a build process, several open source tools are available and a few of them are widely used in different development environments. **Make** is the standard UNIX tool to automate the steps required to create the required binary images from the sources, checking the dependencies for each component, and executing the steps in the right order. Make is a standard POSIX tool, and it is part of many UNIX-like systems. In a GNU/Linux distribution, it is implemented as a standalone tool, which is part of the GNU project. From this point on, the GNU Make implementation is simply referred to as Make.

Make is designed to execute the default build by simply invoking the `make` command with no arguments from the command line, provided that a makefile is present in the working directory. A makefile is a special instruction file, containing rules and recipes to build all the files needed until the expected output files are generated. Open source alternatives offering similar solutions for build automation exist, such as Cmake and Scons, but all the examples in this book are built using Make, because it provide a simple and essential enough environment to control the build system, and it is the one standardized by POSIX.

Some integrated development environments use built-in mechanisms to coordinate the building steps, or generate makefiles before invoking the Make automatically when the user requests to build the output files. However, editing makefiles manually gives complete control on the intermediate steps to generate the final images, where the user can customize the recipes and rules used to generate the desired output files.

There is no specific version that needs to be installed in order to cross-compile code for the Cortex-M target, but some extra parameters, such as the location of the toolchain binaries, or the specific flags needed by the compiler, need to be taken care of when writing targets and directives within the makefile. One of the advantages of using a build process is that targets may have implicit dependencies from other intermediate components that are automatically resolved at compile time. If all the dependencies are correctly configured, makefile ensures that the intermediate steps are executed only when needed, reducing the compile time of the whole project when only a few sources are altered, or when single object files have been deleted.

Makefiles have a specific syntax to describe rules. Each rule begins with the expected target files, expected as the output of the rule, a colon, and the list of prerequisites, which are the files necessary to execute the rule. A set of recipe items follow, each one describing the actions that Make will execute to create the desired target:

```
target: [prerequisites]
    recipe
    recipe
    ...
```

By default, Make will execute the first rule encountered while parsing the file if no rule name is specified from the command line. If any of the prerequisites are not available, Make automatically looks for a rule in the same makefile that can create the required file, recursively until the chain of requirements is satisfied.

Makefiles can assign a custom string of text to internal variables while executing. Variable names can be assigned using the = operator, and referred to by prefixing them with $. For example, the following assignment is used to put the name of two object files into the OBJS variable:

```
OBJS = hello.o world.o
```

A few important variables that are assigned automatically within the rules are the following:

Variable	Meaning
$(@)	Name of the target for the currently executing rule
$(^)	List of all the prerequisites for this rule, without duplicates
$(+)	List of all the prerequisites for this rule, with duplicates if any
$(<)	First element in the prerequisites list

These variables are handy to use within the recipe action lines. For example, the recipe to generate a helloworld ELF file from the two object files can be written as follows:

```
helloworld: $(OBJS)
    gcc -o $(@) $(^)
```

Some of the rules are implicitly defined by Make. For example, the rule to create the files hello.o and world.o from their respective source files can be omitted, as Make expects to be able to obtain each one of these object files in the most obvious way, which is by compiling the corresponding C source files with the same name, if present. This means that this minimalist makefile is already able to compile the two objects from the sources, and link them together using the default set of options for the host system.

The linking recipe can also be implicit, if the executable has the same name as one of its prerequisite objects, minus its `.o` extension. If the final ELF file is called `hello`, our makefile could simply become the following one-liner:

```
hello: world.o
```

This would automatically resolve the `hello.o` and `world.o` dependencies, and then link them together using an implicit linker recipe similar to the one we used in the explicit target.

Implicit rules use predefined variables, which are assigned automatically before the rules are executed, but can be modified within makefile. For example, it is possible to change the default compiler by altering the CC variable. Here is a small list of the most important variables that may be used to alter implicit rules and recipes:

Variable	Meaning	Default value
CC	Compiler program	cc
LD	Linker program	ld
CFLAGS	Flags passed to the compiler when compiling sources	<empty>
LDFLAGS	Flags passed to the compiler in the linking step	<empty>

When linking a bare-metal application for embedded platforms, the makefile must be modified accordingly, and as shown later in this chapter, a number of flags are required to properly cross-compile the sources and instruct the linker to use the desired memory layout to organize the memory sections. Moreover, additional steps are generally needed to manipulate the ELF file and translate it to a format that can be transferred to the target system. However, the syntax of makefile is the same and the simple rules shown here are not too different from those used to build the example. The default variables still need to be adjusted to modify the default behavior, if implicit rules are used.

When all the dependencies are correctly configured in the makefile, Make ensures that the rules are only executed when the target is older than its dependencies, thus reducing the compile time of the whole project when only a few sources are altered, or when single object files have been deleted.

Make is a very powerful tool, and its range of possibilities goes far beyond the few features used to generate the examples in this book. Mastering the automation process of the builds may lead to optimized build processes. The syntax of makefile includes useful features, such as conditionals, which can be used to produce different results by invoking makefile using different targets or environment variables. For a better understanding of the capabilities of Make, please refer to the GNU Make manual available at `https://www.gnu.org/software/make/manual`.

Debugger

In the host environment, debugging an application that runs on top of the operating system is done by running a debugger tool, which can attach to an existing process, or spawn a new one given an executable ELF file and its command-line arguments. The default debugging option provided by the GCC suite is called **GDB**, an acronym for the **GNU Debugger**. While GDB is a command-line tool, several frontends have been developed to provide a better visualization of the state of the execution, and some integrated development environments provide built-in frontends for interacting with the debugger while tracing the single lines being executed.

Once again, the situation is slightly changed when the software to debug is running on a remote platform. A version of GDB, distributed with the toolchain and specific for the target platform, can be run on the development machine to connect to a remote debug session. A debug session on a remote target requires an intermediate tool that is configured to translate GDB commands into actual actions on the core CPU, and the related hardware infrastructure, to establish the communication with the core.

Some embedded platforms provide hardware breakpoints, which are used to trigger system exceptions every time the selected instructions are executed.

Later on in this chapter, we'll see how a remote GDB session can be established with the target, in order to interrupt its execution at the current point, proceed to step through the code, place breakpoints and watch points, and inspect and modify the values in memory. A handful of GDB commands are introduced, giving a quick reference to some of the functionalities provided by the GDB command-line interface, which can be effectively used to debug embedded applications.

The debugger gives the best possible understanding of what the software is actually doing at runtime, and facilitates the hunt for programming errors while directly looking at the effects of the execution on memory and CPU registers.

Embedded workflow

If compared to other domains, the embedded development life cycle includes some additional steps. The code must be cross-compiled, the image manipulated then uploaded to a target, tests must be run, and possibly hardware tools are involved in the measurement and verification phases. The life cycle of native, application software, when using compiled languages, looks like this diagram:

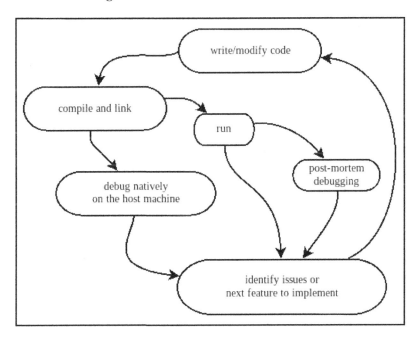

Typical life cycle of application development

When writing software within the same architecture, tests and debugging can be performed right after compiling, and it is often easier to detect issues. This results in a shorter time for the typical loop. Moreover, if the application crashes because of a bug, the underlying operating system is able to produce a core dump, which can be analyzed using the debugger at a later time, by restoring the content of the virtual memory and the context of the CPU registers right at the moment when the bug shows up. Intercepting fatal errors on an embedded target, on the other hand, might be slightly more challenging because of the potential side effect of memory and registers corruption, in the absence of virtual addresses and memory segmentation, which are provided by the operating systems in other contexts. Even if some targets are able to intercept abnormal situations by triggering diagnostic interrupts, such as the Hard Fault handler in Cortex-M, restoring the original context that generated the error is often impossible.

Furthermore, every time new software is generated, there are a few time-consuming steps to perform, such as the translation of the image to a specific format, and uploading the image to the target itself, which may take anywhere from a few seconds up to a minute, depending on the size of the image and the speed of the interface used to communicate with the target:

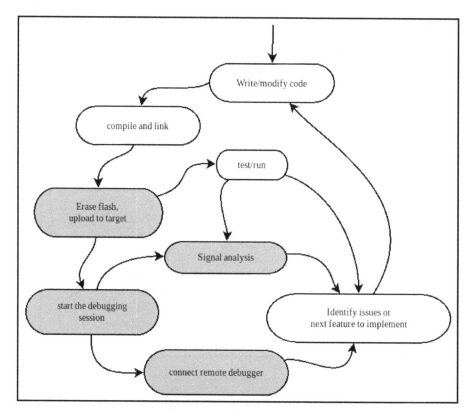

The embedded development life cycle, modified to include the additional steps required by the environment

In some of the phases of the development, when multiple consecutive iterations may be required to finalize a feature implementation or detect a defect, the timing in between compiling and testing the software has an impact on the efficiency of the whole life cycle. Specific tasks implemented in the software, which involve communication through serial or network interfaces, can only be verified with signal analysis, or by observing the effect on the peripheral or the remote system involved. Analyzing the electrical effects on the embedded system requires some hardware setup and instrument configuration, which add more time to the equation.

Finally, developing a distributed embedded system composed of a number of devices running different software images may result in repeating the preceding iterations for each of these devices. Whenever possible, these steps should be eliminated by using the same image and different set configuration parameters on each device, and by implementing parallel firmware upgrade mechanisms. Protocols such as JTAG support uploading the software image to multiple targets sharing the same bus, significantly cutting down the time required for the firmware upgrades, especially in those distributed systems with a larger numbers of devices involved.

No matter how complex the project is expected to be, it is in general worth spending as much time as needed to optimize the life cycle of the software development at the beginning, in order to increase the efficiency later on. No developer likes to switch the focus away from the actual coding steps for too long, and it might be frustrating to work in a suboptimal environment where stepping through the process requires too much time or human interaction.

In the following section, a cross-compiling GCC toolchain is examined, through the analysis of its components and the steps required to build an embedded application.

The GCC toolchain

An embedded toolchain is a set of software tools aimed to build software for a specific platform. While, in some cases, the complexity of the toolchain can be abstracted through a GUI, it is often distributed as a set of standalone applications, each one serving a specific purpose. Understanding the single tools and learning how to use them properly speeds up the development process and gives us a closer look at how things work under the hood.

GCC is nowadays one of the reference toolchains to build embedded systems, due to its modular structure allowing backends for multiple architectures. Thanks to its open source model, and the flexibility in building tailored toolchains from it, GCC-based toolchains are among the most popular development tools in embedded systems.

Building software using a command-line-based toolchain has several advantages, including the possibility of automating the intermediate steps that would build all the modules up from the source code into the final image. This is particularly useful when it is required to program multiple devices in a row, or to automate builds on a continuous integration server.

ARM distributes the GNU Arm Embedded Toolchain for all the most popular development hosts. Toolchains are prefixed with a triplet describing the target. In the case of the GNU Arm Embedded Toolchain, the prefix is `arm-none-eabi`, indicating that the cross-compiler backend is configured to produce objects for ARM, with no specific support for an operating system API, and with the embedded ABI.

The cross-compiler

The cross-compiler distributed with a toolchain is in fact a variant of GCC, with the backend configured to build object files that contain machine code for a specific architecture. The output of the compilation are object files containing symbols that can only be interpreted by the specific target. `arm-none-eabi-gcc` is able to compile C code into machine instructions and CPU optimizations for several different targets.

The GCC backend for the ARM architecture supports a number of machine-specific options, to select the correct instruction set for the CPU, and the machine-specific optimization parameters.

The following table lists some of the ARM-specific machine options available on the GCC backend as `-m` flags:

Option	Description
`-marm` / `-mthumb`	Selects ARM or Thumb instruction set
`-march=name`	Selects the architecture name within the family (for example, `armv7`)
`-mtune=name`	Selects the CPU name for which GCC is optimized (for example, `cortex-m3`)
`-mcpu=name`	Selects the CPU name for optimizations and architecture (can be used instead of `-march` and `-mtune`)

To compile code that is compatible with a generic ARM Cortex M4, the `-mthumb` and `-mcpu=cortex-m4` options must be specified every time the compiler is invoked:

```
$ arm-none-eabi-gcc -c test.c -mthumb -mcpu=cortex-m4
```

The `test.o` file that is the result of this compile step is very different from the one that can be compiled, from the same source, using the host `gcc`. The difference can be better appreciated if instead of the two object files, the intermediate assembly code is compared. The compiler is in fact capable of creating intermediate assembly code files, instead of compiled and assembled objects, when it is invoked with the `-S` option.

Similarly to the host GCC compiler, there are different levels of possible optimization. In some cases, it makes sense to activate the size optimization to generate smaller object files. It is preferable, though, that the non-optimized image can fit the flash during the development, in order to facilitate the debugging procedures, as optimized code flow is more difficult to follow when the compiler may change the order of the execution of the code and hide away the content of some variables. The optimization parameter can be provided at the command line to select the desired optimization level:

Option	Effect
-O0	Do not optimize—turn off optimizations
-O1	Optimize for performance
-O2	Optimize even more
-O3	Maximum level of performance optimization
-Os	Optimize for size

Another generic GCC command-line option that is often used while debugging and prototyping is the -g flag, which instructs the compiler to keep the debugging-related data in the final object, in order to facilitate the access to functions' and variables' readable handles while running within the debugger.

To inform the compiler that we are running a bare-metal application, the -ffreestanding command-line option is used. In GCC jargon, a freestanding environment is defined by the possible lack of a standard library in the linking step, and most importantly, this option alerts the compiler that it should not expect to use the main function as the entry point of the program or provide any preamble code before the beginning of the execution. This option is required when compiling code for the embedded platforms, as it enables the boot mechanism described in Chapter 4, *The Boot-up Procedure*.

The GCC program supports many more command-line options than those quickly introduced here. For a more complete overview of the functionalities offered, please refer to the GNU GCC manual, available at https://gcc.gnu.org/onlinedocs/.

To integrate the cross-compiling toolchain in the automated build using Make, a few changes are required in the makefile.

Assuming that the toolchain is correctly installed on the development host and reachable in its executing path, it is sufficient to change the default compiler command using the CC Make variable in the makefile:

```
CC=arm-none-eabi-gcc
```

The custom command-line options required to run the compile options may be exported through the CFLAGS variable:

```
CFLAGS=-mthumb -mcpu=cortex-m4 -ffreestanding
```

Using default makefile variables, such as CC and CFLAGS, enables implicit makefile rules, building object files from C sources with the same name and a custom compiler configuration.

Compiling the compiler

Binary distributions of the GCC toolchain are available to download for a number of specific targets and host machines. To compile the code for the ARM Cortex-M microprocessors, the arm-none-eabi toolchain is made available for most GNU/Linux distributions. However, in some cases, it might be handy to build the toolchain entirely from the sources. This might be, for example, when the compiler for a certain target does not exist yet or is not shipped in binary format for our favorite development environment. This process is also useful to better understand the various components that are required to build the tools.

Crosstool-NG is an open source project, which consists of a set of scripts aimed to automate the process of creating a toolchain. The tool retrieves the selected version of each and every component, then creates an archive of the toolchain that can be redistributed in binary form. This is normally not necessary, while sometimes useful when it is necessary to modify the sources for a specific component, such as, for example, the C libraries that are finally integrated in the toolchain. It is easy to create a new configuration in crosstool-NG, thanks to its configurator, based on the Linux kernel menuconfig. After installing crosstool-NG, the configurator can be invoked by using:

```
$ ct-ng menuconfig
```

Once the configuration has been created, the build process can be started. Since the operation requires retrieving all the components, patching them, and building the toolchain, it may take several minutes, depending on the speed of the host machine and the internet connection, to retrieve all the components. The build process can be started by issuing:

```
$ ct-ng build
```

Predefined configurations are available for compiling commonly used toolchains, mostly for targets running Linux. When compiling a toolchain for a Linux target, there are a few C libraries to choose from. In our case, since we want a bare-metal toolchain, `newlib` is the default choice. Several other libraries provide an implementation of a subset of the C standard library, such as `uClibc` and `musl`. The `newlib` library is a small cross-platform C library mostly designed for embedded systems with no operating system on board, and it is provided as the default in many GCC distributions, including the `arm-none-eabi` cross-compiler distributed by ARM.

Linking the executable

Linking is the last step in the creation of the ELF file. The cross-compiling GCC groups all the object files together and resolves the dependencies among symbols. By passing the `-T filename` option at the command line, the linker is asked to replace the default memory layout for the program with a custom script, contained in the filename.

The linker script is a file containing the description of the memory sections in the target, which need to be known in advance in order for the linker to place the symbols in the correct sections in flash, and instruct the software components about special locations in the memory mapping area that can be referenced in the code. The file is recognizable by its `.ld` extension, and it is written in a specific language. As a rule of thumb, all the symbols from every single compiled object are grouped in the sections of the final executable image.

The script can interact with the C code, exporting symbols defined within the script, and following indications provided in the code using GCC-specific attributes associated with symbols. The `__attribute__` keyword is provided by GCC to be put in front of the symbol definition, to activate GCC-specific, non-standard attributes for each symbol.

Some GCC attributes can be used to communicate to the linker about:

- Weak symbols, which can be overridden by symbols with the same name
- Symbols to be stored in a specific section in the ELF file, defined in the linker script
- Implicitly used symbols, which prevent the linker from discarding the symbol because it is referred to nowhere in the code

The weak attribute is used to define weak symbols, which can be overridden anywhere else in the code by another definition with the same name. Consider, for example, the following definition:

```
void __attribute__(weak) my_procedure(int x) { /* do nothing */ }
```

In this case, the procedure is defined to do nothing, but it is possible to override it anywhere else in the code base by defining it again, using the same name, but this time without the weak attribute:

```
void my_procedure(int x) { y = x; }
```

The linker step ensures that the final executable contains exactly one copy of each defined symbol, which is the one without the attribute, if available. This mechanism introduces the possibility of having several different implementations of the same functionality within the code, which can be altered by including different object files in the linking phase. This is particularly useful when writing code that is portable to different targets, while still maintaining the same abstractions.

Besides the default sections required in the ELF description, custom sections may be added to store specific symbols, such as functions and variables, at a fixed memory addresses. This is useful when storing data at the beginning of a flash page, which might be uploaded to flash at a different time than the software itself. This is the case for target-specific settings in some cases.

Using the custom GCC attribute section when defining a symbol ensures that the symbol ends up at the desired position in the final image. Sections may have custom names, as long as an entry exists in the linker to locate them. The section attribute can be added to a symbol definition as follows:

```
const uint8_t
__attribute__((section(".keys")))
private_key[KEY_SIZE] = {0};
```

In this example, the array is placed in the .keys section, which requires its own entry in the linker script as well.

It is considered good practice to have the linker discard the unused symbols in the final image, especially when using third-party libraries that are not completely utilized by the embedded application. This can be done in GCC using the linker garbage collector, activated via the -gc-sections command-line option. If this flag is provided, the sections that are unused in the code are automatically discarded, and the unused symbols will in fact be kept out of the final image.

To prevent the linker from discarding symbols associated with a particular section, the `used` attribute marks the symbol as implicitly used by the program. Multiple attributes can be listed in the same declaration, separated by commas, as follows:

```
const uint8_t
__attribute__((used,section(".keys")))
private_key[KEY_SIZE] = {0};
```

In this example, the attributes indicate both that the `private_key` array belongs to the `.keys` section, and that it must not be discarded by the linker garbage collector, because it is marked as used.

A simple linker script for an embedded target defines at least the two sections relative to `RAM` and `FLASH` mapping, and exports some predefined symbols to instruct the assembler of the toolchain about the memory areas. A bare-metal system based on the GNU toolchain usually starts with a `MEMORY` section, describing the mapping of the two different areas in the system, such as:

```
MEMORY {
    FLASH(rx) : ORIGIN = 0x00000000, LENGTH=256k
    RAM(rwx) : ORIGIN = 0x20000000, LENGTH=64k
    }
```

The preceding code snippet describes two memory areas used in the system. The first block is `256k` mapped to `FLASH`, with the `r` and `x` flags, indicating that the area is accessible for read and execute operations. This enforces the read-only attribute of the whole area, and ensures that no variant sections are placed there. `RAM`, on the other hand, can be accessed in write mode directly, which means that variables are going to be placed in a section within that area. In this specific example, the target maps the `FLASH` at the beginning of the address space, while the `RAM` is mapped starting at 512 MB. Each target has its own address space mapping and flash/RAM size, so the linker script is definitely target-specific.

As mentioned earlier in this chapter, the `.text` and `.rodata` ELF sections can only be accessed for reading, so they can safely be stored in the `FLASH` area, since they will not be modified while the target is running. On the other hand, both `.data` and `.bss` must be mapped in `RAM` to ensure that they are modifiable.

Additional custom sections can be added in the script, in the case where it is necessary to store additional sections at a specific location in memory. The linker script can also export symbols related to a specific position in memory, or to the length of dynamically sized sections in memory, which can be referred to as external symbols and accessed in the C source code.

The second block of statements in the linker script is called SECTIONS, and contains the allocation of the sections in specific positions of the defined memory areas. The . symbol, when associated with a variable in the script, represents the current position in the area, which is filled progressively from the lower addresses available. Each section must specify the area where it has to be mapped. The following example, though still incomplete to run the binary executable, shows how the different sections can be deployed using the linker script. The .text and .rodata sections are mapped in the flash memory:

```
SECTIONS
{
    /* Text section (code and read-only data) */
    .text :
{
    . = ALIGN(4);
    _start_text = .;
    *(.text*) /* code */
    . = ALIGN(4);
    _end_text = .;
    *(.rodata*) /* read only data */
    . = ALIGN(4);
    _end_rodata = .;
} > FLASH
```

The modifiable sections are mapped in RAM, with two special cases to notice here.

The AT keyword is used to indicate the load address to the linker, which is the area where the original values of the variables in .data are stored, while the actual addresses used in the execution are in a different memory region. More details about the load address and the virtual address for the .data section are explained in Chapter 4, *The Boot-Up Procedure.*

The NOLOAD attribute used for the .bss section ensures that no predefined values are stored in the ELF file for this section. Uninitialized global and static variables are mapped by the linker in the RAM area, which is allocated by the linker:

```
_stored_data = .;
.data: AT(__stored_data)
{
    . = ALIGN(4);
    _start_data = .;
    *(.data*)
    . = ALIGN(4);
    _start_data = .;
} > RAM
```

```
.bss (NOLOAD):
{
    . = ALIGN(4);
    _start_bss = .;
    *(.bss*)
    . = ALIGN(4);
    _end_bss = .;
} > RAM
}
```

The alternative way to force the linker to keep sections in the final executable, avoiding their removal due to the linker garbage collector, is the use of the KEEP instruction to mark sections. Please note that this is an alternative to the __attribute__((used)) mechanism explained earlier:

```
.keys :
{
    . = ALIGN(4);
    *(.keys*) = .;
    KEEP(*(.keys*));
} > FLASH
```

It is useful, and advisable in general, to have the linker create a .map file alongside the resultant binary. This is done by appending the -Map=filename option to the link step, such as in:

```
$ arm-none-eabi-ld -o image.elf object1.o object2.o -T linker_script.ld -Map=map_file.map
```

The map file contains the location and the description of all the symbols, grouped by sections. This is useful to look for the specific location of symbols in the image, as well as for verifying that useful symbols are not accidentally discarded due to a misconfiguration.

Cross-compiling toolchains provide standard C libraries for generic functionalities, such as string manipulation or standard types declarations. These are substantially a subset of the library calls available in the application space of an operating system, including standard input/output functions. The backend implementation of these functions is often left to the applications, so that calling a function from the library that requires interaction with the hardware, such as printf, implies that a write function is implemented outside of the library, providing the final transfer to a device or peripheral.

The implementation of the backend write function determines which channel would act as the standard output for the embedded application. The linker is capable of resolving the dependencies towards standard library calls automatically, using the built-in `newlib` implementation. To exclude the standard C library symbols from the linking process, the `-nostdlib` option can be added to the options passed to GCC during the linking step.

Binary format conversion

Despite containing all the compiled symbols in binary format, an ELF file is prefixed with a header that contains a description of the content, and pointers to the position where the sections start within the file. All this extra information is not needed to run on an embedded target, so the ELF file produced by the linker has to be transformed into a plain binary file. A tool in the toolchain, called `objcopy`, converts images from one standard format to others, and what is generally done is a conversion of the ELF into a raw binary image, without altering the symbols. To transform the image from ELF to binary format, invoke:

```
$ arm-none-eabi-objcopy -I elf -O binary image.elf image.bin
```

This creates a new file, called `image.bin`, from the symbol contained in the original ELF executable, which can be uploaded to the target.

Even if not suitable in general for direct upload on the target with third-party tools, it is possible to load the symbols through the debugger and upload them to the flash address. The original ELF file is also useful as the target of other diagnostic tools in the GNU toolchain, such as `nm` and `readelf`, which display the symbols in each module, with their type and relative address within the binary image. Furthermore, by using the `objdump` tool on the final image, or even on single object files, several details about the image can be retrieved, including the visualization of the entire assembly code, using the `-d` disassemble option:

```
arm-none-eabi-objdump -d image.elf
```

Interacting with the target

For development purposes, embedded platforms are usually accessed through a JTAG or an SWD interface. Through these communication channels, it is possible to upload the software onto the flash of the target, and access the on-chip debug functionalities. There are several self-contained JTAG/SWD adapters on the market that can be controlled through USB from the host, while some development boards are equipped with an extra chip controlling the JTAG channel, that connects to the host through USB.

A powerful generic open source tool to access JTAG/SWD functionalities on the target is the **Open On-Chip Debugger (OpenOCD)**. Once properly configured, it creates local sockets that can be used as a command console and for the interaction with the debugger frontend. Some development boards are distributed with additional interfaces to communicate with the core CPU. For example, STMicroelectronics prototyping boards for Cortex-M are rarely shipped without a chip technology called **ST-Link**, which allows direct access to debug and flash manipulation functionalities. Thanks to its flexible backend, OpenOCD can communicate with these devices using different transport types and physical interfaces, including ST-Link and other protocols. Several different boards are supported and the configuration files can be found by OpenOCD.

When started, OpenOCD opens two local TCP server sockets, on preconfigured ports, providing the communication services with the target platform. One socket provides an interactive command console that can be accessed through Telnet, while the other is a GDB server, used for remote debugging, as described in the next section.

In order to configure OpenOCD for the STM32F746-Discovery target, we can use the following `openocd.cfg` configuration file:

```
telnet_port 4444
gdb_port 3333
source [find board/stm32f7discovery.cfg]
```

The board-specific configuration file, imported from `openocd.cfg` through the `source` directive, instructs OpenOCD to use the ST-Link interface to communicate with the target, and sets all the CPU-specific options.

The two ports specified in the main configuration file, using the `telnet_port` and `gdb_port` directives, instruct OpenOCD to open two listening TCP sockets.

The first socket, often referred to as the monitor console, can be accessed connecting to the local `4444` TCP port, using a Telnet client from the command line:

```
$ telnet localhost 4444
Open On-Chip Debugger
>
```

The sequence of OpenOCD directives to initialize, erase the flash, and transfer the image starts with:

```
> init
> halt
> flash probe 0
```

The execution is stopped at the beginning of the software image. After the probe command, the flash is initialized, and OpenOCD will print out some information, including the address mapped to write on the flash. The following information shows up with the STM32F746:

```
device id = 0x10016449
flash size = 1024kbytes
flash "stm32f2x" found at 0x08000000
```

The geometry of the flash can be retrieved using the command:

```
> flash info 0
```

Which on the STM32F746 shows:

```
#0 : stm32f2x at 0x08000000, size 0x00100000, buswidth 0, chipwidth 0
# 0: 0x00000000 (0x8000 32kB) not protected
# 1: 0x00008000 (0x8000 32kB) not protected
# 2: 0x00010000 (0x8000 32kB) not protected
# 3: 0x00018000 (0x8000 32kB) not protected
# 4: 0x00020000 (0x20000 128kB) not protected
# 5: 0x00040000 (0x40000 256kB) not protected
# 6: 0x00080000 (0x40000 256kB) not protected
# 7: 0x000c0000 (0x40000 256kB) not protected
STM32F7[4|5]x - Rev: Z
```

This flash contains eight sectors. If the OpenOCD target supports it, the flash can be completely erased issuing the following command from the console:

```
> flash erase_sector 0 0 7
```

Once the flash memory is erased, we can upload a software image to it, linked and converted to raw binary format, using the `flash write_image` directive. As the raw binary format does not contain any information about its destination address in the mapped area, the starting address in the flash must be provided as the last argument, as follows:

```
> flash write_image /path/to/image.bin 0x08000000
```

These directives can be appended to the `openocd.cfg` file, or to different configuration files, in order to automate all the steps needed for a specific action, such as erasing the flash and uploading an updated image.

Some hardware manufacturers offer their own set of tools to interact with the devices. STMicroelectronics devices can be programmed using the ST-Link utilities, an open source project that includes a flash tool (`st-flash`) and a GDB server counterpart (`st-util`). Some platforms have built-in bootloaders that accept alternative formats or binary transfer procedures. A common example is **Device Firmware Upgrade (DFU)**, which is a mechanism to deploy firmware on targets through USB. The reference implementation on the host side is `dfu-util`, which is a free software tool.

Each tool, either generic or specific, tends to meet the same goal of communicating with the device and providing an interface for debugging the code, although often exposing a different interface toward the development tools.

The GDB session

Regardless of the complexity of the project we are working on, most of the development time will be spent trying to understand what our software does, or most likely, what has gone wrong and why the software is not behaving as we would expect when the code was written the first time. The debugger is the most powerful tool in our toolchain, allowing us to communicate directly with the CPU, place breakpoints, control the execution flow instruction by instruction, and check the values of CPU registers, local variables, and memory areas. A good knowledge of the debugger means less time spent trying to figure out what is going on, and a more effective hunt for bugs and defects.

The `arm-none-eabi` toolchain includes a GDB capable of interpreting the memory and the register layout of the remote target, and can be accessed with the same interfaces as the host GDB, provided that its backend can communicate with the embedded platform, using OpenOCD or a similar host tool providing communication with the target through the GDB server protocol. As previously described, OpenOCD can be configured to provide a GDB server interface, which in the proposed configuration is on port `3333`.

After starting `arm-none-eabi-gdb`, we may connect to the running tool using the GDB `target` command. Connecting to the GDB server while OpenOCD is running can be done using the target command:

```
> target remote localhost:3333
```

All GDB commands can be abbreviated, so the command often becomes:

```
> tar rem :3333
```

Once connected, the target would typically stop the execution, allowing GDB to retrieve the information about the instruction that is being currently executed, the stack trace, and the values of the CPU registers.

From this moment on, the debugger interface can be used normally to step through the code, place breakpoints and watchpoints, and inspect and alter CPU registers and writable memory areas at runtime.

GDB can be used entirely from its command-line interface, using shortcuts and commands to start and stop the execution, and access memory and registers.

The following reference table enumerates a few of the GDB commands available in a debug session, and provides a quick explanation of their usage:

Command	Description
`file name`	Load all the symbols from the ELF file on the host filesystem. If the ELF file has been compiled with the GCC `-g` option, it will contain all the data to facilitate debugging.
`load`	Upload the currently loaded symbols to the target. Used to flash new versions of the software during a debug session.
`mon`	Access monitor commands, platform-specific. The OpenOCD monitor interfaces provide commands, such as `mon reset` and `mon init`, to power-cycle the core and initialize the execution.

Break (b) b function_name b line_number b file.c:line_num b address	Place a breakpoint in the code, at the specified location. The location can be specified in different ways. When the execution hits the instruction with the breakpoint, the CPU is temporarily stopped and the control returns to the debugger for inspection.
Watch (w) address	Like break, but instead of placing a breakpoint on a specific location in the code, observe a variable in memory at the given address and interrupt the execution whenever the value changes. Useful to trace the point in the code where a specific value in the memory is altered.
info b	Provide information about the breakpoints and watchpoints currently set in this debugging session.
delete (d) n	Remove breakpoint n.
print (p) ...	Inspect the value of a variable, or a C expression that can be evaluated using variables and memory addresses.
display ...	Like print, but refresh the value of the expression every time that the control returns to the debugger, useful to track the changes while stepping through the code.
Next (n)	Execute the next instruction. If the next instruction is a function call, place an automatic breakpoint on the function return, and return the control to the debugger only when the called function has returned.
Step (s)	Execute the next instruction. If the next instruction is a function call, place an automatic breakpoint on the function return, and return the control to the debugger only when the called function has returned.
Stepi (si)	Like step, but only execute the next machine instruction instead of the whole C line that generated it. Useful to step through single machine instructions.
Continue (c)	Resume the execution on the target from the current position. The control is returned to the debugger if a breakpoint is hit, or if *Ctrl + C* is pressed from the GDB console.
set var=... set $cpu_reg=...	Assign the desired value (or the result of an expression) to a variable or a CPU register, referenced using the $ symbol.
Backtrace (bt)	Inspect the contents of the stack in the reverse order, including the call trace to the current location.
up down	Move the stack pointer through the current call trace, to switch to the context of the caller toward outer functions use up, to switch back to inner functions use down.

GDB is a very powerful and complete debugger, and the commands that have been shown in this section are a small portion of its actual potential. The reader is advised to discover the other features offered by GDB by going through its manual, in order to find the set of commands that best fit their needs.

Validation

Debugging alone, or even simple output analysis, is often not enough when verifying system behavior and identifying issues and unwanted effects in the code. Different approaches may be taken to validate the implementation of the single components, as well as the behavior of the entire system under different conditions. While, in some cases, the results can be directly measurable from the host machine, in more specific contexts, it is often difficult to reproduce the exact scenario, or to acquire the necessary information from the system output.

External tools may come in handy, especially in the analysis of communication interfaces and network devices in a more complex, distributed system. In other cases, single modules can be tested off-target using simulated or emulated environments to run smaller portions of the code base.

Different tests, validation strategies, and tools are considered in this section, to provide solutions for any scenario.

Functional tests

Writing test cases before writing the code is generally considered an optimal practice in modern programming. Writing tests first not only speeds up the development phases, but also improves the structure of the workflow. By setting clear and measurable goals from the beginning, it is harder to introduce conceptual defects in the design of the single components, and also forces a clearer separation among the modules. More specifically, an embedded developer has less possibility to verify the correct behavior of the system through direct interaction, thus **test-driven development** (TDD) is the preferred approach for the verification of the single components as well as the functional behavior of the entire system, as long as the expected results can be directly measurable from the host system.

However, it must be considered that testing often introduces dependencies on specific hardware, and sometimes the output of an embedded system can only be validated through specific hardware tools, or in a very unique and peculiar usage scenario. In all these cases, the usual TDD paradigm is less applicable, and the project can instead benefit from a modular design, to give the possibility to test as many components as possible in a synthetic environment, such as emulators or unit test platforms.

Writing tests often involves programming the host so that it can retrieve information about the running target while the embedded software is executing, or alongside an ongoing debugging session, while the target executes in between breakpoints. The target can be configured to provide immediate output through a communication interface, such as a UART-based serial port, which can in turn be parsed by the host. It is usually more convenient to write test tools on the host using a higher-level interpreted programming language, to better organize the test cases and easily integrate the parsing of test results using regular expressions. Python, Perl, Ruby, and other languages with similar characteristics, are often a good fit for this purpose, also thanks to the availability of libraries and components designed for collecting and analyzing test results and interacting with continuous integration engines. A good organization of the test and verification infrastructure contributes more than everything else to the stability of the project, because regressions can be detected at the right time only if all the existing tests are repeated at every modification. Constantly running all the test cases while the development is ongoing not only improves the efficiency of detecting undesired effects as early as possible, but helps keep the development goals visible at all times, by directly measuring the number of failures, and makes the refactoring of components more affordable at any stage in the project lifetime.

Efficiency is the key, because embedded programming is an iterative process with a number of steps being repeated over and over, and the approach required from the developers is much more predictive than reactive.

Hardware tools

If there is a tool that is absolutely indispensable to assist embedded software developers, it is the logic analyzer. By scoping the input and output signals involving the microcontroller, it is possible to detect the electrical behavior of the signals, their timing, and even the digital encoding of the single bits in the interface protocols. Most logic analyzers are able to identify and decode sequences of symbols by sensing the voltage of the wires, which is often the most effective way to verify that protocols are correctly implemented and compliant with the contracts to communicate with peripherals and network endpoints. While historically available only as standalone dedicated computers, a logic analyzer is often available in other forms, such as electronic instruments that can be connected to the host machine using USB or Ethernet interfaces, and use PC-based software to capture and decode the signals. The result of this process is a complete discrete analysis of the signals involved, which are sampled at a constant rate and then visualized on a screen.

While a similar task can be performed by oscilloscopes, they are often more complex to configure than logic analyzers when dealing with discrete signals. Nevertheless, an oscilloscope is the best tool for the analysis of analog signals, such as analog audio and communication among radio transceivers. Depending on the task, it might be better to use one or the other, but in general, the biggest advantage of a logic analyzer is that it provides better insight for discrete signals. Mixed-signal logic analyzers are often a good compromise between the flexibility of an oscilloscope, with the simplicity and the insights of a discrete signal-logic analysis.

Oscilloscopes and logic analyzers are often used to capture the activity of signals in a specific time window, which might be challenging to synchronize with the running software. Instead of capturing those signals continuously, the beginning of the capture can be synchronized with a physical event, such as a digital signal changing its value for the first time, or an analog signal crossing a predefined threshold. This is done by configuring the instrument to initiate the capture using a trigger, which guarantees that the information being captured only contains a time slice that is interesting for the ongoing diagnostic.

Testing off-target

Another efficient way to speed up the development is limiting the interaction, as much as possible, with the actual target. This is of course not always possible, especially when developing device drivers that require to be tested on actual hardware, but tools and methodologies to partially test the software directly on the development machine exist.

Portions of code that are not CPU-specific can be compiled for the host machine architecture and run directly, as long as their surroundings are properly abstracted to simulate the real environment. The software to test can be as small as a single function, and in this case a unit test can be written specifically for the development architecture. Unit tests are in general small applications that verify the behavior of a single component by feeding them with well-known input, and verifying their output. Several tools are available on a Linux system to assist in writing unit tests. The check library provides an interface for defining unit tests by writing a few preprocessor macros. The result is small self-contained applications that can be run every time the code is changed, directly on the host machine. Those components of the system that the function under test depends on are abstracted using mocks. For example, the following code detects and discards a specific escape sequence, *Esc + C*, from the input from a serial line interface, reading from the serial line until the \0 character is returned:

```
int serial_parser(char *buffer, uint32_t max_len)
{
    int pos = 0;
```

```
    while (pos < max_len) {
        buffer[pos] = read_from_serial();
        if (buffer[pos] == (char)0)
            break;
        if (buffer[pos] == ESC) {
            buffer[++pos] = read_from_serial();
        if (buffer[pos] == 'c')
            pos = pos - 1;
        continue;
        pos++;
        }
    return pos;
}
```

A set of unit tests to verify this function using a check test suite may look like the following:

```
START_TEST(test_plain) {
    const char test0[] = "hello world!";
    char buffer[40];
    set_mock_buffer(test0);
    fail_if(serial_parser(buffer, 40) != strlen(test0));
    fail_if(strcmp(test0,buffer) != 0);
}
END_TEST
```

Each test case can be contained in its START_TEST()/END_TEST block, and provide a different initial configuration:

```
START_TEST(test_escape) {
    const char test0[] = "hello world!";
    const char test1[] = "hello \033cworld!";
    char buffer[40];
    set_mock_buffer(test1);
    fail_if(serial_parser(buffer, 40) != strlen(test0));
    fail_if(strcmp(test0,buffer) != 0);
}
END_TEST


START_TEST(test_other) {
    const char test2[] = "hello \033dworld!";
    char buffer[40];
    set_mock_buffer(test2);
    fail_if(serial_parser(buffer, 40) != strlen(test2));
    fail_if(strcmp(test2,buffer) != 0);
}
END_TEST
```

This first `test_plain` test ensures that a string with no escape characters is parsed correctly. The second test ensures that the escape sequence is skipped, and the third one verifies that a similar escape string is left untouched by the output buffer. Serial communication is simulated using a mock function that replaces the original `serial_read` functionality, which is provided by the driver when running the code on the target. This is a simple mock that feeds the parser with a constant buffer that can be reinitialized using the `set_serial_buffer` helper function. The mock code looks like this:

```
static int serial_pos = 0;
static char serial_buffer[40];


char read_from_serial(void) {
    return serial_buffer[serial_pos++];
}


void set_mock_buffer(const char *buf)
{
    serial_pos = 0;
    strncpy(serial_buffer, buf, 20);
}
```

Unit tests are very useful to improve the quality of the code, but of course achieving a high code coverage consumes a large amount of time and resources in the economy of the project. Functional tests can also be run directly in the development environment, by grouping functions into self-contained modules and implementing simulators that are slightly more complex than mocks for specific test cases. In the example of the serial parser, it would be possible to test the entire application logic on top of a different serial driver on the host machine, which is also able to simulate an entire conversation over the serial line, and interact with other components in the system, such as virtual terminals and other applications generating input sequences. While covering a larger portion of the code within a single test case, the complexity of the simulated environment increases, and so does the amount of work required to reproduce the surroundings of the embedded system on the host machine. Nevertheless, it is good practice, especially when they could be used as verification tools throughout the whole development cycle, and even integrated in the automated test process. Sometimes, implementing a simulator allows for a much more complete set of tests, or it might be the only viable option. Think, for example, about those embedded systems using a GPS receiver for positioning: testing the application logic with negative latitude values would be impossible while sitting in the northern hemisphere, so writing a simulator that imitates the data coming from such a receiver is the quickest way to verify that our final device will not stop working across the equator.

Emulators

Another valid approach to run the code on the development machine, which is much less invasive for our code base and does not have specific portability requirements, is emulating the whole platform on the host PC. An emulator is a software that can replicate the functionality of an entire system, including its core CPU, memory, and a set of peripherals. Some of the modern virtualization hypervisors for PCs are derived from QEMU, a free software emulator capable of virtualizing entire systems, even with a different architecture from those of the machine where it runs. Since it contains the full implementation of the instruction set of many different targets, QEMU can run the firmware image, which had been compiled for our target, in a process on top of the development machine's operating system. One of the supported targets that can run ARM Cortex-M3 microcode is LM3S6965EVB, a Cortex-M-based microcontroller that is fully supported by QEMU. Once a binary image has been created using LM3S6965EVB as a target, and properly converted to raw binary format using `objcopy`, a fully emulated system can be run by invoking QEMU as follows:

```
$ qemu-system-arm -M lm3s6965evb --kernel image.bin
```

The `--kernel` option instructs the emulator to run the image at startup, and while it might sound misnamed, it is called `kernel` because QEMU is widely used to emulate headless Linux systems on other synthetic targets. Similarly, a convenient debugging session can be started by using QEMU's built-in GDB server, through the `-gdb` option, which can also halt the system until our GDB client is connected to it:

```
$ qemu-system-arm -M lm3s6965evb --kernel image.bin -nographic -S -gdb tcp
::3333
```

In the same way as with the real target, we can connect `arm-none-eabi-gdb` to TCP port `3333` on localhost, and start debugging the software image exactly as it was running on the actual platform.

The limit of the emulation approach is that QEMU can only be used to debug generic features that do not involve interaction with actual hardware. The platform emulated is quite specific, and does not match the system layout of a real hardware platform. Nevertheless, running QEMU with a Cortex-M3 target can be a fast way to learn about generic Cortex-M features, such as memory management, system interrupt handling, and processor modes, because many features of the Cortex-M CPU are accurately emulated.

The approach proposed for the definition of test strategies takes into account different scenarios. The idea has been to propose a range of possible solutions for software validation, from lab equipment to tests off-target in simulated and emulated environments, for the developer to choose from in a specific scenario.

Summary

This chapter introduced the tools for working on the development of embedded systems. A hands-on approach has been proposed, to get the reader up and running with the toolchain and the utilities required to communicate with the hardware platform. Using appropriate tools can make embedded development easier and shorten the workflow iterations.

In the next chapter, we provide indications on the organization of the workflow when working with larger teams. Based on real-life experiences, we propose solutions for splitting and organizing tasks, executing tests, iterating throughout the phases of design, and the definition and implementation of an embedded project.

Architectural Patterns 3

Starting an embedded project from scratch means progressively stepping toward the final solution, through the research and development phases, and the synergy among all the parts involved. Software development needs to evolve accordingly throughout these phases. In order to get the best results without excessive overhead, there are a few best practices to follow and tools to discover. This chapter provides the description of a possible approach toward configuration-management tools and design patterns, which is based on real-life experiences. Describing this approach may help you to understand the dynamics of working in a team focused on producing an embedded device or solution.

We will discuss the following topics in this chapter:

- Configuration management
- Source code organization
- The life cycle of an embedded project

Configuration management

When working as a team, coordination and synchronization can be optimized to improve efficiency. Tracking and controlling the development life cycle smoothens the development flow, cutting down time and costs. The most important tools known to help manage the software life cycle are:

- Revision control
- Issue tracking
- Code reviews
- Continuous integration

Different options exist for the four categories. The source code is synchronized among developers through a revision control system. **Issue tracking systems (ITSs)** usually consist of web platforms that keep track of the activities and known bugs of the system. Code reviews can be encouraged with specific web-based tools, and enforced through rules on the revision control systems.

Continuous integration tools ensure that build and test execution tasks are scheduled to automatically execute, periodically or upon changes in the code, collecting test results, and notifying the developers about regressions.

Revision control

No matter whether you are working alone or in a large development team, properly keeping track of the development progress is extremely important. Revision control tools allows developers to roll back failed experiments at any time with the press of a button, and visiting its history gives a clear view on how the project is evolving at any time.

A revision control system, also known as **version control system**, or **VCS**, encourages cooperation by making merge operations easier. The most updated official version is referred to as a **trunk** or **master** branch, depending on the VCS in use.

One of the most modern and widely used open source VCSs is Git. Originally created as the VCS for the Linux kernel, Git offers a range of features, but most importantly provides a flexible mechanism to allow switching among different versions and feature branches quickly and reliably, and facilitates the integration of conflicting modifications in the code. Git terminology is used in this book when describing specific activities related to the VCS.

A **commit** is a VCS action that results in a new version of the repository. The repository keeps track of the sequence of commits and the changes introduced on each version, in a hierarchical structure. A linear sequence of commits is a **branch**. The latest version in a branch is called **HEAD**.

Git refers to the main development branch as master. The master branch is the main focus of the development. Bug fixes and minor changes are committed directly on the master. Feature branches are created for self-contained tasks in progressing and ongoing experiments, which will be eventually merged into the master. When not abused, feature branches are a perfect fit when working in a smaller sub-team on a task, and can simplify the code review process, reducing it to validating completed tasks as single **merge** requests.

A merge operation consists of joining together two versions from two different branches that may have diverged and present conflict in the code through the development. Some merges are trivial and automatically resolved by the VCS, while others may require manual fixing.

Using meaningful and verbose commit messages improves the readability of the history of the repository, and can help to track regressions later on. Tags can be used to track intermediate versions that are released and distributed.

Tracking activities

Keeping track of the activities and the tasks can be simplified by using ITSs. Some tools can be directly linked to the revision control system, so tasks can be linked to specific commits in the repository and vice versa. This is, in general, a good idea, as it is possible to have a good overview of what has been changed to accomplish a specific task.

At first, tasking out the specifications into short activities facilitates the approach to development. Ideally, tasks are as small as possible, and may be grouped by category. Later on, priorities can be set based on intermediate goals, and taking into account the availability of the final hardware. Tasks created should be grouped together into intermediate milestones, which some tools refer to as blueprints, so that the overall progress towards an intermediate deliverable can be measured on the basis of the progress made on the single tasks.

ITS can of course be used to track actual issues in the project. A bug report should be extensive enough for other developers to understand the symptoms and reproduce the behavior that proves that there is a defect in the code. Ideally, final users and early adopters should be able to add new issues to the tracking system, so the tracking system itself can be used to track all the communication with the development team. Community-based open source projects should provide a publicly accessible ITS interface to the users.

Bug-fixing activities in general get a higher priority than development tasks, except in a few cases, for instance, when the bug is the effect of a temporary approximation done by an intermediate prototype, which is expected to be fixed on the next iteration. When a bug affects a behavior of the system, which was proven to work beforehand, it must be marked as regression. This is important because regressions can usually be handled in a different way than normal bugs, as it is possible to track them down to a single commit using revision control tools.

Repository control platforms exist nowadays to provide several tools, including source code history browsing, and the issue-tracking features described earlier. GitLab is a free and open source implementation of such repository control platforms, which can be installed to run as a self-hosted solution. Community projects are often hosted on social coding platforms, such as GitHub, which aim to facilitate contributions to open source and free software projects.

Code reviews

Often integrated in ITS tools nowadays, code reviews facilitate team cooperation by encouraging the critical analysis of the changes proposed to the code base, it can be useful to detect potential issues before the proposed changes make it to the master branch. Depending on the project requirements, code reviews may be recommended, or even enforced to the team, with the purpose of increasing the quality of the code and early detection of defects by human inspection.

When properly integrated with the VCS, it is possible to set a threshold of mandatory positive reviews from other members in the team before the commit is actually considered for merging. It is possible to mandate the reviews of each single commit in the master branch, using tools such as **Gerrit**, integrated with the VCS. Depending on the size of the commits, this mechanism can introduce some unnecessary overhead, so, in most cases, it may be more appropriate to review the changes introduced by a branch altogether when the branch is proposed for a merge in master. Mechanisms based on merge requests give the reviewers an overview of the changes introduced during the entire development of the modification proposed.

Continuous integration

As previously mentioned, the test-driven approach is crucial in an embedded environment. Automating the tests is the best way to promptly detect regressions, and defects in general, while the development is ongoing. Using an automation server, such as **Jenkins**, it is possible to plan several actions, or *jobs*, to run responsively (such as at every commit), periodically (such as every Tuesday at 1 a.m.), or manually, upon user requests. Here are a few examples of jobs that can be automated to improve the efficiency of an embedded project:

- Unit tests on the development machine
- System validation tests
- Functional tests on a simulated environment

- Functional tests on a physical target platform
- Stability tests
- Static code analysis
- Generating documentation
- Tagging, versioning, packaging

The desired level of quality must be decided during design, and test cases must be coded accordingly. Unit test code coverage can be measured using `gcov` upon each test execution. Some projects intended for life-critical applications may require a very high percentage of coverage for unit tests, but writing a complete set of tests for a complex system has a great impact on the total programming effort, and may increase the cost of the development significantly, so researching the right balance between efficiency and quality is advisable in most cases.

A different approach has to be taken with functional tests. All the functionalities implemented on the target should be tested, and tests prepared in advance should be used to define performance indicators and acceptance thresholds. Functional tests should be run in an environment that is as close as possible to the real use case scenario, in all those cases where it is impossible to recreate the full use case on the target system and its surroundings.

Source code organization

The code base should contain all the source code, third-party libraries, data, scripts, and automations needed to build the final image. It is a good idea to keep self-contained libraries in separate directories, so that they can be easily updated to newer versions by replacing the subdirectory itself. Makefiles and other scripts can be placed in the project's root directory. Application code should be short and synthetic, and access the modules abstracting the macro functionalities. Functional modules should describe a process while hiding the details of the underlying implementation, such as reading data from a sensor after it has been properly sampled and processed. Aiming for small, self-contained, and adequately abstracted modules also makes the components of the architecture easier to test. Keeping the majority of the logic for the application components separated from their hardware-specific implementation improves portability across different platforms, and allows us to change the peripherals and the interfaces used on the target even during the development phase. Abstracting too much, though, impacts costs, in terms of development effort and resources needed, so the right balance should be researched.

Hardware abstraction

General-purpose prototyping platforms are built and distributed by silicon manufacturers to evaluate microcontrollers and peripherals, so part of the software development may be often performed on these devices even before the design of the final product begins.

The software that can be run on the evaluation board is usually distributed as reference implementation, in the form of source code or proprietary precompiled libraries. These libraries can be configured and adapted for the final target, so they can be used as reference hardware abstraction from the beginning, and their settings updated to match changes in the hardware configuration.

On our reference target, the support for the hardware components of a generic Cortex-M microcontroller is provided in the form of a library called **Cortex Microcontroller Software Interface Standard** (**CMSIS**), distributed by ARM as a reference implementation. Silicon manufacturers derive their specific hardware abstractions by extending CMSIS. An application linked to a target-specific hardware abstraction can access peripherals through its specific API calls, and core MCU functionalities through CMSIS.

For code to be portable across different MCUs in the same family, drivers may require an additional level of abstraction on top of the vendor-specific API calls. If the HAL implements multiple targets, it can provide the same API to access generic features across multiple platforms, hiding the hardware-specific implementation under the hood. The goal of CMSIS and other free software alternatives, such as **libopencm3** and **unicore-mx**, is to group together all the generic Cortex-M abstractions and the vendor-specific code for the most common Cortex-M silicon manufacturers, while masking the difference among platform-specific calls when controlling the system and the peripherals.

Regardless of the hardware abstraction, some of the code required at the earliest stage of the boot is very specific to each target the software is intended to run on. Each platform has its own specific address space segmentation, interrupt vector, and configuration registers displacement. This means that while working on code that is supposed to be portable among different platforms, makefiles and scripts automating the build must be configurable to link using the correct startup code and linker scripts.

The examples contained in this book do not depend on any specific hardware abstraction, as they are aimed to introduce the control of the system components by directly interacting with the system registers, implementing platform-specific device drivers while focusing on the interaction with the hardware component.

Middleware

Some of the features may already have a well-known solution that has been previously implemented by a single developer, a community, or an enterprise. Solutions may be generic, or perhaps designed for a different platform, or even coming from outside the embedded world. In any case, it is always worth looking for libraries for any data transformation, protocol implementation, or subsystem model that might already have been coded and is waiting to be integrated in our project.

A number of open source libraries and software components are ready be included in embedded projects and allow us to implement a broader set of functionalities. Integrating components from open source projects is particularly useful to deliver standard functionalities. There is a vast choice of well-established open source implementations designed for embedded devices that can be easily integrated on embedded projects. These include:

- Real-time operating systems
- Cryptography libraries
- TCP/IP, 6LoWPAN, and other network protocols
- **Transport Layer Security (TLS)** libraries
- Filesystems
- IoT message queue protocols
- Parsers

Some components from these categories are described in more detail later in this book.

Basing the software upon an operating system allows us to manage memory areas and thread execution. In this case, threads execute independently from each other, and it is even possible to implement memory separation among threads, and between running threads and the kernel. This approach is advisable when the complexity of the design increases, or when there are well-known blocking points in the modules that cannot be redesigned. If an operating system is used, other libraries usually require multithreading support, which can be enabled at compile time if present.

The decision of integrating third-party libraries must be evaluated by measuring the resources needed, in terms of code size and memory used, to perform specific tasks on the target platform. As the whole firmware is distributed as a single executable file, all the licenses of the components must be compatible, and the integration must not violate the license terms of any of its single components.

Application code

The role of the application code is to coordinate, from the highest layer in the project design, all the modules involved, and orchestrate the heuristics of the system. A clean main module that is well-designed allows us to keep a clear view of all the macroscopic blocks of the system, how they are related to each other, and the timing of execution of the various components.

Bare-metal applications are built around a main endless loop function, which is in charge of distributing the CPU time among the entry points of the underlying libraries and drivers. The execution happens sequentially, so the code cannot be suspended, except by interrupt handlers. For this reason, all the functions and library calls invoked from the main loop are supposed to return as fast as possible, because stall points hidden inside other modules may compromise the reactivity of the system, or even block forever, with the risk of never returning to the main loop. Ideally, in a bare-metal system, every component is designed to interact with the main loop using the event-driven paradigm, with a main loop constantly waiting for events, and mechanisms to register callbacks to wake up the application on specific events.

The advantage of the bare-metal, single-thread approach is that synchronization among threads is not needed, all the memory is accessible by any function in the code, and it is not necessary to implement complex mechanisms, such as context and execution model switches.

If multiple tasks are meant to run on top of an operating system, each task should be confined as much as possible within its own module, and explicitly export its start function and public variables as global symbols. In this case, tasks can sleep and call blocking functions, which should implement the OS-specific blocking mechanisms. Thanks to the flexibility of the Cortex-M CPU, there are different degrees of threads and process separation that can be activated on the system. The CPU offers multiple tools to facilitate the development of multithreading systems with separation among tasks, multiple execution modes, kernel-specific registers, privilege separation, and memory-segmentation techniques. These options allow architects to define complex systems, more oriented to general-purpose applications, which offer privilege separation and memory segmentation among processes, but also smaller, simpler, more straightforward systems, which don't need these as they are generally designed for a single purpose.

Selecting an executing model that is based on non-privileged threads results in a much more complex implementation of the context changes in the system, and may impact the latency of the real-time operations, which is the reason why bare-metal, single-threaded solutions are still preferred for most real-time applications.

The life cycle of an embedded project

Modern development frameworks, such as agile software development methodologies, recommend, among other best practices, splitting the work into smaller action points, and marking milestones through the project development, producing intermediate working deliverables. Each deliverable focuses on giving a prototype of the entire system, with the missing features temporarily replaced using dummy code.

These recommendations seem particularly effective on embedded projects. In an environment where every error could be fatal to the entire system, working on small action points, one at a time, is an efficient way to promptly identify defects and regressions while working on the code base, provided that a CI mechanism is in place from the early stages of the development. Intermediate milestones should be as frequent as possible, and for this reason, it is advisable to create a prototype of the final system as soon as possible in the development phase. This has to be taken into account when actions are identified, prioritized, and distributed to the team.

Once the steps to reach the goal are defined, we need to find the optimal sequence to produce working prototypes for the intermediate milestones. The dependencies among the development actions are taken into account to sort the priorities for the assignments of the work.

Facing unexpected issues along the path, a progressive understanding of the system behavior and hardware constraints may change the view on the architecture of the system while it is under development. Changing specifications as a reaction to measurements and evaluations performed on the intermediate prototype may require a major code rework. Throwing away consistent parts of the project to replace them with a new, improved design is often definitely beneficial for the quality of the project and may result in improved productivity in the later stages. This process, known as **refactoring**, must not be seen as development overhead whenever it is aimed to improve the design and behavior of the system.

Finally, the process of creating system software includes the necessity of defining a clear API for the applications to be able to interact with the system in the desired way. Embedded system provide specific APIs to access system resources most of the time, however, some operating systems and libraries may provide POSIX-like interfaces to access functionalities. In any case, the API is the entry point for the system interfaces, and must be designed for usability and well documented.

Defining project steps

When analyzing the specifications, defining the required steps, and assigning priorities, several factors may have to be taken into account. Consider having to design an air quality monitor device, with a PM10 air quality serial sensor, which collects the measurements done hourly into the internal flash, then transmits all the statistics daily to a gateway using a wireless transceiver. The target system is a custom board based on Cortex-M MCU, which is adequately sized to run the final software. The final hardware design will not be available until some real-life measurements are done on the transceiver transmitting data to the gateway.

The list of steps to be performed to reach the final goal, resulting from these specifications, may look like the following:

1. Boot a minimal system on the target (empty main loop)
2. Set up serial port 0 for logging
3. Set up serial port 1 for the communication to the sensor
4. Set up a timer
5. Write the PM10 sensor driver
6. Application that wakes up every hour and reads from sensor
7. Write flash submodule to store/restore measurements
8. Set up an SPI port to communicate to the radio chip
9. Write the radio driver
10. Implement protocol to communicate with the gateway
11. Every 24 measurements, the application sends daily measurements to the gateway

Note that some of the steps may depend on others, so there are constraints on the order of execution. Some of these dependencies can be removed by using simulators or emulators. For example, we might want to implement the communication protocol without having a working radio only if there is a way to test the protocol against the agent running on the gateway by using a simulated radio channel on the gateway itself. Keeping the modules self-contained and with a minimal set of API calls exposed to the outside makes it easier to detach the single modules to run and test them on different architectures, and under a controlled environment, before integrating them on the target system.

Prototyping

As it is part of the specifications, we know that we should prioritize the activities related to the radio communication to allow the hardware team to progress on the design, so in this case, the first prototype must:

- Boot a minimal system on the target (empty main loop)
- Set up serial port 0 for logging
- Set up an SPI port to communicate to the radio chip
- Write the radio driver
- Set up the timer
- Write the main application to test the radio channel (sending raw packets at regular intervals)

This first prototype will already start to look like the final device, even if it does not know how to communicate with the sensor yet. Some test cases can already be implemented to run on a mock gateway, checking that messages are received and valid.

Moving ahead to the next prototype definition, we can start by adding a few additional features. Real sensor readings are not necessary to progress on the protocol with the gateway, as it is possible to use constant test values instead. This allows us to progress on other tasks when the real hardware is not available.

Whether the development team is adopting pure agile software development, or is working with a different methodology, fast prototyping in an embedded development environment allows to respond faster to the uncertainties on the path, which often depend on the behavior of the hardware and the actions that need to be taken in software.

Providing workable intermediate deliverables is a common practice in embedded development teams, which directly derives from the agile methodologies. Agile software development foresees the delivery of working software on a regular basis, and within short intervals of time. Like in the preceding example, an intermediate prototype does not have to implement all the logic of the final software image, but instead must be used to prove concepts, make measurements, or provide examples on top of a reduced part of the system.

Refactoring

Too often considered a drastic remedy for a failure, refactoring is actually a healthy practice that improves the software while the system takes its final shape, and the support for software components and the peripherals evolves through time.

Refactoring works better if all the tests are up and running on the old code. Unit tests should be adapted to the new function signatures while redesigning the module internals. On the other hand, existing functional tests for the module that is being refactored should not change if the API of the module stays unchanged, and will provide continuous feedback about the status and the accuracy of the process, as long as the interface towards other modules remains the same.

Smaller portions of the code base are exponentially easier to refactor than larger ones, which gives us yet another reason to keep each module small and dedicated to a specific function on the system. Progressing through intermediate deliverable prototypes implies constant alterations in the application code, which should requires less effort when the subsystems are designed to be independent from each other and from the application code itself.

API and documentation

We all know that a book should not be judged by its cover. However, a system can often be judged by its API, which may reveal many aspects of the internal implementation and the design choices of the system architects. A clear, readable, and easy-to-understand API is one of the most important features for an embedded system. Application developers expect to understand how to access functionalities quickly, to use the system in the most efficient way possible. The API represents the *contract* between the system and the applications, and for this reason, it must be designed beforehand and modified as little as possible, if at all, while the development moves towards the final delivery.

Some interfaces in the API may describe complex subsystems and abstract more elaborate characteristics, so it is always a good idea to provide adequate documentation to help application developers move around and exploit all the system capabilities. There are different ways to provide documentation along with the code, either distributing user manuals in the repository as separate files, or including the explanation of the different interfaces directly in the code.

The amount of comments in the code is not an indicator of quality. Comments have a tendency to *age* whenever the code they refer to gets modified, because of the possibility that the developer forgets to update the comment to match the new behavior in the code. Moreover, not all code needs to be commented: good habits, such as keeping functions short and low in complexity or using expressive symbol names, would make code comments redundant in most cases, as the code can explain itself. There are exceptions for lines of code that contain complex calculations, bit shifting, elaborate conditions, or side effects that are not easy to spot when reading the code for the first time. Some portions of code may also require a description at the beginning, for example, those functions with multiple return values and specific error handling. Switch/case statements not containing the break instruction between two cases must always have a comment to indicate that the fall-through is intended, and not a mistake. They should also possibly explain why some actions are grouped together between two or more cases. Adding superfluous comments that do not provide any valuable explanation of the code only contributes to make the code itself harder to read.

On the other hand, describing the behavior of a module with a separate editor and tools requires dedication, as all the documentation must be updated every time there are significant changes in the code, and the developers are asked to switch the focus away from the actual code.

Usually, the important part to document is the description of the contract mentioned previously, enumerating and explaining the functions and the variables that the applications and the other components involved can access at runtime. Since these declarations can be grouped within header files, it is possible to describe the entire contract by adding extended comments on top of the declaration of each exported symbol. Software tools exist that convert these comments into formatted documentation. A popular example is **Doxygen**, a free and open source document-generation tool that parses comments matching a specific syntax in the whole code base to produce hypertexts, structured PDF manuals, and many other formats. If the documentation is in the code base, updating and keeping track of its results is easier and less invasive for the developers' workflow. Integrating the generation of the documentation on the automation server can provide a freshly generated copy of the manuals for all the APIs at every commit on the master branch.

Summary

The methodologies that have been proposed are meant as an example of reference patterns used to design and manage the development of embedded projects. While it is possible that some of the patterns described may not apply to all projects, the goal of this chapter is to encourage embedded architects to look for improvements in the process that may result in a more efficient and less expensive software life cycle.

In the next chapter, we'll analyze what happens at boot time inside the embedded system, and how to prepare a bootable application using a simple, bare-metal, main-loop approach.

4
The Boot-Up Procedure

Now that mechanisms, tools, and methodologies are in place, it is finally time to start looking at the procedures required to run the software on the target. Booting up an embedded system is a process that often requires knowledge of the specific system, and the mechanisms in play. Depending on the target, there are a few indications we need to look for in the manual to find out what the system expects from the developer to successfully boot executables from the flash memory. This chapter focuses on the description of the boot process, with emphasis on the case of the Cortex-M microcontroller, which we decided to use as a reference platform. In particular, it covers:

- The interrupt vector table
- Memory layout
- Building and running the boot code
- Multiple boot stages

The interrupt vector table

The **interrupt vector table**, often abbreviated to **IVT** or simply **IV**, is an array of pointers to functions, associated by the CPU to handle specific *exceptions*, such as faults, system service requests from the application, and interrupt requests from peripherals. The IVT is usually located at the beginning of the binary image, and thus stored starting from the lowest address in the flash memory.

An interrupt request from a hardware component or peripheral will force the CPU to abruptly suspend the execution, and execute the function at the associated position in the vector. For this reason, these functions are called **interrupt service routines** (or simply **ISR**). Runtime exceptions and faults can be handled in the same way as hardware interrupts, so special service routines are associated to internal CPU triggers through the same table.

The order of the ISR enumerated in the vector and their exact positions depend on the CPU architecture, the microcontroller model, and the peripherals supported. Each interrupt line corresponds to a predefined interrupt number and, depending on the microcontroller features, may be assigned a priority.

In a Cortex-M microcontroller, the first 16 positions in memory are reserved to store the pointers to system handlers, that are architecture dependent, associated to different types of CPU runtime exceptions. The lowest address is used to store the initial value of the stack pointer, and the next 15 positions are reserved for system services and fault handlers. However, some of these positions are reserved and not connected to any event. The system exceptions that can be handled using separate service routines in a Cortex-M CPU are:

- Reset
- NMI
- Hard fault
- Memory exceptions
- Bus fault
- Usage fault
- Supervisor call
- Debug monitor
- PendSV call
- System tick

The order of the hardware interrupts, starting from position 16, depends on the microcontroller configuration, and thus on the specific silicon model, as the interrupt configuration refers to specific components, interfaces, and external peripheral activities.

A fully populated vector of external interrupt handlers for STM32F407 and LM3S targets can be found in the examples repository online.

Startup code

In order to boot a workable system, we need to define the interrupt vector, and associate pointers to defined functions. A typical startup code file for our reference platform places the interrupt vector in a dedicated section, using the GCC attribute `section`. As the section will be put at the beginning of the image, we must define our interrupt vector starting with the reserved space for the initial stack pointer, followed by the system exception handlers.

The zeros correspond to the positions of the reserved/unused slots:

```c
__attribute__ ((section(".isr_vector")))
void (* const IV[])(void) =
{
    (void (*)(void))(END_STACK),
    isr_reset,
    isr_nmi,
    isr_hard_fault,
    isr_mem_fault,
    isr_bus_fault,
    isr_usage_fault,
    0, 0, 0, 0,
    isr_svc,
    isr_dbgmon,
    0,
    isr_pendsv,
    isr_systick,
```

From this position on, we define the interrupt lines for the external peripherals, such as:

```c
    isr_uart0,
    isr_ethernet,
    /* ... many more external interrupts follow */
};
```

The startup code must also include the implementation of every symbol referenced in the array. The handler can be defined as `void` procedures with no arguments, the same format as the signature of the IV:

```c
void isr_bus_fault(void) {
    /* Bus error. Panic! */
    while(1);
}
```

The interrupt handler in this example never returns, as a result of an unrecoverable bus error, and hangs the system forever. Empty interrupt handlers can be associated to both system and external interrupts using weak symbols that can be overridden in the device driver modules by simply defining them again in the relevant code section.

Reset handler

When the microcontroller is powered on, it starts the execution from the reset handler. This is a special ISR which does not return, but it rather performs initialization of the .data and .bss sections, and then calls the entry point of the application. The initialization of the .data and .bss sections consists of copying the initial value of the variables in the .data section in flash onto the actual section in RAM where variables are accessed at runtime, and filling the .bss section in RAM with zeros, so that the initial value of static symbols is guaranteed to be zero as per C convention.

Source and destination addresses of the .data and .bss sections in RAM are computed by the linker when generating the binary image, and exported as pointers using the linker script. The implementation of isr_reset may look similar to the following:

```
void isr_reset(void)
{
    unsigned int *src, *dst;
    src = (unsigned int *) &_stored_data;
    dst = (unsigned int *) &_start_data;
    while (dst != (unsigned int *)&_end_data) {
        *dst = *src;
        dst++;
        src++;
    }
    dst = &_start_bss;
    while (dst != (unsigned int *)&_end_bss) {
        *dst = 0;
        dst++;
    }
    main();
}
```

Once the variables in the .bss and .data section have been initialized, it is finally possible to call the main function, which is the entry point of the application. The application code ensures that main never returns, by implementing an infinite loop.

Allocating the stack

In order to comply with the **application binary interface (ABI)** of the CPU, it is required to assign space in memory for the execution stack. This can be done in different ways, but usually it is preferable to mark the end of the stack space in the linker script, and associate the stack space to a specific area in RAM not in use by any section.

The address obtained through the END_STACK symbol, exported by the linker script, points to the end of an unused area in RAM. As mentioned earlier, its value must be stored at the beginning of the vector table, at address 0 in our case, just before the IV. The address of the end of the stack has to be constant, and cannot be calculated at runtime, because the IV content is stored in the flash memory and thus cannot be modified later on.

Properly sizing the execution stack in memory is a delicate task that includes the assessment of the whole code base, keeping in mind stack usage from local variables and the depth of the call trace at any time during the execution. The analysis of all the factors related to stack usage and troubleshooting are part of a wider topic that is covered in the next chapter. Our simple startup code provided here has a stack size that is big enough to contain the local variables and the functions call stack, as it is mapped by the linker script as far as possible from the .bss and .data sections. More aspects about the placement of the stack are considered through Chapter 5, *Memory Management*.

Fault handlers

Fault-related events are triggered by the CPU in the case of execution errors, or policy violations. The CPU is able to detect a number of runtime errors such as:

- Attempting to execute code outside the memory areas marked as executable
- Fetching data or next instruction to execute from an invalid location
- Illegal load or store using an unaligned address
- Division by zero
- Trying to access unavailable coprocessor functionalities
- Attempting to read/write/execute outside the memory areas allowed for the current running mode

Some core microcontrollers support different types of exceptions depending on the type of error. Cortex-M3/M4 is able to distinguish among bus errors, usage faults, memory access violations and generic faults, triggering the related exception. In other, smaller systems, fewer details are available on the type of runtime error.

Very often, a fault will make the system unusable or unable to continue the execution, due to the CPU register values or the stack being corrupted. In some cases, even placing a breakpoint inside the exception handler is not sufficient to detect the cause of the problem, making the debugging harder. Some CPUs support extended information on the cause of the fault, which is available through memory-mapped registers after the exception occurs. In the case of Cortex-M3/M4, this information is available through the **Configurable Fault Status Register** (**CFSR**), which is mapped at address `0xE000ED28` on all Cortex-M3/M4 CPUs.

Memory violations may be non-fatal if the corresponding exception handler implements some kind of recovery strategy, and can be useful to detect and react to the fault at runtime, which is especially useful in multithreaded environments, as we will see in more detail in `Chapter 9`, *Distributed Systems and IoT Architecture*.

Memory layout

The linker script, as we already know, contains the instructions for the linker on how to assemble together the components of an embedded system. More specifically, it describes the sections mapped in memory and how they are deployed into the flash and the RAM of the target, as in the example provided in `Chapter 2`, *Work Environment and Workflow Optimization*.

In most embedded devices, and in particular our reference platform, the `.text` area, which contains all the executable code, should include the special subsection dedicated to store the IV at the very beginning of the executable image.

We integrate the linker script by adding the `.isr_vector` section at the beginning of `.text` area, before the rest of the code:

```
.text :
{
    *(.isr_vector)
    *(.text*)
    *(.rodata*)
} > FLASH
```

Defining a read-only section in flash which is dedicated to the vector table is the only strict requirement for our system to boot up properly, as the address of the `isr_reset` function is retrieved by the CPU at boot time from address `0x04` in memory.

Right after the definition for the text and read-only areas in flash, the linker script should export the value of the current address, which is the beginning of the .data section stored in flash. This area contains the initial value of all the global and static variables that have been initialized in the code. In the example linker script, the beginning of the .data section is marked by the linker script variable _stored_data, as follows:

```
_stored_data = .;
```

The data section will eventually be mapped in RAM, but its initialization is done manually in the isr_reset function by copying the content from flash to the actual .data region in RAM. The linker script provides a mechanism to separate the **Virtual Memory Address (VMA)** and the **Load Memory Address (LMA)** for a section, using the keyword AT in the definition of the section. If no AT word is specified, the LMA is by default set to the same address as the VMA. In our case, the VMA of the .data region is in RAM, and exported using the _start_data pointer, which will be used by the isr_vector as destination address when copying the values of the symbols stored from flash. The LMA of .data, though, is located in the flash memory, so we set the LMA address to the _stored_data pointer in flash while defining the .data region:

```
.data : AT (_stored_data)
{
    _start_data = .;
    *(.data*)
    . = ALIGN(4);
    _end_data = .;
} > RAM
```

For .bss, there is no LMA, as no data is stored in the image for this section. When including the .bss region, its VMA will automatically be set to the end of the .data section:

```
.bss :
{
    _start_bss = .;
    *(.bss*)
    . = ALIGN(4);
    _end_bss = .;
    _end = .;
} > RAM
```

Finally, in this design, the linker is expected to provide the initial value for the execution stack. Using the highest address in memory is a common choice for a single-threaded application, even though, as discussed in the next chapter, this may cause problems in the case of stack overflow. For this example, however, this is an acceptable solution, and we define the symbol END_STACK by adding the following line to the linker script:

```
END_STACK = ORIGIN(RAM) + LENGTH(RAM);
```

To better understand where each symbol will be placed in memory, variable definitions can be added to the startup file in different places within the code. This way, we can check the locations where the variables are stored in memory when running the executable in the debugger for the first time. Supposing that we have variables stored in both the .data and .bss sections, the memory layout for the example startup code may look like the following:

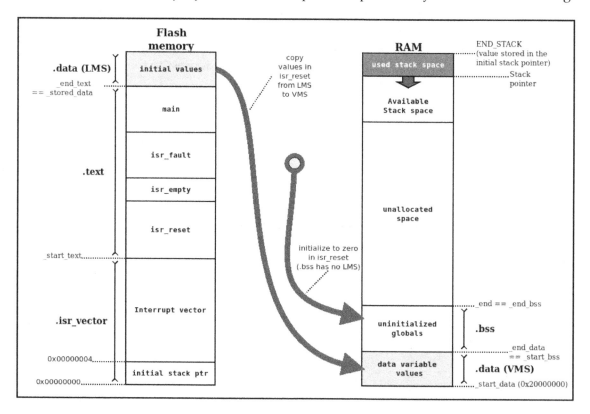

Memory layout in the example startup code

When the executable is linked, the symbols are automatically set at compile time to indicate the beginning and the end of each section in memory. In our case, variables indicating the beginning and the end of each section are automatically assigned to the right value, depending on the size of the sections that the linker will include when creating the executable. Since the size of each section is known at compile time, the linker is able to identify those situations where the .text and .data do not fit into the flash, and a linker error is generated at the end of the build. Creating a .map file is useful to check the size and the location of each symbol. In our boot-up example code, here is how the .text section appears within the .map file:

```
.text 0x0000000000000000 0x168
0x0000000000000000 _start_text = .
*(.isr_vector)
.isr_vector 0x0000000000000000 0xf0 startup.o
0x0000000000000000 IV
*(.text*)
.text 0x00000000000000f0 0x78 startup.o
0x00000000000000f0 isr_reset
0x0000000000000134 isr_fault
0x000000000000013a isr_empty
0x0000000000000146 main
```

Similarly, we can find the boundaries of each section, exported by the linker script at compile time:

```
0x0000000000000000 _start_text = .
0x0000000000000168 _end_text = .
0x0000000020000000 _start_data = .
0x0000000020000004 _end_data = .
0x0000000020000004 _start_bss = .
0x0000000020000328 _end_bss = .
0x0000000020000328 _end = .
```

The section .rodata, which is empty in this minimalist example, is mapped in the flash memory area, in between .text and the data LMA. This is reserved for constant symbols, because constants do not have to be mapped in RAM. It is advisable to enforce the C modifier const when defining constant symbols, because RAM is often our most precious resource, and in some cases even sparing a few bytes of writable memory by moving constant symbols to the flash can make the difference in the project development, as flash memory is usually much bigger, and its usage can be easily determined at linking time.

Building and running the boot code

The example provided here is one of the simplest executable images that can be run on the target. To assemble, compile and link everything together, we can use a simple makefile that automates all the steps and allows us to focus on our software life cycle.

When the image is ready, we can transfer it to the real target, or alternatively, run it using an emulator.

The makefile

A very basic makefile to build our startup application describes the final target (`image.bin`) and the intermediate steps required to build it. Makefile syntax is in general very vast, and covering all the functions provided by **Make** is outside the scope of this book. However, the few concepts explained here should be sufficient to get up and running on automating the build process.

The typical syntax to define a `target` in the makefile is:

```
target: dependencies
    recipe
```

A `target` is the name of the output file being built, followed by `:`. Dependencies are input files, expected to be found, and checked for existence when Make is invoked. If any of the files listed among dependencies is not available, or is newer than the target itself, Make will look for another `target` that can satisfy that dependency.

Defining the targets for our makefile in this case is quite simple. The source file `startup.c`, containing the IV, some exception handlers, the main and the global variables we used in the example, can be compiled and assembled into an object file `startup.o`. The linker uses the indications provided in the linker script `target.ld` to deploy the symbols in the correct sections, producing the executable image `.elf`.

Finally, `objcopy` is used to transform the `.elf` executable into a binary image, which can be transferred to the target, or run using QEMU:

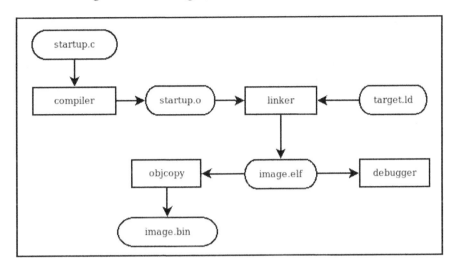

Build steps and dependencies

The makefile should contain a few configuration variables to describe the toolchain. The assignment operator = allows you to set values for the variables when invoking the `make` command. Some of these variables are implicitly used during compilation and linking, unless a recipe for the target is explicitly given. It is common practice to define the toolchain prefix using the `CROSS_COMPILE` variable, and use that as a prefix for the tools involved in the build process:

```
CROSS_COMPILE=arm-none-eabi-
CC=$(CROSS_COMPILE)gcc
LD=$(CROSS_COMPILE)ld
OBJCOPY=$(CROSS_COMPILE)objcopy
```

Changing the default cross compiler for this project can be done by running `make` and assigning a different `CROSS_COMPILE`. All the names of the tools are prefixed by the `CROSS_COMPILE` variable expansion, so that the build steps will use the components from the given toolchain. In the same way, we can define our default flags for the compiler and the linker:

```
CFLAGS=-mcpu=cortex-m3 -mthumb -g -ggdb -Wall -Wno-main
LDFLAGS=-T target.ld -gc-sections -nostdlib -Map=image.map
```

When invoked with no arguments, Make builds the first target defined in the makefile, `image.bin`. A new target for `image.bin` can be defined as follows:

```
image.bin: image.elf
    $(OBJCOPY) -O binary $^ $@
```

The variables `$@` and `$^` will be replaced in the recipe with the target and the list of dependencies, respectively. This means that, in the example, the makefile will process the recipe as:

```
arm-none-eabi-objcopy -O binary image.elf image.bin
```

This is the command we need to produce a raw binary image from the `.elf` executable.

Similarly, we can define the recipe for `image.elf`, which is the linking step, depending on the compiled object file `startup.o`, and the linker script:

```
image.elf: startup.o target.ld
    $(LD) $(LDFLAGS) startup.o -o $@
```

In this case, we are not going to use the `$^` variable for the list of dependencies, as the recipe includes the linker script in the linker command line using `LDFLAGS`. The recipe for the linking step will be expanded by `main` as:

```
arm-none-eabi-ld -T target.ld -gc-sections -nostdlib -Map=image.map
startup.o -o image.elf
```

Using `-nostdlib` ensures that no default C libraries are linked automatically to the project, among those available in the toolchain, that would by default be linked in to produce the executables. This ensures that no symbols are automatically pulled.

The last step for resolving dependencies is compiling the source code into the object file. This target can have an implicit recipe that is automatically expanded. So, to generate the target file `startup.o`, Make will implicitly look for the file `startup.c`. The recipe gets implicitly defined as:

```
$(CC) -c -o $@ $^ $(CFLAGS)
```

This in turn gets translated to the following, when using the project default values:

```
arm-none-eabi-gcc -c -o startup.o startup.c -mcpu=cortex-m3 -mthumb -g -
ggdb -Wall -Wno-main
```

Using the `-mcpu=cortex-m3` flag ensures that the code produced is compatible with Cortex-M targets from Cortex-M3 on. The same binary can in fact eventually be run on any Cortex-M3, M4, or M7 target, and it is generic until we do not decide to use any CPU-specific feature, or define hardware interrupt handlers, as the order of those depends on the specific microcontroller.

By defining a `clean` target, at any point in time it is possible to start over from a clean slate, by removing the intermediate targets and the final image and running `make` again. The `clean` target is also often included in the same makefile. In our example it looks as follows:

```
clean:
    rm -f image.bin image.elf *.o image.map
```

The target `clean` usually has no dependencies. Running `make clean` removes all the intermediate and final targets as instructed in the recipe, leaving the sources and the linker script untouched.

Running the application

Once the image is built, we can run it on a real target or using `qemu-system-arm`, as explained in `Chapter 2`, *Work Environment and Workflow Optimization*. Since the application will produce no output while running on the emulator, to investigate more on the actual behavior of the software it is required to attach a debugger to it. When running the emulator, `qemu-system-arm` must be invoked with the `-S` option, meaning stop, so that it will not start the execution until the debugger is connected. Since the `CFLAGS` variable in the previous step contains the `-g` option, all the symbol names will be kept in the `.elf` so that the debugger can follow the execution through the code line by line, placing breakpoints and checking the values for the variables.

Following the procedures step by step, and comparing addresses and values with those in the `.map` files, can be helpful to understand what is happening and how the context changes through the entire boot sequence.

Multiple boot stages

Booting a target through a bootloader is useful in several cases. In a real-life scenario, being able to update the running software on devices in a remote location means that developers are able to fix bugs and introduce new features after the first version of the embedded system has been deployed.

This represents a huge advantage for maintenance when a bug is discovered in the field, or when the software has to be re-engineered to adapt to changes in requirements. Bootloaders may implement automatic remote upgrade and other useful features, such as:

- Loading of the application image from an external storage
- Verification of the integrity of the application image before boot
- Failover mechanisms in case of corrupted application

Multiple bootloaders can be chained to perform a multiple-stage boot sequence. This allows you to have separate software images for the multiple boot stages, which can be uploaded to the flash independently. A first-stage boot, when present, is usually very simple and used to simply select the entry point for the next stage. However, in some cases, early stages benefit from slightly more complex designs to implement software upgrade mechanisms or other features. The example proposed here shows the separation between two boot stages, achieved using the functionalities available in many Cortex-M processors. The only purpose of this simple bootloader is to initialize the system for booting the application in the next stage.

Bootloader

The first stage bootloader starts up as a normal standalone application. Its IV must be located at the beginning of the flash, and the `reset` handler initializes the associated `.data` and `.bss` memory sections, like in a normal single-stage boot. A partition at the beginning of the flash should be reserved for the bootloader `.text` and `.data` sections. To do so, the linker script for the bootloader will only include the beginning of the flash memory, and that of the application will have an offset of the same size.

The bootloader and the application will be in fact built into two separate binaries. This way, the two linker scripts can have the same name for sections, and differ only by the description of the `FLASH` partition in the linker memory. Nevertheless, the method suggested next is only one of the possible configurations: a more complex setup may benefit from exporting the full geometry using start addresses and sizes of all the partitions.

If we want to reserve 4 KB for the bootloader partition, we can hardcode the `FLASH` area in the bootloader linker script as follows:

```
FLASH (rx) : ORIGIN = 0x00000000, LENGTH = 0x00001000
```

Similarly, the linker script of the application has an offset in the origin, hardcoded to the size of the bootloader, so that the `.text` section of the application always starts at the address `0x1000`. From the application point of view, the whole `FLASH` area starts from address `0x00001000`:

```
FLASH (rx) : ORIGIN = 0x00001000, LENGTH = 0x0003F000
```

The geometry of the flash in this case would be the following:

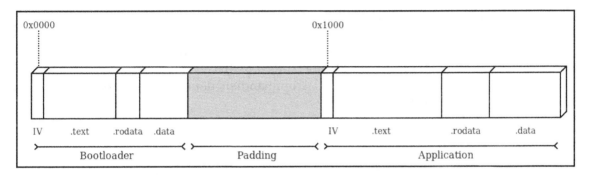

Layout of the flash content, showing the sections of both Bootloader and Application

Bootloader and **Application** run separate code, and both can define their own **IV**, based on the handler that will be used in the respective stage. The simplest example of a working bootloader can be realized by hardcoding the address of the application, and jumping to the entry point, being the `reset` handler in the IV of the application, stored with offset 4 inside the vector table.

The application may enforce its own memory layout. At startup it will be able to initialize the new `.data` and `.bss` sections according to the new geometry, and even define a new initial stack pointer and IV. The bootloader can obtain these two pointers by reading the first two words of the IV stored at address `0x1000`:

```
uint32_t app_end_stack = (*((uint32_t *)(APP_OFFSET)));
void (* app_entry)(void);
app_entry = (void *)(*((uint32_t *)(APP_OFFSET + 4)));
```

Before jumping to the entry point of the application, we want to reset the main execution stack pointer to the end address of the stack. Since MSP is a special-purpose CPU register in the ARMv7-M architecture, it can only be written using the assembly instruction **move special from register (msr)**. The following code is inlined in the bootloader to set the correct application stack pointer to the value stored in flash at the beginning of the application image:

```
asm volatile("msr msp, %0" ::"r"(app_end_stack));
```

In Cortex-M3 and other, more powerful, 32-bit Cortex-M CPUs, a control register is present within the system control block area, which can be used to specify an offset for the vector table at runtime. This is the **Vector Table Offset Register (VTOR)**, which is located at address `0xE000ED08`. Writing the application offset to this register means that, from that moment, the new IV is in place and the interrupt handlers defined in the application will be executed upon exceptions:

```
uint32_t * VTOR = (uint32_t *)0xE000ED08;
*VTOR = (uint32_t *)(APP_OFFSET);
```

When this mechanism is not available, like in Cortex-M0 microcontrollers which do not have a VTOR, the application will still share the interrupt vector with the bootloader after it is started. To provide a different set of interrupt handlers, the relevant function pointers can be stored in a different area of the flash, and the bootloader can check whether the application had been started or not at every interrupt, and in case it was, call the respective handler from the table in the application space.

When handling pointers to interrupt handlers and other exception routines, it is important to consider that an exception can occur at any time while running the code, especially if the bootloader has enabled peripherals or activated timers in the CPU. To prevent unpredictable jumps to interrupt routine, it is advisable to disable all the interrupts while the pointers are being updated.

The instruction set provides mechanisms to temporarily mask all the interrupts. While running with interrupt globally disabled, the execution cannot be interrupted by any exception, excluding NMI. In Cortex-M, interrupts can be temporarily disabled by using the assembly statement `cpsid i`:

```
asm volatile ("cpsid i");
```

To enable the interrupt again, the `cpsie i` instruction is used:

```
asm volatile ("cpsie i");
```

Running code with interrupts disabled should be done as much as strictly necessary, and only in special cases where other solutions are not available, because it impacts on the latency of the entire system. In this special case, it is used to ensure that no service routines are invoked while the IV is being relocated.

The last action performed by the bootloader in its short life is a direct jump to the reset handler in the application IV. Since the function will never return, and a brand new stack space has been just allocated, we force an unconditional jump by setting the value CPU program counter register to start executing from the address of app_entry, that is pointed by the isr_reset:

```
asm volatile("mov pc, %0" :: "r"(app_entry));
```

In our example, this function will never return, since we replaced the execution stack pointer value. This is compatible with the behavior foreseen by the reset handler, which will in turn jump to the main function in the application.

Building the image

Since the two executables will be built in separate .elf files, there are mechanisms to join the content of the two partitions together into a single image, to upload to the target or to use in the emulator. The bootloader partition can be filled with zeros upto its size by using the --pad-to option of objcopy when converting from the .elf executable to the binary image. Wearing the flash can be reduced by using the value 0xFF to fill the padding area, which can be obtained by passing the option --gap-fill=0xFF. The resultant bootloader.bin will be exactly 4096 bytes, so that application image can be concatenated at the end of it. The steps to compose an image containing the two partitions are the following:

```
$ arm-none-eabi-objcopy -O binary --pad-to=4096 --gap-fill=0xFF
bootloader.elf bootloader.bin
$ arm-none-eabi-objcopy -O binary app.elf app.bin
$ cat bootloader.bin app.bin > image.bin
```

Looking at the resultant image.bin file with a hexadecimal editor, it should be possible to identify the end of the bootloader within the first partition by recognizing the zero pattern that is used by objdump as padding, and the application code starting at address 0x1000.

By aligning the application offset to the start of a physical page in flash instead, it is even possible to upload the two images in separate steps, allowing you for instance to upgrade the application code, leaving the bootloader partition untouched.

Debugging a multi-stage system

The separation between two or more stages implies that the symbols of the two executables are linked into different .elf files. Debugging using both sets of symbols is still possible, but the symbols from both .elf files must be loaded in the debugger in two steps. When the debugger is executed using the symbols from the bootloader, by adding the bootloader.elf file as an argument, or using the file command from the GDB command line, the symbols of the bootloader are loaded in the symbol table for the debugging session. To add the symbols from the application .elf file, we can add the corresponding .elf at a later stage, using add-symbol-file.

The directive add-symbol-file, unlike file, ensures that the symbols of a second executable are loaded without overwriting the ones previously loaded, and it requires to specify the address where the .text section is stored in the application .elf file as argument. In the system composed in this example, there is no clash between the two sets of symbols, as the two partitions do not share any area on the flash. The debugger can continue the execution normally and still have all the symbols available after the bootloader jumps to the application entry point:

```
> add-symbol-file app.elf 0x1000
add symbol table from file "app.elf" at
    .text_addr = 0x1000
(y or n) y
Reading symbols from app.elf...done.
```

Sharing the same names for sections and symbols between the two executables is legal, as the two executables are self-contained and not linked together. The debugger is aware of duplicate names when we refer to a symbol by its name during debug. For example, if we place a breakpoint on main, and we have correctly loaded the symbols from both executables, the breakpoint will be set on both locations:

```
> b main
Breakpoint 1 at 0x14e: main. (2 locations)
> info b
Num Type Disp Enb Address What
1 breakpoint keep y <MULTIPLE>
1.1 y 0x0000014e in main at startup_bl.c:53
1.2 y 0x00001158 in main at startup.c:53
```

Separate boot stages are completely isolated from each other, and do not share any executable code. For this reason, software distributed with different licenses, even if not compatible with each other, can run in separate boot stages. As seen in the example, the two software images can use the same symbol names without creating conflicts, as they would have been running on two separate systems.

In some cases, however, multiple boot stages may have functionalities in common that can be implemented using the same library. Unfortunately, there is no simple way to access the symbols of the library from separate software images. The mechanism described in the next example provides access to shared libraries between the two stages, by storing the symbols needed only once in the flash.

Shared libraries

Suppose that there is a small library providing general-purpose utilities or device drivers, which is in use by both the bootloader and the application. Even when the footprint is small, it is preferable not to have duplicate definitions of the same functions in the flash memory. The library can instead be linked in a dedicated section of the bootloader, and referred to in a later stage. In our preceding two-stage example, we can safely place the API function pointers in an array starting at address $0x400$, which is past the end of the interrupt vector we are currently using. In a real project, the offset must be high enough to be after the actual vector table in memory. The .utils section is placed in the linker script in between the vector table and the start of .text in the bootloader:

```
.text :
{
    _start_text = .;
    KEEP(*(.isr_vector))
    . = 0x400;
    KEEP(*(.utils))
    *(.text*)
    *(.rodata*)
    . = ALIGN(4);
    _end_text = .;
} > FLASH
```

The actual function definitions can be placed in a different source file, and linked in the bootloader. What is actually in the .utils section is a table containing the pointers to the actual address of the functions inside the bootloader .text section:

```
__attribute__((section(".utils"),used))
    static void *utils_interface[4] = {
    (void *)utils_open,
```

```
        (void *)utils_write,
        (void *)utils_read,
        (void *)utils_close
};
```

The layout of the bootloader now has this extra `.utils` section, aligned at address `0x400`, containing a table with the pointers to the library functions that are meant to be exported for use from other stages:

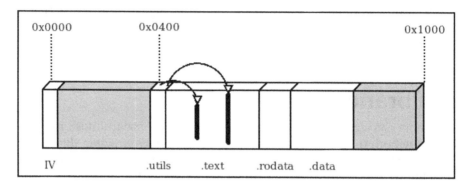

Bootloader partition with the .utils section

The application expects to find the function table at the given address:

```
static void **utils_interface = (void**)(0x00000400);
```

The address of the single functions that have been stored in the bootloader are now available, but there is no information about the signature of these functions. For this reason, the application can only access the API properly if the pointers are converted to match the expected function signature. An inline wrapper can then be provided so that the application code can access the function directly:

```
static inline int utils_read(void *buf, int size) {
    int (*do_read)(void*, int) = (int (*)(void*,int))
    (utils_interface[2]);
    return do_read(buf, size);
}
```

In this case, the contract is implicitly shared between the two modules, and the correspondence between the function signatures is not checked at compile time, nor is the validity of the function pointer stored in flash. On the other hand, it is a valid approach to avoid binary code duplication and might be an effective way to reduce flash usage by sharing symbols across separate contexts.

Summary

Understanding the boot procedure is a key step towards the development of an embedded system. We have seen how to boot straight into the bare-metal application, and we have examined the structures involved in a multi-stage system boot.

In the next chapter, we will explore mechanisms and approaches for memory management, that represent the most important factor to take into account while developing safe and reliable embedded systems.

5
Memory Management

Handling memory is one of the most important tasks for an embedded system programmer, and surely the most delicate to take into account in every phase of the development of the system. This chapter is about the models commonly used to manage the memory in an embedded system, the geometry and the mapping of the memory, and how to prevent issues that could compromise the stability and the safety of the software running on the target. The chapter is divided into four parts:

- Memory mapping
- The execution stack
- Heap management
- The memory protection unit

Memory mapping

Application software usually benefits from a number of abstractions available in the environment, for the handling of memory. In modern operating systems for personal computers, each process can access its own memory space, which can also be relocated by the system, to resize or move memory blocks using a different physical location. Moreover, dynamic memory allocations are possible through virtual memory pools provided by the kernel. Embedded devices do not rely on these mechanisms, as there is no way to assign virtual addresses to physical memory locations. In all contexts and running modes, all the symbols can be accessed only by pointing at physical addresses.

As we have seen in the previous chapter, booting a bare-metal embedded application requires defining the sections at compile time within the assigned regions in the available address space using the linker script. In order to properly configure the memory sections in our embedded software, it is important to analyze the properties of the various regions and the techniques that we can use to organize and manage the memory areas.

Memory model and address space

The total amount of available addresses depends on the size of memory pointers. 32-bit machines can reference a contiguous memory space of 4 GB, which is segmented to host all the memory-mapped devices in the system. This may include:

- Internal RAM
- Flash memory
- System control registers
- Components internal to the microcontroller
- External peripheral bus
- Additional external RAM

Every region has a fixed physical address that may depend on the characteristics of the platform. All the locations are hardcoded, and some of them are platform-specific.

In the ARM Cortex-M, the total addressable space is divided into six macro regions. Depending on their purpose, the regions have different permissions, so that there are areas of memory that can only be accessible for read operations at runtime, or that are not allowed to execute in place. These constraints are implemented in hardware, but might be configurable at runtime on microcontrollers that include an MPU:

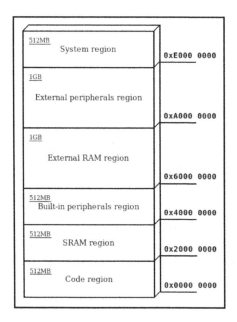

The ARM Cortex-M address space

In general, only small sections (of the same size as physical components) are mapped within these regions. Trying to access memory that is not mapped to any hardware triggers an exception in the CPU. When approaching a target platform, it is important to know the locations and the sizes of the memory sections corresponding to the hardware on board, in order to properly describe the geometry of the available address space in the linker script, and in the source code.

The code region

The lowest 512 MB of the addressing space in a Cortex-M microcontroller is reserved for executable code. Targets that support XIP always map the flash memory within this area, and the memory is generally not writable at runtime. In our previous examples, the `.text` and `.rodata` sections are mapped within this region as they remain constant during the execution of the software. Additionally, the initial values of all non-zero defined symbols are placed in this area and need to be explicitly copied and re-mapped to a writable segment in order to modify their value at runtime. As we already know, the **interrupt vector table (IVT)** is usually located at the beginning of the mapped section, starting at address `0`. Multiple flash memory banks may be mapped into the code region. The regions associated to physical devices must be known in advance and are dependent on the hardware design.

The RAM regions

Internal RAM banks are mapped to addresses in the second 512 MB block, starting at address `0x20000000`. External memory banks may be mapped anywhere in the 1 GB region, starting at address `0x60000000`. Depending on the geometry of the internal SRAM inside the Cortex-M microcontroller, or the displacement of external memory banks, actually accessible memory areas can be mapped in non-contiguous, different parts of the memory within the allowed range. Memory management must take into account discontinuity in the physical mapping and refer to each section separately. The STM32F407 MPU, for example, has two non-contiguously mapped blocks of internal SRAM:

- 128 KB of SRAM at address `0x20000000` (in two contiguous blocks of 112 KB and 16 KB)
- A separate bank of 64 KB **Core-Coupled Memory (CCM)**, mapped at address `0x10000000`

This second memory is tightly coupled to the CPU, and optimized for time-critical operations, which allows for zero-wait states access from the CPU itself.

In this case, we may reference the two blocks as two separate areas in the linker script:

```
FLASH (rx)  : ORIGIN = 0x08000000, LENGTH = 256K
SRAM (rwx)  : ORIGIN = 0x20000000, LENGTH = 128K
CCMSRAM(rwx) : ORIGIN = 0x10000000, LENGTH = 64K
```

While the RAM region is designed for data, it generally keeps execution permissions, so sections of code can be loaded into RAM and executed at runtime. Executing code in RAM expands the flexibility of the system, allowing us to process code sections before loading them to memory. Binaries that are not meant to be executed in place can be stored to any device in other formats too, even using compression or encryption algorithms. While sometimes handy, the possibility of using sections in RAM to store executable code takes away precious runtime memory from the system. The benefits must be carefully taken into account beforehand when designing the system, especially from the point of view of actual runtime memory demands coming from the application.

Peripheral-access regions

The 512 MB area following the internal RAM region, starting at address `0x40000000`, is reserved for peripherals that are normally built into the microcontroller. The 1 GB area starting at address `0xA0000000` is instead used to map external memory chips and other devices that can be memory-mapped in the MCU addressing space, but are not part of the original chip package. In order to correctly access the peripherals, the configuration of the internal components within the MCU packaging and the addresses of the memory-mapped devices must be known in advance. Code execution is never allowed in these regions.

The system region

The highest 512 MB of the Cortex-M memory mapping is reserved for accessing system configuration and private control blocks. This region contains the system control registers, which are the registers used to program the processor, and the peripheral control registers, used to configure devices and peripherals. Code execution is not allowed, and the region is uniquely accessible when the processor is running in *privileged level*, as explained in more detail in `Chapter 10`, *Parallel Tasks and Scheduling*.

Accessing hardware registers by de-referencing their well-known addresses is useful to set and get their values at runtime. However, there is no way for the compiler to tell the difference between an assignment of a variable mapped in RAM and a configuration register in the system control block. For this reason, the compiler often thinks that it is a good idea to optimize the code by altering the order of the memory transactions, which might in fact result in unpredictable effects when the next operation depends on the correct conclusion of all the memory transfer from the previous ones. For this reason, extra care is needed when accessing configuration registers to ensure that the memory transfer operation is concluded before the next one is executed.

Order of memory transactions

On ARM CPUs, the memory system does not guarantee that the memory transactions are executed in the same order of the instructions that generate them. The order of memory transactions can be altered to adjust to the characteristics of the hardware, such as the wait states required to access underlying physical memory, or by the speculative branch prediction mechanisms implemented at microcode level. While Cortex-M microcontrollers guarantee a strict ordering of the transactions involving the peripherals and the system regions, in all other cases the code must be instrumented accordingly, by putting adequate memory barriers to ensure that the previous memory transactions have been executed before executing the next instruction. The Cortex-M instruction set includes three kinds of barriers:

- The **data memory barrier (DMB)**
- The **data synchronization barrier (DSB)**
- The **instruction synchronization barrier (ISB)**

The DSB is a *soft* barrier, invoked to ensure that all the pending transactions are executed before the next memory transaction occurs. The DSB is used to actually suspend the execution until all the pending transactions have been executed. The ISB, in addition, also flushes the CPU pipeline and ensures that all the new instructions are fetched again after the memory transactions, thus preventing any side effects caused by the outdated memory content. There are a number of cases where using a barrier is required:

- After updating the VTOR to change the address of the IV
- After updating the memory mapping
- During execution of code that modifies itself

The execution stack

As seen in the previous chapter, a bare-metal application starts executing with an empty stack area. The execution stack grows backwards, from the high address provided at boot towards lower addresses every time a new item is stored. The stack keeps track of the chain of function calls at all times by storing the branching point at each function call, but also serves as temporary storage during function executions. Variables within the local scope of each function are stored inside the stack while the function is executing. For this reason, keeping stack usage under control is one of the most critical tasks while developing an embedded system.

Embedded programming requires us to be aware at all times about stack usage while coding. Placing big objects in the stack, such as communication buffers or long strings, is in general not a good idea, considering that the space for the stack is always very limited. The compiler can be instructed to produce a warning every time the stack space required by a single function exceeds a certain threshold, as, for example, in this code:

```
void function(void)
{
    char buffer[200];
    read_serial_buffer(buffer);
}
```

If compiled with the GCC option -Wstack-usage=100, it will produce the following warning:

```
main.c: In function 'function':
main.c:15:6: warning: stack usage is 208 bytes [-Wstack-usage=]
```

That can be intercepted at compile time.

While this mechanism is useful to identify local stack overuses, it is not effective to identify all the potential stack overflows in the code, as the function calls may be nested and their stack usage added up. Our function uses 208 bytes of stack whenever it is invoked, 200 to host the *buffer* local variable in the stack, and 8 additional bytes to store two pointers: the origin of the call in the code section, that is stored as return point, and the frame pointer, which contains the old location of the stack pointer before the call.

By design, the stack grows every time a function is called and shrinks again when functions return. In a given case, it is particularly difficult to make estimations about the runtime stack usage, and that is the use of recursive functions. For this reason, the use of recursion in the code should be avoided whenever possible, or reduced to the minimum and kept under strict control otherwise, knowing that the memory area reserved to the stack in the target is small:

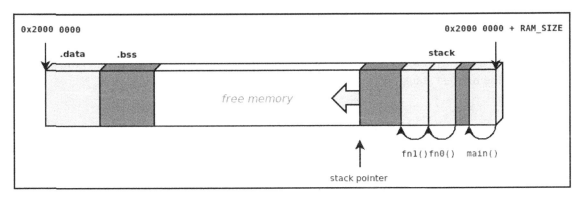

The stack pointer moves down when a function is called, to store frame pointers and local variables

Stack placement

The initial pointer to the stack area can be selected at boot, by setting the desired memory address in the first word of the IV table, which corresponds to the beginning of the binary image loaded in flash.

This pointer may be set at compile time, in different ways. The simple example from `Chapter 4`, *The Boot-Up Procedure*, shows how it is possible to assign a specific area for the stack, or using symbols exported from the linker script.

Using the linker script as a central point to describe memory regions and segments makes the code more portable across similar platforms.

Since our STM32F407 provides an additional, tightly coupled, 64 KB memory bank at address `0x10000000`, we may want to reserve its lower 16 KB for the execution stack, and keep the rest in a separate section for later use. The linker script must define the region on top, in the `MEMORY` block:

```
MEMORY
{
    FLASH (rx) : ORIGIN = 0x00000000, LENGTH = 1M
```

```
    SRAM (rwx) : ORIGIN = 0x20000000, LENGTH = 128K
    CCRAM(rwx) : ORIGIN = 0x10000000, LENGTH = 64K
}
```

Two symbols may now be exported at the end of the file, by assigning constant, pre-defined values:

```
_stack_size = 16 * 1024;
_stack_end = ORIGIN(CCRAM) + _stack_size;
```

The values of _stack_size and _stack_end can be accessed by the application as ordinary C symbols. _stack_end is placed at address 0 when the vector table is initialized, to indicate the highest stack address:

```
__attribute__ ((section(".isr_vector")))
void (* const IV[])(void) =
{
    (void (*)(void))(&_end_stack),
    isr_reset, // Reset
    isr_fault, // NMI
    isr_fault, // HardFault
/* more interrupt routines follow */
```

A common strategy used to organize memory in a bare-metal application running with a single contiguous area in RAM is to place the initial stack pointer at the highest available address at the end of the memory. This way, the stack is free to grow from the top of the memory down, while the application can still use the memory to allocate dynamic objects from the lowest address that is not used by any other section. While this mechanism is considered the most efficient, giving the illusion that it is possible to use up until the last byte of RAM available, it is dangerous because the two areas growing in opposite directions may collide, leading to unpredictable results.

Stack overflows

The main problem with stack sizing and placement is that it is very difficult, if not impossible, to recover from a situation of stack overflow in a single-thread bare-metal application. When the stack is self-contained in its own physical region, such as a separate memory bank, if its lower bound is a region not mapped to any device, a stack overflow will cause a hard fault exception, which can be trapped to halt the target.

In other cases, such as when adjacent memory is used for other purposes, the stack pointer might overflow into other segments, with a concrete risk of corrupting other memory areas, with catastrophic consequences including even opening the door to malicious code injections and arbitrary code execution attacks on the target. The best strategy usually consists of assigning adequate stack space at boot, isolating the stack as much as possible from the other memory sections, and checking the stack usage at runtime. Configuring the stack to use the lowest available addresses in RAM ensures that a stack overflow would result in a hard fault, rather than accessing valid pointers in adjacent areas in memory. The most classic approach for a bare-metal system with a single contiguous region of memory-mapped RAM is putting the initial stack pointer at the highest address available and having it grow backward toward lower addresses. The linker script exports the highest address mapped as the initial stack pointer:

```
_end_stack = ORIGIN(RAM) + LENGTH(RAM);
```

The available memory between the end of the `.bss` section and the lowest address in the stack may be used for dynamic allocations by the application, and at the same time the stack is allowed to grow in the opposite direction. This is a very efficient way to utilize all the available memory, because the stack does not require a lower boundary, and it is safe until the total amount of memory used from both sides fits inside the designated area at all times. On the other hand, if the sections are allowed to dynamically grow towards higher addresses, there is always a possibility of collisions in case of overlap from both sides:

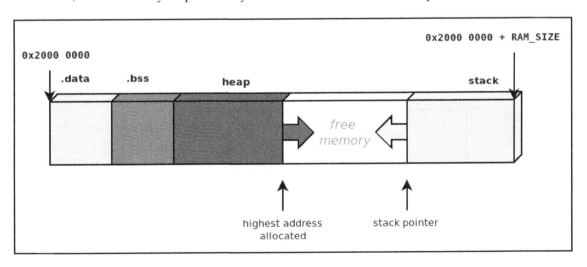

Heap allocations and the execution stack growing in opposite directions

Stack painting

An effective way to measure the amount of stack space needed consists of filling the estimated stack space with a well-known pattern. This mechanism, informally referred to as stack painting, reveals the maximum expansion of the execution stack at any time. By running the software with a painted stack, it is in fact possible to measure the amount of stack used by looking for the last recognizable pattern, and assuming that the stack pointer has moved during the execution at most until that point.

We can perform stack painting manually in the reset handler, during memory initialization. To do so, we need to assign an area to paint. In this case it would be the last 8 KB of memory up until _end_stack. Once again, while manipulating the stack in the reset_handler function, local variables should not be used. The reset_handler function will store the value of the current stack pointer into the global variable sp:

```
static unsigned int sp;
```

Within the handler, the following section can be added before invoking main():

```
asm volatile("mrs %0, msp" : "=r"(sp));
dst = ((unsigned int *)(&_end_stack)) - (8192 / sizeof(unsigned int)); ;
while (dst < sp) {
    *dst = 0xDEADC0DE;
    dst++;
}
```

The first assembly instruction is used to store the current value of the stack pointer to the variable sp, to ensure that the painting stops after painting the area, but only up until the last unused address in the stack:

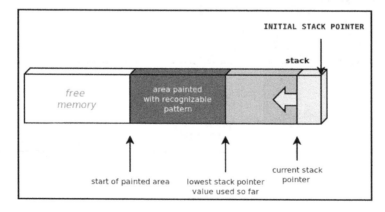

Painting the stack area with a recognizable pattern helps estimating the stack memory used in the prototype

The current stack usage can be checked periodically at runtime, for instance in the main loop, to detect the area painted with the recognizable pattern. The areas that are still painted have never been used by the execution stack so far, and indicate the amount of stack still available.

This mechanism may be used to verify the amount of stack space required by the application to run comfortably. According to the design, this information can be used later on to set a safe lower limit on the segment that can be used for the stack.

Heap management

Safety-critical embedded systems often are designed not to implement any dynamic memory allocation. While this may sound extreme, it minimizes the impact of the most common programming mistakes in the application code, which might lead to catastrophic consequences for the running system.

On the other hand, dynamic allocation is a powerful tool, because it gives complete control over the lifetime and the size of the memory blocks. Many third-party libraries designed for embedded devices expect an existing implementation of dynamic memory allocation. Dynamic memory is managed through a heap structure in memory, by keeping track of the status and the size for each allocation, incrementing the pointer to the next area of free memory and reusing blocks that had been freed if new allocation requests are processed.

A standard programming interface for heap allocation consists of two basic functions:

```
void *malloc(size_t size);
void free(void *ptr);
```

These function signatures are borrowed from the POSIX API found in operating systems, and allow us to request a new memory area of a given size, and free up the previously allocated area referred to the specified pointer, respectively. More complete heap management has support for an additional call, realloc, that would allow us to resize a memory area previously allocated, either in place or by relocating it to a new segment that is large enough to contain an object of the given size:

```
void *realloc(void *ptr, size_t size);
```

While realloc is generally left out from most of the embedded system implementations, it may be useful in some cases to resize objects in memory.

Depending on the implementation, the memory management could be more or less efficient in joining together contiguous blocks that had been freed, in order to create larger available segments without having to allocate new space.

In case we opt for a solution that allows for dynamic allocations, it is important to design it taking into account a few important factors:

- The geometry of the regions where the heap is placed
- The higher boundary of the section dedicated to the heap, in case it is shared with the stack, to prevent heap-stack collisions
- The policy to adopt in case there is not enough memory to satisfy requests for new allocations
- How to deal with memory fragmentation and keep the overhead of unused blocks as small as possible
- Using separate pools to separate the memory used by specific objects and modules
- Spreading a single pool of memory across non-contiguous regions

Custom implementation

Unlike servers and personal computers, where memory allocations are handled using pages of a specific size, in bare-metal embedded systems the heap is usually a contiguous area of physical memory that can be divided internally using any alignment. Building heap-based memory allocation based on the `malloc/free` interface consists of keeping track of the requested allocations in memory. This is usually done by prepending a small header in front of each allocation, to track the state and the size of the allocated section, which can be used in the `free` function to validate the allocated block and make it available for the next allocation. A basic implementation, providing dynamic memory starting from the first available address after the end of the `.bss` section, might represent each block in memory using a preamble, like the following:

```
struct malloc_block {
    unsigned int signature;
    unsigned int size;
};
```

Two different signatures can be assigned to identify valid blocks, and differentiate between blocks still in use versus blocks that have already been freed:

```
#define SIGNATURE_IN_USE (0xAAC0FFEE)
#define SIGNATURE_FREED (0xFEEDFACE)
#define NULL (((void *)0))
```

The `malloc` function should keep track of the highest address in the stack. In this example, a static variable is used to mark the current end of the stack. This is set to the start address at the beginning, and will grow every time a new block is allocated:

```
void *malloc(unsigned int size)
{
    static unsigned int *end_heap = 0;
    struct malloc_block *blk;
    char *ret = NULL;
    if (!end_heap) {
        end_heap = &_start_heap;
    }
```

The next two lines ensure that the block requested is 32-bit-aligned, to optimize the access to `malloc_block`:

```
    if (((size >>2) << 2) != size)
        size = ((size >> 2) + 1) << 2;
```

The `malloc` function then first looks in the heap for a memory section that has been previously freed:

```
    blk = (struct malloc_block *)&_start_heap;
    while (blk < end_heap) {
        if ((blk->signature == SIGNATURE_FREED) &&
        (blk->size <= size)) {
            blk->signature = SIGNATURE_IN_USE;
            ret = ((char *)blk) + sizeof(struct malloc_block);
            return ret;
        }
        blk = ((char *)blk) + sizeof(struct malloc_block) + blk->size;
    }
```

If no available slot is found, or if none of them is large enough to satisfy the size required for the allocation, the memory is allocated at the end of the stack and the pointer is updated accordingly:

```
    blk = (struct malloc_block *)end_heap;
    blk->signature = SIGNATURE_IN_USE;
    blk->size = size;
```

```
    ret = ((char *)end_heap) + sizeof(struct malloc_block);
    end_heap = ret + size;
    return ret;
}
```

In both cases, the address returned hides the `malloc_block` control structure that precedes it. The `end_heap` variable always points to the end of the last block allocated in the heap, but it is not an indication of the memory used, as intermediate blocks may have been freed in the meanwhile. This example `free` function, demonstrating a very simple case, is only performing basic checks on the block that needs to be freed, and setting the signature to indicate that the block is no longer being used:

```
void free(void *ptr)
{
    struct malloc_block *blk = (struct malloc_block *)
            (((char *)ptr)-sizeof(struct malloc_block));
    if (!ptr)
        return;
    if (blk->signature != SIGNATURE_IN_USE)
        return;
    blk->signature = SIGNATURE_FREED;
}
```

Although this example is very simplistic, it aims at explaining the basic functionality of heap allocation without taking into account all real-life constraints and limitations. In fact, allocating and freeing objects of different sizes may cause fragmentation. To minimize the impact of this phenomenon in terms of memory usage and wasted space in between active allocations, the `free` function should at least implement some kind of mechanism to join together adjacent areas that are no longer in play. Furthermore, the preceding example `malloc` assumes that the heap section does not have an upper boundary, it does not perform any check on the new location of the `end_heap` pointer, nor does it define a strategy when there is no memory available to allocate.

Although toolchains and libraries often provide a default implementation of `malloc` and `free`, implementing custom heap-based allocation mechanisms still makes sense in those cases where the implementations available do not meet the requirements; for example, if we want to manage separate memory pools, or merge together separate physical memory sections to use in the same pool.

Fragmentation issues cannot be completely resolved on systems with physical memory mapping due to the fact that it is impossible to move around previously allocated blocks to optimize the space available. The issue can, however, be mitigated by keeping the number of allocations under control, reusing allocated blocks as much as possible, and avoiding frequent calls to `malloc/free`, especially to request blocks with different sizes.

The use of dynamic memory, regardless of the implementation, introduces a number of safety concerns, and should be avoided in all life-critical systems, and in general wherever it is not required. Simpler, single-purpose embedded systems may be designed to avoid the use of dynamic memory allocations altogether. In these cases, a simple `malloc` interface can be provided to allow permanent allocations during startup.

Using newlib

Toolchains may provide a set of utilities, which often include dynamic memory allocation mechanisms. GCC-based toolchains for microcontrollers include a reduced set of standard C calls, usually in the built-in standard C library. A popular choice, often included in the ARM-GCC embedded toolchain, is `newlib`. While providing the implementation of many standard calls, `newlib` remains as flexible as possible, by allowing customization of the operations involving the hardware. The `newlib` library can be integrated in both single-thread bare-metal applications and in a real-time operating system, provided that the required system calls are implemented.

In the case of `malloc`, `newlib` requires an existing implementation of the `sbrk` function. This function is expected to move the heap pointer forward at every new allocation, and return the old value of the heap to `malloc`, in order to complete allocations every time an existing, previously freed reusable block is not found in the pool:

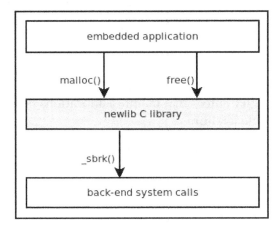

newlib implements malloc and free, and relies on an existing implementation of _sbrk

A possible implementation of the `_sbrk` function may be the following:

```
void * _sbrk(unsigned int incr)
{
    static unsigned char *heap = NULL;
    void *old_heap = heap;
    if (((incr & 0x03) != incr)
        incr = ((incr >> 2) + 1) << 2;
    if (old_heap == NULL)
        old_heap = heap = (unsigned char *)&_start_heap;
    heap += incr;
    return old_heap;
}
```

If the code is linked without the `-nostdlib` flag, the `malloc` and `free` functions, if invoked anywhere in the code, will be automatically found within the `newlib` built in the toolchain, and included to the final binary. Failing to define a `_sbrk` symbol in this case will result in a linking error.

Limiting the heap

In all the allocation functions seen so far, there is no limit imposed by the software on the amount of memory reserved for the heap. While overflowing the stack is often hard to prevent, and extremely difficult to recover from, running out of available heap memory can more often be gracefully handled by the application, for example, by canceling or postponing the operation that required the allocation. In more complex multi-threaded systems, the operating system could actively react to the memory shortage by terminating non-vital processes to free up memory for new allocations. Some advanced systems using page-swapping mechanisms, like Linux, may implement overcommit on the available memory. This mechanism guarantees that memory allocations never fail, and `malloc` will never return `NULL` to indicate a failure.

Memory-consuming processes in the system may be instead terminated at any time by a kernel thread, the out-of-memory killer, to make space for new allocations from other less resource-consuming processes. On an embedded system, especially if there is no multi-threading, the best choice is to have the allocator return `NULL` when there is no physical space left on the heap, so that the system can keep running and the application can possibly recover by recognizing the out-of-memory episode. The section in memory dedicated to the heap can be limited by exporting the address for its upper boundary in the linker script, for example:

```
_heap_end = ORIGIN(RAM) + LENGTH(RAM);
```

The backend for the `newlib malloc` implementation can account for the newly introduced upper bound in the `_sbrk()` function:

```
void * _sbrk(unsigned int incr) {
    static unsigned char *heap = NULL;
        void *old_heap = heap;
    if (((incr & 0x03) != incr)
        incr = ((incr >> 2) + 1) << 2;
    if (old_heap == NULL)
        old_heap = heap = (unsigned char *)&_start_heap;
    if ((heap + incr) >= &_end_heap)
        return (void *)(-1);
    else
        heap += incr;
    return old_heap;
}
```

The special value `(void *)(-1)` that is returned by `sbrk` in case of memory shortage for heap allocation indicates to the calling `malloc` that there is not enough space to perform the requested allocation. `malloc` will then return `NULL` to the caller.

It is very important in this case that the caller always checks the return value at each invocation of `malloc()`, and that the application logic is able to correctly detect that the system is out of memory, and react in the attempt to recover from it.

Multiple memory pools

In some systems, it is useful to keep separate sections as dynamic memory heaps, each dedicated to a specific function in the system. Heap allocation mechanisms using separate pools may be implemented for different reasons, such as ensuring that specific modules or subsystems do not use more memory than the amount that is assigned to them at compile time, or ensuring that allocations with the same size can reuse the same physical space in memory, reducing the impact of fragmentation, or even assigning a pre-defined, fixed area in memory for DMA operations with peripherals or network devices. It is possible to delimit the sections for the different pools as usual, by exporting symbols in the linker script. The example below pre-allocates the space in memory for two pools, of 8 KB and 4 KB respectively, located at the end of the `.bss` section in RAM:

```
PROVIDE(_start_pool0 = _end_bss);
PROVIDE(_end_pool0 = _start_pool0 + 8KB);
PROVIDE(_start_pool1 = _end_pool0);
PROVIDE(_end_pool1 = _start_pool1 + 4KB);
```

A custom allocation function must be defined, since the `malloc` interface does not support the selector of the pool, but the functions can be made generic for both pools. A global structure can be populated with the values exported by the linker:

```
struct memory_pool {
    void *start;
    void *end;
    void *cur;
};
static struct memory_pool mem_pool[2] = {
    {
        .start = &_start_pool0;
        .end = &_end_pool0;
    },
    {
        .start = &_start_pool1;
        .end = &_end_pool1;
    },
};
```

The function must take an extra argument to specify the pool. Then, the allocation is performed with the same algorithm, only changing the current pointer and the boundaries of the selected pool. In this version, the out-of-memory errors are detected before moving the current heap value forward, returning NULL to notify the caller:

```
void *mempool_alloc(int pool, unsigned int size)
{
    struct malloc_block *blk;
    struct memory_pool *mp;
    char *ret = NULL;
    if (pool != 0 && pool != 1)
        return NULL;
    mp = mem_pool[pool];
    if (!mp->cur)
        mp->cur = mp->start;
    if (((size >>2) << 2) != size)
        size = ((size >> 2) + 1) << 2;
    blk = (struct malloc_block *)mp->start;
    while (blk < mp->cur) {
        if ((blk->signature == SIGNATURE_FREED) &&
        (blk->size <= size)) {
            blk->signature = SIGNATURE_IN_USE;
            ret = ((char *)blk) + sizeof(struct malloc_block);
            return ret;
        }
        blk = ((char *)blk) + sizeof(struct malloc_block) + blk->size;
    }
```

```
    blk = (struct malloc_block *)mp->cur;
    if (mp->cur + size >= mp→end)
        return NULL;
    blk->signature = SIGNATURE_IN_USE;
    blk->size = size;
    ret = ((char *)mp->cur) + sizeof(struct malloc_block);
    mp->cur = ret + size;
    return ret;
}
```

Once again, this mechanism does not account for memory fragmentation, so the `mempool_free` function can have the same implementation as the `free` for the simplified `malloc`, as the only necessary thing to do is to mark the blocks being freed as unused.

In more complete cases, where `free` or a separate garbage collector routine takes care of merging contiguous freed blocks, it might be required to keep track of the freed blocks in each pool, in a list or another data structure that can be visited to check if merging is possible.

Common heap usage errors

The use of dynamic memory allocation is considered unsafe in some environments, as it is widely known to be the source of nasty bugs, which are in general both critical and very hard to identify and fix. Dynamic allocations may be difficult to track, especially when the code grows in size and complexity and there are many dynamically allocated data structures. This is already very serious in multi-threaded environments, where it is still possible to implement fallback mechanisms, such as terminating a misbehaving application, but it becomes critical on single-threaded embedded systems, where these kinds of errors are often fatal for the system. The most common types of errors when programming with heap allocations are:

- `NULL` pointer dereference
- Double `free`
- Use after `free`
- Failure to call `free`, resulting in memory leaks

Some of these can be avoided by following a few simple rules. malloc returns the value that should always be checked before using the pointer. This is particularly important in environments where resources are limited, and the allocator can return NULL pointers to indicate that there is no memory available for the allocation. The preferred approach is ensuring that there is a defined strategy to follow when the required memory is not available. In any case, all dynamic pointers must be checked to be not NULL in the code, before attempting to de-reference.

Freeing NULL pointers is a legal operation that must be identified when free is called. By including a check at the beginning of the function, if the pointer is NULL, no action is performed and the call is ignored.

Immediately after, we can also check that the memory has not been freed before. In our free function, we implement a simple check against the signature of the malloc_block structure in memory. It would be possible to add a log message, or even a breakpoint to debug the origin of the second free function:

```
if (blk->signature != SIGNATURE_IN_USE) {
    /* Double free detected! */
    asm("BKPT #0") ;
    return;
}
```

Unfortunately, this mechanism may only work in some cases. In fact, if the block that was previously freed is assigned again by the allocator, it would be impossible to detect further uses of its original reference, and a second free would cause the second reference to be lost as well. For the same reason, use-after-free errors are hard to diagnose, as there is no way to tell that a memory block freed has been accessed again. There is a possibility to paint the freed blocks with a recognizable pattern, so that if the content of the block is altered after the free has been called, the next invocation of the malloc on that block can detect the alteration. However, this again does not guarantee detection of all the cases, and only works for write accesses to a freed pointer; additionally, it would not be able to identify all the cases where the freed memory is accessed for reading.

Memory leaks are easy to diagnose, but sometimes difficult to locate. With limited resources, it is often the case that forgetting to free allocated memory uses up all the available heap very quickly. While there are techniques used to track down the allocations, it is often sufficient to break into the software with the debugger and look for repeated allocations with the same size to track down the buggy caller.

In conclusion, due to their catastrophic and hideous nature, dynamic memory bugs may be one of the biggest challenges on embedded systems. Therefore, writing safer application code is often less expensive in terms of resources than hunting for memory bugs at system level, for example, instrumenting the allocator. Analyzing the lifetime of each allocated object thoroughly, and making the logic as clear and readable as possible, may prevent most of the problems related to pointer handling, and save a lot of time that would otherwise be spent debugging.

The memory protection unit

In a system without virtual address mapping, it is harder to create a separation among sections that can be accessed by the software at runtime. The memory protection unit, often referred to as the MPU, is an optional component present in many ARM-based microcontrollers. The MPU is used to separate sections in memory by setting local permissions and attributes. This mechanism has several uses in real-life scenarios, such as preventing access to the memory when the CPU is running in user mode, or preventing fetching code to execute from writable locations in RAM. When the MPU is enabled, it enforces the rules by triggering a memory exception interrupt when those are violated.

While commonly used by operating systems to create process stack separation and enforce privileged access to system memory, the MPU can be useful in a number of other cases, including bare-metal applications.

MPU configuration registers

In Cortex-M, the control block region related to MPU configuration is located in the system control block, starting at address `0xE000ED90`. Five registers are used to access the MPU:

- The **MPU Type Register** (`offset = 0x00`) contains information about the availability of the MPU system and the number of regions supported. This register is also available on systems without an MPU to indicate that the functionality is not supported.
- The **MPU Control Register** (offset is `0x04`) is used to activate the MPU system, and to enable the default background mapping for all the regions that are not explicitly mapped in the MPU. If the background mapping is not enabled, accessing non-mapped regions is not allowed.
- The **MPU Region Number Register** (`RNR`, offset is `0x08`) is used to select the region to configure.

- The **MPU Region Base Address Register** (RBAR, offset is 0x0C) can be accessed to change the base address of the selected region.
- The **MPU Region Attribute and Size Register** (RASR, offset is 0x10) defines the permissions, attributes, and size of the selected region.

Programming the MPU

The MPU of Cortex-M microcontrollers support up to eight different programmable regions. A function that enables the MPU and sets up all the regions can be implemented and invoked at the beginning of the program. The MPU registers are mapped in HAL libraries, but in this case, we decided to define our own version and access them directly:

```
#define MPU_BASE 0xE000ED90
#define MPU_TYPE (*(volatile uint32_t *)(MPU_BASE + 0x00))
#define MPU_CTRL (*(volatile uint32_t *)(MPU_BASE + 0x04))
#define MPU_RNR (*(volatile uint32_t *)(MPU_BASE + 0x08))
#define MPU_RBAR (*(volatile uint32_t *)(MPU_BASE + 0x0c))
#define MPU_RASR (*(volatile uint32_t *)(MPU_BASE + 0x10))
```

In our example, we used the following defined bit-field value definitions to set the right attributes in the RASR:

```
#define RASR_ENABLED (1)
#define RASR_RW (1 << 24)
#define RASR_RDONLY (5 << 24)
#define RASR_NOACCESS (0 << 24)
#define RASR_SCB (7 << 16)
#define RASR_SB (5 << 16)
#define RASR_NOEXEC (1 << 28)
```

The possible sizes, which should end up in the size field of the RASR in bits 1:5, are coded as follows:

```
#define MPUSIZE_1K (0x09 << 1)
#define MPUSIZE_2K (0x0a << 1)
#define MPUSIZE_4K (0x0b << 1)
#define MPUSIZE_8K (0x0c << 1)
#define MPUSIZE_16K (0x0d << 1)
#define MPUSIZE_32K (0x0e << 1)
#define MPUSIZE_64K (0x0f << 1)
#define MPUSIZE_128K (0x10 << 1)
#define MPUSIZE_256K (0x11 << 1)
#define MPUSIZE_512K (0x12 << 1)
#define MPUSIZE_1M (0x13 << 1)
```

```
#define MPUSIZE_2M (0x14 << 1)
#define MPUSIZE_4M (0x15 << 1)
#define MPUSIZE_8M (0x16 << 1)
#define MPUSIZE_16M (0x17 << 1)
#define MPUSIZE_32M (0x18 << 1)
#define MPUSIZE_64M (0x19 << 1)
#define MPUSIZE_128M (0x1a << 1)
#define MPUSIZE_256M (0x1b << 1)
#define MPUSIZE_512M (0x1c << 1)
#define MPUSIZE_1G (0x1d << 1)
#define MPUSIZE_2G (0x1e << 1)
#define MPUSIZE_4G (0x1f << 1)
```

The first thing to do when we enter the `mpu_enable` function is to ensure that the feature is available on our target, by checking the `MPU_TYPE` register:

```
int mpu_enable(void)
{
    volatile uint32_t type;
    volatile uint32_t start;
    volatile uint32_t attr;
    type = MPU_TYPE;
    if (type == 0) {
        /* MPU not present! */
        return -1;
    }
}
```

In order to configure the MPU, we must ensure that it is disabled while we change the base addresses and the attributes of each region:

```
    MPU_CTRL = 0;
```

The flash region that contains the executable code can be marked as read-only region 0. The values for the `RASR` attributes are as follows:

```
    start = 0;
    attr = RASR_ENABLED | MPUSIZE_256K | RASR_SCB | RASR_RDONLY;
    mpu_set_region(0, start, attr);
```

The whole RAM region can be mapped as read-write. If we do not need to execute code from RAM, we can set the XN (execute-never) bit in the region attributes. RAM is mapped as region 1 in this case:

```
    start = 0x20000000;
    attr = RASR_ENABLED | MPUSIZE_64K | RASR_SCB |
    RASR_RW | RASR_NOEXEC;
    mpu_set_region(1, start, attr);
```

Since memory mapping is processed in the same order as memory regions numbers, we can use region 2 to create an exception within region 1. Regions with higher numbers have priority over regions with lower numbers, so exceptions can be created within an existing mapping with a lower number.

Region 2 is used to define a guard region as a lower boundary for the stack growing backwards, whose purpose is to intercept stack overflows. In fact, if at any moment the program tries to access the guard region, it triggers an exception and the operation fails. In this case, the guard region occupies 1 KB at the bottom of the stack. It has no access permissions configured in its attributes. The MPU ensures that the region is not accessible at runtime:

```
start = (uint32_t)(&_end_stack) - (STACK_SIZE + 1024);
attr = RASR_ENABLED | MPUSIZE_1K | RASR_SCB |
RASR_NOACCESS | RASR_NOEXEC;
mpu_set_region(2, start, attr);
```

Finally, we describe the system area as a read-write, non-executable, non-cacheable area, so that the program will still be able to access the system registers after the MPU has been activated again. We use region 3 for this:

```
start = 0xE0000000;
attr = RASR_ENABLED | MPUSIZE_256M | RASR_SB
RASR_RW | RASR_NOEXEC;
mpu_set_region(3, start, attr);
```

As a final step, we enable the MPU again. The MPU will allow us to define a *background region*, setting the default permissions for those areas that are not covered in the active region configurations. In this case, the absence of the definition for a background policy results in prohibited access to all the areas that are not explicitly mapped:

```
MPU_CTRL = 1;
return 0;
}
```

The helping function that sets address and attributes for the memory regions looks like the following:

```
static void mpu_set_region(int region, uint32_t start, uint32_t attr)
{
    MPU_RNR = region;
    MPU_RBAR = start;
    MPU_RNR = region;
    MPU_RASR = attr;
}
```

The value used to set attributes and sizes in MPU_RASR in this example is defined according to the structure of the register itself. MPU_RASR is a bit-field register, containing the following fields:

- **Bit 0**: Enable/disable region.
- **Bits 1:5**: Size of the partition (see the special values to assign to this field).
- **Bits 16:18**: Indicates if the memory is bufferable, cacheable, and shared, respectively. Devices and system registers should be marked as non-cacheable at all times, to guarantee the strict order of the transaction, as explained at the beginning of this chapter.
- **Bits 24:26**: Access permissions (read/write), separated for user and supervisor mode.
- **Bit 28**: Disable execution (XN flag).

It is now possible to write a program that overflows the stack, and see the difference in the debugger when the mpu_enable function is called, and when it is not. If the MPU is available on the target, it is now able to intercept stack overflows, triggering an exception in the CPU:

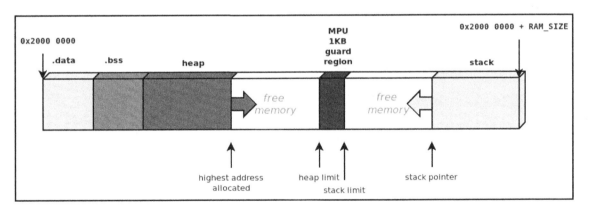

The guard region is marked as inaccessible in the MPU to prevent stack overflows

The configuration we used in this case for the MPU is very strict, not allowing access to any memory, except for the regions mapping flash and RAM. The extra 1 KB guard region ensures that we can detect stack overflows at runtime. In real applications, the MPU configuration may be more complex, and even updated at runtime. In Chapter 11, *Embedded Operating Systems* for example, we explain how the MPU can be used to isolate thread-address spaces in a real-time operating system.

Summary

Memory management in an embedded system is the source of the most critical bugs, and for this reason particular attention must be dedicated to designing and implementing the correct solutions for the platform in use, and application purposes. The execution stack should be carefully placed, sized, and delimited when possible.

Systems not providing dynamic allocations are safer, but most embedded systems benefit from dynamic allocation techniques. Programmers must be aware that errors in memory handling can be critical for the system, and very difficult to spot, so extra care is required when the code handles dynamically allocated pointers.

The MPU can be a valid tool to enforce access permissions and attributes on memory regions, and can be used for several purposes. In the example shown, we implemented an MPU-based mechanism to enforce a physical boundary for the stack pointer.

In the next chapter, we examine other common components included in modern microcontrollers. We learn how to handle clock settings, interrupt priorities, general-purpose I/O communication, and other optional features.

General-Purpose Peripherals

6

Modern microcontrollers integrate a number of features that help in building stable and reliable embedded systems. Once the system is up and running, memory and peripherals can be accessed, and basic functionalities are in place. Only then can all the components of the system be initialized by activating the associated peripherals through the system registers, setting the correct frequencies for the clock lines, and configuring and activating interrupts. In this chapter, we describe the interface exposed by the microcontroller to access built-in peripherals and some basic system functionalities. In particular, we focus on the following:

- The interrupt controller
- System time
- Generic timers
- General-purpose I/O
- The watchdog

While these peripherals are often accessible through the hardware-support libraries implemented and distributed by chip manufacturers, our approach here involves fully understanding the hardware components and the meaning of all the registers involved, by configuring and using the functionalities in the microcontroller straight through the interface exported by the hardware logic.

When designing drivers for a specific platform, it is necessary to study the interface provided by the microcontroller to access peripherals and CPU features. In the examples provided, the STM32F4 is used as a reference microcontroller for implementing platform-specific features. Nevertheless, inspecting a possible implementation on our reference platform allows to get better insight into how to interact with generic targets exposing similar functionalities, using the documentation provided by the silicon manufacturer.

The interrupt controller

Real-time systems have improved their accuracy thanks to the rapid evolution of modern embedded systems, and in particular from the research on interrupt controllers. Assigning different priorities to interrupt lines guarantees a lower interrupt latency for higher-priority interrupt sources, and makes the system react faster to prioritized events. Interrupts may, however, occur at any time while the system is running, including during the execution of another interrupt service routine. In this case, the interrupt controller provides a way to chain the interrupt handlers, and the order of execution depends on the priority levels assigned to the interrupt source.

One of the reasons for the popularity of the Cortex-M family of microprocessors among real-time and low-power embedded applications is perhaps the design of its programmable real-time controller, namely the **Nested Vector Interrupt Controller**, or **NVIC** for short. The NVIC supports up to 240 interrupt sources, which can be grouped into up to 256 priority levels, depending on the bits reserved to store the priority in the microprocessor logic. These characteristics make it very flexible, as the priorities can also be changed while the system is running, maximizing the freedom of choice for the programmer. As we already know, the NVIC is connected to the vector table located at the beginning of the code region. Whenever an interrupt occurs, the current state of the executing application is pushed into the stack automatically by the processor, and the service routine associated to the interrupt line is executed.

Systems that do not have an interrupt-priority mechanism implement back-to-back interrupt handling. In these cases, chaining interrupts implies that the context is restored at the end of the execution of the first service routine in line, and then saved again while entering the following one. The NVIC implements a tail-chaining mechanism to execute nested interrupts. If one or more interrupts occur while another service routine is executing, the pull operation normally occurring at the end of the interrupt to restore the context from the stack will be canceled, and the controller will instead fetch the location of the second handler in the interrupt vector and ensure it is executed immediately after the first. Because of the increased pace of the stack save and restore operations being implemented in hardware, the interrupt latency results significantly reduced in all those cases where interrupts are chained. Thanks to its implementation, NVIC allows us to change parameters while the system is running, and is able to reshuffle the order of execution of the interrupt service routines associated to the pending signals, according to the priority levels. Moreover, the same interrupt is not allowed to run twice in the same chain of handlers, which may be caused by altering the priorities in the other handlers. This is intrinsically enforced by the NVIC logic, which ensures that no loops are possible in the chain.

Peripherals interrupt configuration

Each interrupt line can be enabled and disabled through the NVIC Interrupt Set/Clear Enable registers, NVIC_ISER, NVIC_ICER, located at address 0xE000E100 and 0xE000E180, respectively. If the target supports more than 32 external interrupts, arrays of 32-bit registers are mapped at the same locations. Each bit in the registers is used to activate a predefined interrupt line, associated to the bit position in that specific register. For example, on an STM32F4 microcontroller, in order to activate the interrupt line for the SPI controller SPI1, which is associated with number 35, the fourth bit should be set on the second register in the NVIC_ISER area.

The generic NVIC function, to enable the interrupt, activates the flag corresponding to the NVIC interrupt number for the source, in the associate NVIC_ISER register:

```
#define NVIC_ISER_BASE (0xE000E100)

static inline void nvic_irq_enable(uint8_t n)
{
    int i = n / 32;
    volatile uint32_t *nvic_iser =
    ((volatile uint32_t *)(NVIC_ISER_BASE + 4 * i));
    *nvic_iser |= (1 << (n % 32));
}
```

Similarly, to disable the interrupt, the nvic_irq_disable function activates the corresponding bit in the interrupt clear register:

```
#define NVIC_ICER_BASE (0xE000E180)
static inline void nvic_irq_disable(uint8_t n)
{
    int i = n / 32;
    volatile uint32_t *nvic_icer =
    ((volatile uint32_t *)(NVIC_ICER_BASE + 4 * i));
    *nvic_icer |= (1 << (n % 32));
}
```

The interrupt priorities are mapped in an array of 8-bit registers, each containing the priority value for the corresponding interrupt line, starting at address 0xE000E400, so that they can be accessed independently to change the priority at runtime:

```
#define NVIC_IPRI_BASE (0xE000E400)
static inline void nvic_irq_setprio(uint8_t n, uint8_t prio)
{
    volatile uint8_t *nvic_ipri = ((volatile uint8_t *)
    (NVIC_IPRI_BASE + n));
```

```
        *nvic_ipri = prio;
    }
```

These functions will come in handy to route and prioritize interrupt lines whenever an interrupt is enabled for a peripheral.

System time

Timekeeping is a basic requirement for almost any embedded system. A microcontroller can be programmed to trigger an interrupt at regular intervals, which is commonly used to increment the monotonic system clock. To do so, a few configuration steps must be performed at startup in order to have a stable tick interrupt. Many processors can run at custom frequencies while using the same oscillator as source. The input frequency of the oscillator, which can be internal or external to the CPU, is used to derive the processor main clock. The configurable logic integrated in the CPU is implemented by a PLL that multiplies the input clock from an external stable source, and produces the desired frequencies used by the CPU and integrated peripherals.

Adjusting the flash wait states

If the initialization code is running from flash, it might be necessary to set the wait state for the flash memory before altering the system clocks. If the microprocessor runs at high frequencies, it might require a few wait states in between two consecutive access operations to persistent memory with XIP capabilities. Failing to set the correct wait states, and matching the ratio between the CPU speed and the access time of the flash, would most likely result in a hard fault. The configuration registers for the flash memory are located in a platform-specific location within the internal peripheral's region. On STM32F407, the flash configuration registers are mapped starting at address $0x40023800$. The Access Control Register, which is the one we need to access to set the wait states, is located at the beginning of the area:

```
#define FLASH_BASE (0x40023C00)
#define FLASH_ACR (*(volatile uint32_t *)(FLASH_BASE + 0x00))
```

The lowest three bits in the `FLASH_ACR` register are used to set the number of wait states. According to the STM32F407 datasheet, the ideal number of wait states to access the flash while the system is running at 168 MHz is 5. At the same time, we can enable the data and instruction cache by activating bits 10 and 9, respectively:

```
void flash_set_waitstates(void) {
    FLASH_ACR = 5 | (1 << 10) | (1 << 9);
}
```

After the wait states are set, it is safe to run the code from the flash after setting the CPU frequency at a higher speed, so we can proceed with the actual clock configuration and distribution to the peripherals.

Clock configuration

The configuration of the clocks in Cortex-M microcontrollers happens through the **Reset and Clock Control** (**RCC**) registers, located at a specific address within the internal peripheral region. The RCC configuration is vendor-specific, as it depends on the logic of the PLL implemented in the microcontroller. The registers are described in the documentation of the microcontroller, and often, example source code is provided by the chip manufacturer to demonstrate how to properly configure the clocks on the microcontroller. On our reference target, STM32F407, assuming that an external 8 MHz oscillator is used as a source, the following procedure configures a 168 MHz system clock, and ensures that the clock is also distributed to each peripheral bus. The following code ensures that the PLL is initialized with the required value, and that the CPU clock is ticking at the desired frequency. This procedure is common among many STM Cortex-M microcontrollers, and the values for the PLL configurations can be obtained from the chip documentation, or calculated using software tools provided by ST.

The software examples provided after this point will make use of a system-specific module, exporting the functions needed to configure the clock and set the flash memory latency. We now analyze two possible implementations for the PLL configuration, on two different Cortex-M microcontrollers.

To access the configuration of the PLL in the STM32F407-Discovery, first we define some shortcut macros to the addresses of the registers provided by the RCC:

```
#define RCC_BASE (0x40023800)
#define RCC_CR (*(volatile uint32_t *)(RCC_BASE + 0x00))
#define RCC_PLLCFGR (*(volatile uint32_t *)(RCC_BASE + 0x04))
#define RCC_CFGR (*(volatile uint32_t *)(RCC_BASE + 0x08))
#define RCC_CR (*(volatile uint32_t *)(RCC_BASE + 0x00))
```

For the sake of readability, and to ensure that the code is maintainable in the future, we also define the mnemonics associated to the single-bit values in the corresponding registers:

```
#define RCC_CR_PLLRDY (1 << 25)
#define RCC_CR_PLLON (1 << 24)
#define RCC_CR_HSERDY (1 << 17)
#define RCC_CR_HSEON (1 << 16)
#define RCC_CR_HSIRDY (1 << 1)
#define RCC_CR_HSION (1 << 0)

#define RCC_CFGR_SW_HSI 0x0
#define RCC_CFGR_SW_HSE 0x1
#define RCC_CFGR_SW_PLL 0x2
#define RCC_PLLCFGR_PLLSRC (1 << 22)

#define RCC_PRESCALER_DIV_NONE 0
#define RCC_PRESCALER_DIV_2 8
#define RCC_PRESCALER_DIV_4 9
```

Finally, we define the platform-specific constant values used to configure the PLL:

```
#define CPU_FREQ (168000000)
#define PLL_FULL_MASK (0x7F037FFF)
#define PLLM 8
#define PLLN 336
#define PLLP 2
#define PLLQ 7
#define PLLR 0
```

One additional macro invoking the DMB assembly instruction is defined, for brevity, as it will be used in the code to ensure that any pending memory transfer towards the configuration registers is completed before the execution of the next statement:

```
#define DMB() asm volatile ("dmb");
```

The next function will then ensure that the PLL initialization sequence is performed, in order to set the correct CPU frequency. First, it will enable the internal high-speed oscillator, and will wait until it is ready by polling the CR:

```
void rcc_config(void)
{
    uint32_t reg32;
    RCC_CR |= RCC_CR_HSION;
    DMB();
    while ((RCC_CR & RCC_CR_HSIRDY) == 0)
        ;
```

The internal oscillator is then selected as a temporary clock source:

```
reg32 = RCC_CFGR;
reg32 &= ~((1 << 1) | (1 << 0));
RCC_CFGR = (reg32 | RCC_CFGR_SW_HSI);
DMB();
```

The external oscillator is then activated in the same way:

```
RCC_CR |= RCC_CR_HSEON;
DMB();
while ((RCC_CR & RCC_CR_HSERDY) == 0)
    ;
```

On this device, the clock can be distributed to all the peripherals through three system buses. Using prescalers, the frequency of each bus can be scaled by a factor of two or four. In this case, we set the clock speed for HPRE, PPRE1, and PPRE2 to be 168, 84 and 46 MHz respectively on this target:

```
reg32 = RCC_CFGR;
reg32 &= ~0xF0;
RCC_CFGR = (reg32 | (RCC_PRESCALER_DIV_NONE << 4));
DMB();
reg32 = RCC_CFGR;
reg32 &= ~0x1C00;
RCC_CFGR = (reg32 | (RCC_PRESCALER_DIV_2 << 10));
DMB();
reg32 = RCC_CFGR;
reg32 &= ~0x07 << 13;
RCC_CFGR = (reg32 | (RCC_PRESCALER_DIV_4 << 13));
DMB();
```

The PLL configuration register is set to contain the parameters to correctly scale the external oscillator frequency to the desired value:

```
reg32 = RCC_PLLCFGR;
reg32 &= ~PLL_FULL_MASK;
RCC_PLLCFGR = reg32 | RCC_PLLCFGR_PLLSRC | PLLM |
(PLLN << 6) | (((PLLP >> 1) - 1) << 16) |
(PLLQ << 24);
DMB();
```

The PLL is then activated, and the execution is suspended until the output is stable:

```
RCC_CR |= RCC_CR_PLLON;
DMB();
while ((RCC_CR & RCC_CR_PLLRDY) == 0);
```

The PLL is selected as final source for the system clock:

```
reg32 = RCC_CFGR;
reg32 &= ~((1 << 1) | (1 << 0));
RCC_CFGR = (reg32 | RCC_CFGR_SW_PLL);
DMB();
while ((RCC_CFGR & ((1 << 1) | (1 << 0))) != RCC_CFGR_SW_PLL);
```

The internal oscillator is no longer in use, and can be disabled. The control returns to the caller, and all the clocks are successfully set.

As mentioned earlier, the procedure for the clock initialization is strictly dependent on the PLL configuration in the microcontroller. To properly initialize the system clocks required for the CPU and the peripherals to operate at the desired frequencies, it is always advised to refer to the datasheet of the microcontroller provided by the silicon manufacturer. As a second example, we can verify how QEMU is capable of emulating the behavior of the LM3S6965 microcontroller. The emulator provides a virtual clock, which is configurable using the same initialization procedure as described on the manufacturer datasheet. On this platform, two registers are used for clock configuration, referred to as RCC and RCC2:

```
#define RCC     (*(volatile uint32_t*))(0x400FE060)
#define RCC2    (*(volatile uint32_t*))(0x400FE070)
```

To reset the RCC to a known state, the reset value must be written to these registers at boot:

```
#define RCC_RESET   (0x078E3AD1)
#define RCC2_RESET  (0x07802810)
```

This microcontroller uses a raw interrupt to notify that the PLL is locked to the requested frequency. The interrupt status can be checked by reading the bit 6 in the Raw Interrupt Status Register:

```
#define RIS (*(volatile uint32_t*))(0x400FE050)
#define PLL_LRIS (1 << 6)
```

The clock configuration routine in this case starts by resetting the RCC registers, and setting the appropriate values to configure the PLL. The PLL is configured to generate a 400 MHz clock from an 8 MHz oscillator source:

```
void rcc_config(void)
{
    RCC = RCC_RESET;
    RCC2 = RCC2_RESET;
    DMB();
    RCC = RCC_SYSDIV_50MHZ | RCC_PWMDIV_64 |
    RCC_XTAL_8MHZ_400MHZ | RCC_USEPWMDIV;
```

The resultant 50 MHz CPU frequency is derived from this master 400 MHz clock using the system divider. The clock is pre-divided by two, and then a factor of 4 is applied:

```
RCC2 = RCC2_SYSDIV2_4;
DMB();
```

The external oscillators are powered on:

```
RCC  &= ~RCC_OFF;
RCC2 &= ~RCC2_OFF;
```

And, the system clock divider as well. As long as the bypass bit is set, the oscillator is used as a source for the system clock, and the PLL is bypassed:

```
RCC |= RCC_BYPASS | RCC_USESYSDIV;
DMB();
```

The execution is held until the PLL is stable and has locked on the desired frequency:

```
while ((RIS & PLL_LRIS) == 0);
```

Disabling the bypass bits in the RCC registers at this point is sufficient to connect the PLL output to the system clock:

```
RCC  &= ~RCC_BYPASS;
RCC2 &= ~RCC2_BYPASS;
}
```

Clock distribution

Once the bus clocks are available, the RCC logic can be programmed to distribute the clock to single peripherals. To do so, the RCC exposes bit-mapped peripheral clock source registers. Setting the corresponding bit in one of the registers enables the clock for each mapped peripherals in the microcontroller. Each register can control clock gating for 32 peripheral.

The order of the peripherals, and consequently the corresponding register and bit, are strictly dependent on the specific microcontrollers. The STM32F4 has three registers dedicated to this purpose. For example, to enable the clock source for the internal watchdog, it is sufficient to set the bit number 9 in the clock enable register at address 0x40021001c:

```
#define APB1_CLOCK_ER (*(uint32_t *)(0x4002001c))
#define WDG_APB1_CLOCK_ER_VAL (1 << 9)


APB1_CLOCK_ER |= WDG_APB1_CLOCK_ER_VAL;
```

Keeping the clock source off for a peripheral that is not in use saves power, thus, if the target supports clock gating, it can implement optimization and fine-tuning of power consumption by disabling the single peripherals at runtime through their clock gates.

Enabling the SysTick

Once a stable CPU frequency has been set up, we can configure the main timer on the system, the SysTick. Since the implementation of a specific system timer is not mandatory on all Cortex-M, sometimes it is necessary to use an ordinary auxiliary timer to keep track of the system time. In most cases, though, the SysTick interrupt can be enabled by accessing its configuration, which is located in the system control block within the system configuration region. In all Cortex-M microcontrollers that include a system tick, the configuration can be found starting at address 0xE000E010, and exposes four registers:

- The control/status register (SYSTICK_CSR) at offset 0
- The reload value register (SYSTICK_RVR) at offset 4
- The current value register (SYSTICK_CVR) at offset 8
- The calibration register (SYSTICK_CALIB) at offset 12

The SysTick works as a countdown timer. It holds a 24-bit value, which is decreased at every CPU clock tick. The timer reloads the same value every time it reaches 0, and triggers the SysTick interrupt if it is configured to do so.

As a shortcut to access the SysTick registers, we define their locations:

```
#define SYSTICK_BASE  (0xE000E010)
#define SYSTICK_CSR   (*(volatile uint32_t *)(SYSTICK_BASE + 0x00))
#define SYSTICK_RVR   (*(volatile uint32_t *)(SYSTICK_BASE + 0x04))
#define SYSTICK_CVR   (*(volatile uint32_t *)(SYSTICK_BASE + 0x08))
#define SYSTICK_CALIB (*(volatile uint32_t *)(SYSTICK_BASE + 0x0C))
```

Since we know the frequency of the CPU in Hz, we can define the system tick interval by setting the value in the **Reload Value Register (RVR)**. For a 1 ms interval in between two consecutive ticks, we simply divide the frequency by 1,000. We can also set the current value for the `timer` to 0, so that the first interrupt is immediately triggered after we enable the countdown. The SysTick can finally be enabled by configuring the control/status register. The meaning of the least significant three bits of the CSR are as follows:

- **Bit 0**: Enables countdown. After this bit is set, the counter in the SysTick timer is automatically decreased at every CPU clock interval.
- **Bit 1**: Enables interrupt. If this bit is set when the counter reaches 0, a SysTick interrupt will be generated.
- **Bit 2**: Source clock selection. If this bit is reset, an external reference clock is used as source. The CPU clock is used as source when this bit is set.

We are going to define a custom SysTick interrupt handler, so we want to set bit 1 as well. Because we configured the CPU clock correctly, and we are scaling the system tick interval reload value on that, we also want bit 2 to be set. The last line of our `systick_enable` routine will enable the three bits together in the CSR:

```
void systick_enable(void) {
    SYSTICK_RVR = ((CPU_FREQ / 1000) - 1);
    SYSTICK_CVR = 0;
    SYSTICK_CSR = (1 << 0) | (1 << 1) | (1 << 2);
}
```

The system timer that we have configured is the same as that used by real-time operating systems to initiate process switches. In our case, it might be helpful to keep a monotonic system wallclock, measuring the time elapsed since the clock configuration. A minimalist implementation of the interrupt service routine for the system timer could be as follows:

```
volatile unsigned int jiffies = 0;
void isr_systick(void)
{
    ++jiffies;
}
```

This simple function, and the associated global `volatile` variable associated, are sufficient to keep track of the time transparently while the application is running. In fact, the system tick interrupt happens independently, at regular intervals, when the `jiffies` variable is incremented in the interrupt handler, without altering the flow of the main application. What actually happens is that every time the system tick counter reaches 0, the execution is suspended, and the interrupt routine quickly executes. When `isr_systick` returns, the flow of the main application is resumed by restoring exactly the same context of execution stored in memory a moment before the interrupt occurred.

The reason why the system timer variable must be defined and declared everywhere as `volatile` is that its value is supposed to change while executing the application in a way that is independent of the behavior possibly predicted by the compiler for the local context of execution. The keyword `volatile` in this case ensures that the compiler is forced to produce code that checks the value of the variable every time it is instantiated, by disallowing the use of optimizations based on the false assumption that the variable is not being modified by the local code.

Here is an example main program that uses the previous functions to boot the system, configure the master clock, and enable the SysTick:

```
void main(void) {
    flash_set_waitstates();
    clock_config();
    systick_enable();
    while(1) {
        WFI();
    }
}
```

The shortcut for the assembly instruction **WFI**, short for **wait for interrupt**, is defined. It is used in the main application to keep the CPU inactive until the next interrupt occurs:

```
#define WFI() asm volatile ("wfi")
```

To verify that the SysTick is actually running, the program can be executed with the debugger attached, and stopped after a while. If the system tick has been configured correctly, the variable `jiffies` should always be displaying the time in milliseconds elapsed since boot.

Generic timers

Providing a SysTick timer is not mandatory for low-end microcontrollers. Some targets may not have a system timer, but all of them expose some kind of interface to program a number of general-purpose timers for the program to be able to implement time-driven operations. Timers in general are very flexible and easy to configure, and are generally capable of triggering interrupts at regular intervals. The STM32F4 provides up to 17 timers, each with different characteristics. Timers are in general independent from each other, as each of them has its own interrupt line and a separate peripheral clock gate. On the STM32F4, for example, these are the steps needed to enable the clock source and the interrupt line for timer 2. The timer interface is based on a counter that is incremented at every tick. The interface exposed on this platform is very flexible and supports a number of features, including the selection of a different clock source for input, the possibility to concatenate timers, and even the internals of the timer implementation that can be programmed. It is possible to configure the timer to count up or down, and trigger interrupt events on different values of the internal counter. Timers can be one-shot or continuous.

An abstraction of the timer interface can usually be found in support libraries provided by the silicon vendor, or in other open source libraries. However, in order to understand the interface exposed by the microcontroller, the example provided here is once again directly communicating with the peripherals using the configuration registers.

This example mostly uses the default settings for a general-purpose timer on the STM32F407. By default, the counter is increased at every tick, up to its automatic reload value, and continuously generates interrupt events on overflow. A prescaler value can be set to divide the clock source to increase the range of the possible intervals. To generate interrupts spread at a constant given interval, only a few registers need to be accessed:

- **Control registers 1** and **2 (CR1, CR2)**
- The **DMA/Interrupt enable register (DIER)**
- The **status register (SR)**
- The **prescaler counter (PSC)**
- The **auto-reload register (ARR)**

In general, the offsets for these registers are the same for all the timers, so that, given the base address, they can be calculated using a macro. In this case, only the register, for the timer in use are defined:

```
#define TIM2_BASE (0x40000000)
#define TIM2_CR1 (*(volatile uint32_t *)(TIM2_BASE + 0x00))
#define TIM2_DIER (*(volatile uint32_t *)(TIM2_BASE + 0x0c))
```

```
#define TIM2_SR (*(volatile uint32_t *)(TIM2_BASE + 0x10))
#define TIM2_PSC (*(volatile uint32_t *)(TIM2_BASE + 0x28))
#define TIM2_ARR (*(volatile uint32_t *)(TIM2_BASE + 0x2c))
```

Also, for readability, we define some relevant bit position in the registers that we are going to configure:

```
#define TIM_DIER_UIE (1 << 0)
#define TIM_SR_UIF (1 << 0)
#define TIM_CR1_CLOCK_ENABLE (1 << 0)
#define TIM_CR1_UPD_RS (1 << 2)
```

First of all, we are going to define a service routine. The `timer` interface requires us to clear one flag in the status register. In this simple case, all we do is increment a local variable, so that we can verify that the `timer` is being executed by inspecting it in the debugger. We mark the `timer2_ticks` variable as `volatile` so it does not get optimized out by the compiler, since it is never used in the code:

```
void isr_tim2(void)
{
    static volatile uint32_t timer2_ticks = 0;
    TIM2_SR &= ~TIM_SR_UIF;
    timer2_ticks++;
}
```

The service routine must be associated, by including a pointer to the function in the right position within the interrupt vector defined in `startup.c`:

```
isr_tim2 , // TIM2_IRQ 28
```

If the timer is connected to a different branch in the clock tree, as in this case, we need to account for the additional scaling factor between the clock bus that feeds the timer, and the actual CPU clock frequency, while calculating the values for the prescaler and the reload threshold. Timer 2 on STM32F407 is connected to the APB bus, which runs at half of the CPU frequency.

This initialization is an example of a function that automatically calculates `TIM2_PSC` and `TIM2_ARR` values, and initializes a timer based on the given interval, expressed in milliseconds. The clock variable must be set to the frequency of the clock source for the timer, which may differ from the CPU frequency.

The following definitions are specific for our platform, mapping the address for the clock gating configuration and the interrupt number of the device we want to use:

```
#define APB1_CLOCK_ER (*(volatile uint32_t *)(0x40023840))
#define APB1_CLOCK_RST (*(volatile uint32_t *)(0x40023820))
#define TIM2_APB1_CLOCK_ER_VAL (1 << 0)
#define NVIC_TIM2_IRQN (28)
```

And, here is the function to invoke from `main` to enable a continuous `timer` interrupt at the desired interval:

```
int timer_init(uint32_t clock, uint32_t interval_ms)
{
    uint32_t val = 0;
    uint32_t psc = 1;
    uint32_t err = 0;
    clock = (clock / 1000) * interval_ms;
    while (psc < 65535) {
        val = clock / psc;
        err = clock % psc;
        if ((val < 65535) && (err == 0)) {
            val--;
            break;
        }
        val = 0;
        psc++;
    }
    if (val == 0)
        return -1;
    nvic_irq_enable(NVIC_TIM2_IRQN);
    nvic_irq_setprio(NVIC_TIM2_IRQN, 0);
    APB1_CLOCK_RST |= TIM2_APB1_CLOCK_ER_VAL;
    DMB();
    APB1_CLOCK_RST &= ~TIM2_APB1_CLOCK_ER_VAL;
    APB1_CLOCK_ER |= TIM2_APB1_CLOCK_ER_VAL;
    TIM2_CR1 = 0;
    DMB();
    TIM2_PSC = psc;
    TIM2_ARR = val;
    TIM2_CR1 |= TIM_CR1_CLOCK_ENABLE;
    TIM2_DIER |= TIM_DIER_UIE;
    DMB();
    return 0;
}
```

The example presented here is only one of the possible applications of system timers.

General-purpose I/O

The majority of the pins of a microcontroller chip represents configurable input/output lines. Each pin can be configured to represent a logic level by driving the voltage of the pin as a digital output, or to sense the logic state by comparing the voltage as a digital input. Some of the generic pins, though, can be associated to alternate functions, such as analog input, a serial interface, or the output pulse from a timer. Pins may have several possible configurations, but only one is activated at a time. The GPIO controller exposes the configuration of all the pins, and manages the association of the pins to the subsystems when alternate functions are in use.

Pin configuration

Depending on the logic of the GPIO controller, the pins can be activated all together, separately, or in groups. In order to implement a driver to set up the pins and use them as needed, it is possible to refer to the datasheet of the microcontroller, or any example implementation provided by the silicon vendor.

In the case of the STM32F4, general-purpose I/O pins are divided in groups. Each group is connected to a separate clock gate, so, to use the pins associated to a group, the clock gate must be enabled. The following code will distribute the clock source to the GPIO controller for the group D:

```
#define AHB1_CLOCK_ER (*(volatile uint32_t *)(0x40023840))
#define GPIOD_AHB1_CLOCK_ER (1 << 3)
AHB1_CLOCK_ER |= GPIOD_AHB1_CLOCK_ER;
```

The configuration registers associated to the GPIO controllers are mapped to a specific area in the peripherals region as well. In the case of the GPIOD controller, the base address is at 0x40020C00. On the STM32F4 microcontrollers, there are 10 different registers for configuring and using each digital I/O group. As groups are composed of at most 16 pins, some registers may use a representation of two bits per pin:

- Mode register (offset 0 in the address space) selects the mode (among digital input, digital output, alternate function or analog input), using two bits per pin
- Output type register (offset 4) selects the output signal driving logic (push-pull or open-drain)
- Output speed register (offset 8) selects output drive speed

- Pull-up register (offset 12) enables or disables the internal pull-up or pull-down resistor
- Port input data (offset 16) is used to read the state of a digital input pin
- Port output data (offset 20) containing the current value of the digital output
- Port bit set/reset (offset 24) used to drive a digital output signal high or low
- Port configuration lock (offset 28)
- Alternate function low bit register (offset 32), four bits per pin, pins 0-7
- Alternate function high bit register (offset 36), four bits per pin, pins 8-15

The pin must be configured before use, and the clock gating configured to route the source clock to the controller for the group. The configurations available on this GPIO controller can be better explained by looking at specific examples.

Digital output

Enabling a digital output is possible by setting the mode to output in the mode register bits corresponding to the given pin. To be able to control the level of pin D13, which is also connected to an LED on our reference platform, we need to access the following registers:

```
#define GPIOD_BASE    0x40020c00
#define GPIOD_MODE    (*(volatile uint32_t *)(GPIOD_BASE + 0x00))
#define GPIOD_OTYPE   (*(volatile uint32_t *)(GPIOD_BASE + 0x04))
#define GPIOD_PUPD    (*(volatile uint32_t *)(GPIOD_BASE + 0x0c))
#define GPIOD_ODR     (*(volatile uint32_t *)(GPIOD_BASE + 0x14))
#define GPIOD_BSRR    (*(volatile uint32_t *)(GPIOD_BASE + 0x18))
```

In later examples, alternate functions are used to change the pin assignment. The two registers containing the alternate function settings are:

```
#define GPIOD_AFL    (*(volatile uint32_t *)(GPIOD_BASE + 0x20))
#define GPIOD_AFH    (*(volatile uint32_t *)(GPIOD_BASE + 0x24))
```

The following simple functions are meant to control the output of the pin D15 connected to the blue LED on the STM32F4. The main program must call `led_setup` before any other function call, in order to configure the pin as output, and activate the pull-up/pull-down internal resistor:

```
#define LED_PIN (15)
void led_setup(void)
{
    uint32_t mode_reg;
```

First, the clock gating is configured to enable the clock source for the GPIOD controller:

```
AHB1_CLOCK_ER |= GPIOD_AHB1_CLOCK_ER;
```

The mode register is altered to set the mode for GPIO D15 to digital output. The operation is done in two steps. Any previous value set in the two bits corresponding to the position of the pin mode within the register is erased:

```
GPIOD_MODE &= ~ (0x03 << (LED_PIN * 2));
```

In the same position, the value 1 is set, meaning that the pin is now configured as digital output:

```
GPIOD_MODE |= 1 << (LED_PIN * 2);
```

To enable the pull-up and pull-down internal resistors, we do the same. The value to set in this case is 2, corresponding to the following:

```
    GPIOD_PUPD &= 0x03 << (LED_PIN * 2);
    GPIOD_PUPD |= 0x02 << (LED_PIN * 2);
}
```

After the setup function is invoked, the application and the interrupt handlers can call the functions exported, to set the value of the pin high or low, by acting on the bit set/reset register:

```
void led_on(void)
{
    GPIOD_BSRR |= 1 << LED_PIN;
}
```

The highest half of the BSRR is used to reset the pins. Writing 1 in the reset register bit drives the pin logic level to low:

```
void led_off(void)
{
    GPIOD_BSRR |= 1 << (LED_PIN + 16);
}
```

A convenience function is defined, to toggle the LED value, from on to off, and vice versa:

```
void led_toggle(void)
{
    if ((GPIOD_ODR & (1 << LED_PIN)) == (1 << LED_PIN))
        led_off();
    else
        led_on();
}
```

Using the `timer` configured in the previous section, it is possible to run a small program that blinks the blue LED on the STM32F407-Discovery. The `led_toggle` function can be called from inside the service routine of the `timer` implemented in the previous section:

```
void isr_tim2(void)
{
    TIM2_SR &= ~TIM_SR_UIF;
    led_toggle();
}
```

In the main program, the LED driver must be initialized before starting the timer:

```
void main(void) {
    flash_set_waitstates();
    clock_config();
    led_setup();
    timer_init(CPU_FREQ, 1, 1000);
    while(1)
        WFI();
}
```

The main loop of the program is empty. The `led_toggle` action is invoked every second to blink the LED.

PWM

Pulse Width Modulation, or **PWM** for brevity, is a commonly used technique to control different types of actuators, encode messages into signal with different pulse duration, and in general to generate pulses with fixed frequency and variable duty cycles on digital output lines for different purposes.

The `timer` interface may allow associating pins to output a PWM signal. On our reference microcontroller, four output compare channels can be associated to general-purpose timers, and the pins connected to the OC channels may be configured to output the encoded output automatically. On the STM32F407-Discovery board, the blue LED pin PD15, used in the previous example to demonstrate digital output functionality, is associated to the OC4 that can be driven by timer 4. According to the chip documentation, selecting the alternate function 2 for the pin directly connects the output pin to OC4.

The following diagram shows the pin configuration to use alternate function 2 to connect it to the output of the timer:

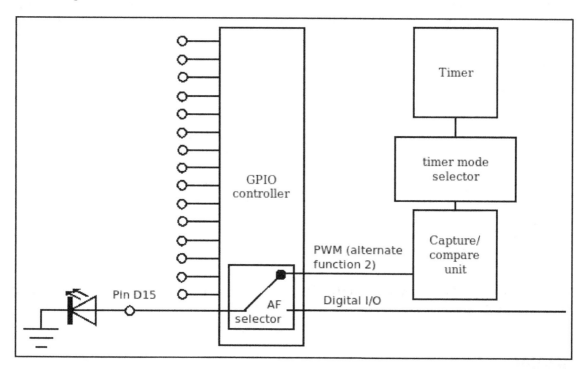

Configuring pin D15 to use alternate function 2 connects it to the output of the timer

The pin is initialized, and set to use the alternate configuration instead of the plain digital output, by clearing the `MODE` register bits and setting the value to `2`:

```
GPIOD_MODE &= ~ (0x03 << (LED_PIN * 2));
GPIOD_MODE |= (2 << (LED_PIN * 2));
```

Pins from 0 to 7 in this GPIO group use four bits each in the AFL register of the `GPIOD` controller. Higher pins, in the range 8-15, use four bit each in the AFH register. Once the alternate mode is selected, the right alternate function number is programmed into the four bits associated to pin 15, so using the AFH register in this case:

```
uint32_t value;
if (LED_PIN < 8) {
    value = GPIOD_AFL & (~(0xf << (LED_PIN * 4)));
    GPIOD_AFL = value | (0x2 << (LED_PIN * 4));
} else {
    value = GPIOD_AFH & (~(0xf << ((LED_PIN - 8) * 4)));
    GPIOD_AFH = value |(0x2 << ((LED_PIN - 8) * 4));
}
```

The `pwm_led_init()` function, that we can call from the main program to configure the LED pin PD15, will look like this:

```
void led_pwm_setup(void)
{
    AHB1_CLOCK_ER |= GPIOD_AHB1_CLOCK_ER;
    GPIOD_MODE &= ~ (0x03 << (LED_PIN * 2));
    GPIOD_MODE |= (2 << (LED_PIN * 2));
    GPIOD_OSPD &= ~(0x03 << (LED_PIN * 2));
    GPIOD_OSPD |= (0x03 << (LED_PIN * 2));
    GPIOD_PUPD &= ~(0x03 << (LED_PIN * 2));
    GPIOD_PUPD |= (0x02 << (LED_PIN * 2));
    GPIOD_AFH &= ~(0xf << ((LED_PIN - 8) * 4));
    GPIOD_AFH |= (0x2 << ((LED_PIN - 8) * 4));
}
```

The function that sets up the timer for PWM generation is similar to the one used in the simple interrupt-generating timer in the digital output example, except that configuring the timer to output a PWM involves modifying the value of four additional registers:

- The **capture/compare enable register (CCER)**
- The **capture/compare mode registers 1** and **2 (CCMR1** and **CCMR2)**
- The **capture channel 4 (CC4)** configuration

The signature of the function we will use in the example to configure a PWM with the given duty cycle has the following signature:

```
int pwm_init(uint32_t clock, uint32_t dutycycle)
{
```

Enabling the clock gate to turn on timer 4 is still required:

```
APB1_CLOCK_RST &= ~TIM4_APB1_CLOCK_ER_VAL;
APB1_CLOCK_ER |= TIM4_APB1_CLOCK_ER_VAL;
```

Both the timer and its output compare channels are temporarily disabled to start the configuration from a clean slate:

```
TIM4_CCER &= ~TIM_CCER_CC4_ENABLE;
TIM4_CR1 = 0;
TIM4_PSC = 0;
```

For this example, we can use a fixed PWM frequency of 100 KHz, by setting the automatic reload value to 1/100000 of the input clock, and enforcing no use of the prescaler:

```
uint32_t val = clock / 100000;
```

The duty cycle is calculated according to the value that is passed as second parameter to pwm_init(), expressed as a percentage. To calculate the corresponding threshold level, this simple formula is used, so that, for example, a value of 80 means that the PWM will be active for 4/5 of the time. The resultant value is decremented by one, only if not zero to avoid underflow:

```
lvl = (val * threshold) / 100;
if (lvl != 0)
    lvl--;
```

Comparator value register CCR4, and auto-reload value register ARR, are set accordingly:

```
TIM4_ARR = val - 1;
TIM4_CCR4 = lvl;
```

In order to correctly set up a PWM signal on this platform, we first ensure that the portions of the CCMR1 register we are going to configure are correctly cleared. This includes the capture selection and the mode configuration:

```
TIM4_CCMR1 &= ~(0x03 << 0);
TIM4_CCMR1 &= ~(0x07 << 4);
```

The PWM1 mode selected is just one of the possible alternate configurations that are based on the capture/compare timer. To enable the mode, we set the PWM1 value in CCMR2, after clearing the relevant bits of the registers:

```
TIM4_CCMR1 &= ~(0x03 << 0);
TIM4_CCMR1 &= ~(0x07 << 4);
TIM4_CCMR1 |= TIM_CCMR1_OC1M_PWM1;
```

```
TIM4_CCMR2 &= ~(0x03 << 8);
TIM4_CCMR2 &= ~(0x07 << 12);
TIM4_CCMR2 |= TIM_CCMR2_OC4M_PWM1;
```

Finally, we enable the OC4. The timer is then set up to automatically reload its stored value every time that the counter overflows:

```
TIM4_CCMR2 |= TIM_CCMR2_OC4M_PWM1;
TIM4_CCER  |= TIM_CCER_CC4_ENABLE;
TIM4_CR1   |= TIM_CR1_CLOCK_ENABLE | TIM_CR1_ARPE;
}
```

Using a PWM to drive the voltage applied on the LED modify its brightness, according to the configured duty cycle. An example program such as the following reduces the brightness of the LED to 50%, if compared to that of an LED powered by a constant voltage output, like the one in the digital output example:

```
void main(void) {
    flash_set_waitstates();
    clock_config();
    led_pwm_setup();
    pwm_init(CPU_FREQ, 50);
    while(1)
        WFI();
}
```

The effect of the PWM on the LED brightness can be better visualized by dynamically altering the duty cycle. It is possible, for example, to set up a second timer to generate an interrupt every 50 ms. In the interrupt handler, the duty cycle factor is cycling in the range 0-80% and back, using 16 steps. In the first eight steps the duty cycle is increased by 10% at every interrupt, from 0 to 80%, and in the last eight steps it is reduced at the same rate, bringing the duty cycle back to 0:

```
void isr_tim2(void) {
    static uint32_t tim2_ticks = 0;
    TIM2_SR &= ~TIM_SR_UIF;
    if (tim2_ticks > 16)
        tim2_ticks = 0;
    if (tim2_ticks > 8)
        pwm_init(master_clock, 10 * (16 - tim2_ticks));
    else
        pwm_init(master_clock, 10 * tim2_ticks);
    tim2_ticks++;
}
```

If we initialize timer 2 in the main program to trigger interrupts spread over constant intervals, like in the previous examples, we can see the LED pulsating, rhythmically fading in and out.

In this case, timer 2 is initialized by the main program, and its associated interrupt handler updates the settings for timer 4, 20 times per second:

```
void main(void) {
    flash_set_waitstates();
    clock_config();
    led_pwm_setup();
    pwm_init(CPU_FREQ, 0);
    timer_init(CPU_FREQ, 1, 50);
    while(1)
        WFI();
}
```

Digital input

A GPIO pin configured in input mode detects the logic level of the voltage applied to it. The logic value of all the input pins on a GPIO controller can be read from the **input data register (IDR)**. On the reference board, the pin A0 is connected to the user button, so the status of the button can be read at any time while the application is running.

The GPIOA controller can be turned on by clock gating:

```
#define AHB1_CLOCK_ER (*(volatile uint32_t *)(0x40023830))
#define GPIOA_AHB1_CLOCK_ER (1 << 0)
```

The controller itself is mapped at address 0x40020000:

```
#define GPIOA_BASE 0x40020000
#define GPIOA_MODE (*(volatile uint32_t *)(GPIOA_BASE + 0x00))
#define GPIOA_IDR (*(volatile uint32_t *)(GPIOA_BASE + 0x10))
```

To set up the pin for input, we only ensure that the mode is set to 0, by clearing the two mode bits relative to pin 0:

```
#define BUTTON_PIN (0)
void button_setup(void)
{
    AHB1_CLOCK_ER |= GPIOA_AHB1_CLOCK_ER;
    GPIOA_MODE &= ~ (0x03 << (BUTTON_PIN * 2));
}
```

The application can now check the status of the button at any time by reading the lowest bit of the IDR. When the button is pressed, the reference voltage is connected to the pin, and the value of the bit corresponding to the pin changes from 0 to 1:

```
int button_is_pressed(void)
{
    return (GPIOA_IDR & (1 << BUTTON_PIN)) >> BUTTON_PIN;
}
```

Interrupt-based input

Having to proactively read the value of the pin by constantly polling the IDR is not convenient in many cases, where the application is supposed to react to state changes. Microcontrollers usually provide mechanisms to connect digital input pins to interrupt lines, so that the application can react in real time to events related to the input because the execution is interrupted to execute the associated service routine.

On the reference MCU, the pin A0 can be connected to the external interrupt and event controller, also known as **EXTI**. EXTI offers a number of edge-detection triggers that can be attached to interrupt lines. The number of the pin within the GPIO group determines the number of the EXTI interrupt that is associated to it, so that the EXTI 0 interrupt routine may be connected to the pin 0 of any GPIO group, if needed:

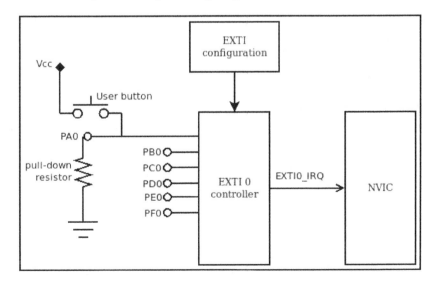

EXTI0 controller associating edge detection triggers to the user button connected to PA0

To associate **PA0** to **EXTI 0**, the **EXTI configuration** register must be modified to set the number of the GPIO group in the bits associated to **EXTI 0**. In the STM32F4, the EXTI configuration registers (EXTI_CR) are located at address 0x40013808. Each register is used to set the interrupt controller associated to an EXTI line. The lowest four bits of the first register are relative to EXTI line 0. The number for the GPIO group A is 0, so we need to ensure that the corresponding bits are cleared in the first EXTI_CR. The goal of the next example is to demonstrate how to enable the **EXTI 0** interrupt and associate it to the pin A0, so the following definitions are provided to access the first EXTI_CR to set the GPIO group A:

```
#define EXTI_CR_BASE (0x40013808)
#define EXTI_CR0 (*(volatile uint32_t *)(EXTI_CR_BASE + 0x00))
#define EXTI_CR_EXTI0_MASK (0x0F)
```

The EXTI0 interrupt is connected to NVIC line number 6, so we add this definition to configure the NVIC:

```
#define NVIC_EXTI0_IRQN (6)
```

The EXTI controller in STM32F4 microcontrollers is located at address 0x40013C00, and provides the following registers:

- **Interrupt mask register (IMR)** at offset 0. Sets/clears the corresponding bit to enable/disable the interrupt for each of the EXTI lines.
- **Event mask register (EMR)** at offset 4. Sets/clears the corresponding bit to enable/disable the event trigger for the corresponding EXTI line.
- **Rising trigger select register (RTSR)** at offset 8. Sets the corresponding bit to generate events and interrupts when the associated digital input level switches from 0 to 1.
- **Falling trigger select register (FTSR)** at offset 12. Sets the corresponding bit to generate events and interrupts when the associated signal falls from a logic value of 1 back to 0.
- **Software interrupt enable register (SWIER)** at offset 16. If a bit is set in this register, the associated interrupt event will be immediately generated, and the service routine executed. This mechanism can be used to implement custom software interrupts.
- **Pending interrupt register (PR)** at offset 20. To clear a pending interrupt, the service routine should set the bit corresponding to the EXTI line, or the interrupt will remain pending. A new service routine will be spawned until the PR bit for the EXTI line is cleared.

For convenience, we may define the registers as follows:

```
#define EXTI_BASE (0x40013C00)
#define EXTI_IMR (*(volatile uint32_t *)(EXTI_BASE + 0x00))
#define EXTI_EMR (*(volatile uint32_t *)(EXTI_BASE + 0x04))
#define EXTI_RTSR (*(volatile uint32_t *)(EXTI_BASE + 0x08))
#define EXTI_FTSR (*(volatile uint32_t *)(EXTI_BASE + 0x0c))
#define EXTI_SWIER (*(volatile uint32_t *)(EXTI_BASE + 0x10))
#define EXTI_PR (*(volatile uint32_t *)(EXTI_BASE + 0x14))
```

The procedure to enable the interrupt on the rising edge of PA0, associated to the button press, is the following:

```
void button_setup(void)
{
    AHB1_CLOCK_ER |= GPIOA_AHB1_CLOCK_ER;
    GPIOA_MODE &= ~ (0x03 << (BUTTON_PIN * 2));
    EXTI_CR0 &= ~EXTI_CR_EXTI0_MASK;
    nvic_irq_enable(NVIC_EXTI0_IRQN);
    EXTI_IMR |= 1 << BUTTON_PIN;
    EXTI_EMR |= 1 << BUTTON_PIN;
    EXTI_RTSR |= 1 << BUTTON_PIN;
}
```

The ISR, IMR, and RTSR corresponding bits have been set, and the interrupt has been enabled in the NVIC. Instead of polling for the value of the digital input to change, we can now define a service routine that will be invoked every time the button is pressed:

```
volatile uint32_t button_presses = 0;
void isr_exti0(void)
{
    EXTI_PR |= 1 << BUTTON_PIN;
    button_presses++;
}
```

In this simple example, the `button_presses` counter is expected to increase by one at every button press event. In a real-life scenario, buttons based on mechanical contact like the one on the STM32F407-Discovery are tricky to control using this mechanism. A single physical button press may in fact trigger the rising front interrupt multiple times during the transitory phase. This phenomenon, known as a button bouncing effect, can be mitigated using specific *debounce* techniques, which are not discussed here.

Analog input

Some pins have the possibility to measure the applied voltage dynamically, and assign a discrete number to the measured value, using an **analog to digital signal converter**, or **ADC**. This is very useful to acquire data from a wide range of sensors, capable of conveying the information as output voltage, or simply using a variable resistor.

The configuration of the ADC subsystem may vary significantly across different platforms. ADCs on modern microcontrollers offer a wide range of configuration options. The reference microcontroller equips three separate ADC controllers, sharing 16 input channels, and each one with a resolution of 12 bits. Multiple features are available, such as DMA transfer of the acquired data, and monitoring the signals in between two watchdog thresholds.

The simplest case consist in the implementation a one-shot read operation for a single conversion. Associating a specific pin to the controller is possible by checking how channels are mapped on the controllers, if the pin supports it and it is connected through a channel to one of the configured as analog input, and reading out the value which results from the conversion of the analog signal. In this example, the pin B1 is used as analog input, and can be connected to the `ADB1` controller through channel 9. The following constants and registers are defined for the configuration of the `ADB1` controller:

```
#define APB2_CLOCK_ER (*(volatile uint32_t *)(0x40023844))
#define ADC1_APB2_CLOCK_ER_VAL (1 << 8)
#define ADC1_BASE (0x40012000)
#define ADC1_SR (*(volatile uint32_t *)(ADC1_BASE + 0x00))
#define ADC1_CR1 (*(volatile uint32_t *)(ADC1_BASE + 0x04))
#define ADC1_CR2 (*(volatile uint32_t *)(ADC1_BASE + 0x08))
#define ADC1_SMPR1 (*(volatile uint32_t *)(ADC1_BASE + 0x0c))
#define ADC1_SMPR2 (*(volatile uint32_t *)(ADC1_BASE + 0x10))
#define ADC1_SQR3 (*(volatile uint32_t *)(ADC1_BASE + 0x34))
#define ADC1_DR (*(volatile uint32_t *)(ADC1_BASE + 0x4c))
#define ADC_CR1_SCAN (1 << 8)
#define ADC_CR2_EN (1 << 0)
#define ADC_CR2_CONT (1 << 1)
#define ADC_CR2_SWSTART (1 << 30)
#define ADC_SR_EOC (1 << 1)
#define ADC_SMPR_SMP_480CYC (0x7)
```

These are the definitions to configure GPIO as usual, this time mapped for `GPIOB`:

```
#define AHB1_CLOCK_ER (*(volatile uint32_t *)(0x40023830))
#define GPIOB_AHB1_CLOCK_ER (1 << 1)
#define GPIOB_BASE (0x40020400)
#define GPIOB_MODE (*(volatile uint32_t *)(GPIOB_BASE + 0x00))
```

```
#define ADC_PIN (1)
#define ADC_PIN_CHANNEL (9)
```

The three ADCs share a few registers for common settings, such as the clock prescale factor, so they will all operate at the same frequency. The prescale factor for the ADC must be set within the working range of the converter recommended by the datasheet. In the target platform, halving the frequency of the APB2 clock through the common prescaler. The common ADC configuration registers start at port 0x40012300:

```
#define ADC_COM_BASE (0x40012300)
#define ADC_COM_CCR (*(volatile uint32_t *)(ADC_COM_BASE + 0x04))
```

Based on these definitions, the initialization function can be written as follows. First, we enable the clock gating for both the ADC controller and the GPIO group:

```
int adc_init(void)
{
    APB2_CLOCK_ER |= ADC1_APB2_CLOCK_ER_VAL;
    AHB1_CLOCK_ER |= GPIOB_AHB1_CLOCK_ER;
```

PB1 is set to analog input mode, corresponding to the value 3 in the mode register:

```
    GPIOB_MODE |= 0x03 << (ADC_PIN * 2);
```

The ADC1 is temporarily switched off to set the desired configuration. The common clock prescaler is set to 0, meaning a divisor of 2 from the input clock. This ensures that the frequency fed to the ADC controller is within its operational range. Scan mode is disabled, and so is continuous mode, as we are not using these features in this example:

```
    ADC1_CR2 &= ~(ADC_CR2_EN);
    ADC_COM_CCR &= ~(0x03 << 16);
    ADC1_CR1 &= ~(ADC_CR1_SCAN);
    ADC1_CR2 &= ~(ADC_CR2_CONT);
```

The sampling frequency can be set using the two registers SMPR1 and SMPR2, depending on the channel in use. Each register represents one channel sample rate using three bits per register, so the channels 0 to 9 are configurable using SMPR1, and all the others through SMPR2. The channel for PB1 is set to 9, so in this case the SMPR1 is used, but to remind about this the generic mechanism to set the sample rate on any channel is provided:

```
if (ADC_PIN_CHANNEL > 9) {
    uint32_t val = ADC1_SMPR2;
    val = ADC_SMPR_SMP_480CYC << ((ADC_PIN_CHANNEL - 10) * 3);
    ADC1_SMPR2 = val;
} else {
    uint32_t val = ADC1_SMPR1;
```

```
        val = ADC_SMPR_SMP_480CYC << (ADC_PIN_CHANNEL * 3);
        ADC1_SMPR1 = val;
}
```

Finally, the channel is enabled in the conversion sequence of the ADC controller using the **sequence registers (SQR)**. The mechanisms foresee that multiple channels can be added to the same sequence on the controller, by populating the registers in inverse order, from SQR3 to SQR1. Each source channel is represented in five bits, so each register contains up to six sources, except SQR1, which stores five, and reserves the higher bits to indicate the length of the stack stored in the registers, minus one. In our case, there is no need to set the length-minus-one field, as it would be zero for a single source in SQR1:

```
    ADC1_SQR3 |= (ADC_PIN_CHANNEL);
```

Finally, the ADC1 is enabled again by setting the enable bit in the CR2, and the initialization function successfully returns:

```
    ADC1_CR2 |= ADC_CR2_EN;
        return 0;
}
```

After the ADC has been initialized and configured to convert the analog signal on PB1, the A/D conversion can be started at any time. A simple blocking read function would initiate the conversion, wait for the conversion to be successfully started, then wait until the conversion is completed by looking at the **end of conversion (EOC)** bit in the status register:

```
int adc_read(void)
{
    ADC1_CR2 |= ADC_CR2_SWSTART;
    while (ADC1_CR2 & ADC_CR2_SWSTART)
        ;
    while ((ADC1_SR & ADC_SR_EOC) == 0)
        ;
```

When the conversion is completed, the corresponding discrete value is available on the lowest 12 bits of the data register, and can be returned to the caller:

```
        return (int)(ADC1_DR);
}
```

The watchdog

Another common feature in many microcontrollers is the presence of a watchdog timer. A watchdog ensures that the system is not stuck within an endless loop or any other blocking situation within the code. This is particularly useful in bare-metal applications that rely on an event-driven loop, where calls are required not to block, and to return to the main event loop within the allowed amount of time.

The watchdog must be seen as the very last resort to recover an unresponsive system, by triggering a forced reboot regardless of the current state of the execution in the CPU.

The reference platform provides one independent watchdog timer, with a counter similar to those of the generic timers, with a 12-bit granularity and a prescaler factor. The prescaler of the watchdog, however, is expressed in multiples of 2, and has a range between 4 (represented by the value 0) and 256 (value 6).

The clock source is connected to a lower-speed oscillator, through an independent branch of the clock distribution. For this reason, the clock gating is not involved in the activation of this peripheral.

The watchdog configuration area is mapped within the peripherals address region, and consists of four registers:

- The key register (offset 0), used to trigger the three operations unlock, start, and reset by writing predefined values in the lowest 16 bits
- The prescale register (offset 4), to set the prescale factor of the counter
- The reload register (offset 8), containing the reload value for the counter
- The status register (offset 12), providing the status flags to synchronize the setup operations

The registers can be referenced using shortcut macros:

```
#define IWDG_BASE (0x40003000)
#define IWDG_KR (*(volatile uint32_t *)(IWDG_BASE + 0x00))
#define IWDG_PR (*(volatile uint32_t *)(IWDG_BASE + 0x04))
#define IWDG_RLR (*(volatile uint32_t *)(IWDG_BASE + 0x08))
#define IWDG_SR (*(volatile uint32_t *)(IWDG_BASE + 0x0c))
```

The three possible operations that can be triggered via the key register are as follows:

```
#define IWDG_KR_RESET     0x0000AAAA
#define IWDG_KR_UNLOCK    0x00005555
#define IWDG_KR_START     0x0000CCCC
```

Two meaningful status bits are provided in the status, and they must be checked to ensure that the watchdog is not busy before unlocking and setting the value for prescale and reload:

```
#define IWDG_SR_RVU (1 << 1)
#define IWDG_SR_PVU (1 << 0)
```

The initialization function to configure and start the watchdog may look like the following:

```
int iwdt_init(uint32_t interval_ms)
{
    uint32_t pre = 0;
    uint32_t counter;
```

In the next line, the input value in milliseconds is scaled to the frequency of the watchdog clock, which is 32 KHz:

```
    counter = interval_ms << 5;
```

The minimum prescaler factor is 4, however, so the value should be divided again. We then look for the minimum prescaler value that results in a counter that fits the 12 bits available, by halving the counter value and increasing the prescaler factor until the counter is appropriately scaled:

```
    counter >>= 2;
    while (counter > 0xFFF) {
        pre++;
        counter >>= 1;
    }
```

The following checks ensure that the interval provided does not result in a zero-counter, or a value that is too large for the available scaling factor:

```
    if (counter == 0)
        counter = 1;
    if (pre > 6)
        return -1;
```

The actual initialization of the registers is done, but the device requires us to initiate the write with an unlock operation, and only after checking that the registers are available for writing:

```
while(IWDG_SR & IWDG_SR_PR_BUSY);
IWDG_KR = IWDG_KR_UNLOCK;
IWDG_PR = pre;
while (IWDG_SR & IWDG_SR_RLR_BUSY);
IWDG_KR = IWDG_KR_UNLOCK;
IWDG_RLR = counter;
```

Starting the watchdog simply consists of setting the START command in the key register to initiate the start operation:

```
IWDG_KR = IWDG_KR_START;
return 0;
}
```

Once started, the watchdog cannot be stopped and will run forever, decreasing the counter until it reaches zero, and rebooting the system.

The only way to prevent the system from being rebooted is resetting the timer manually, an operation often referred to as *kicking the watchdog*. A watchdog driver should export a function that allows the application to reset the counter, for example, at the end of each iteration in the main loop. Here is ours:

```
void iwdt_reset(void)
{
    IWDG_KR = IWDG_KR_RESET;
}
```

As a simple test for the watchdog driver, a watchdog counter of two seconds can be initialized in main():

```
void main(void) {
    flash_set_waitstates();
    clock_config();
    button_setup();
    iwdt_init(2000);
    while(1)
        WFI();
    }
}
```

The watchdog is reset upon button press, in the interrupt service routine of the button GPIO:

```
void isr_exti0(void)
{
    EXTI_PR |= (1 << BUTTON_PIN);
    iwdt_reset();
}
```

In this test, the system will reboot if the user button is not pressed for two seconds in a row, so the only way to keep the system running is by repeatedly pressing the button.

Summary

The general-purpose peripherals shown in this chapter are commonly supported by a wide range of microcontrollers. Although implementation details such as register names and placement may differ on other targets, the mechanisms described in this chapter are available on most embedded platforms, and they are the bricks for building the most basic system functionalities as well as providing means of interaction with sensors and actuators.

In the next chapter, we focus on serial communication channels provided by most microprocessors as communication interfaces towards other devices, and peripherals in the proximity of the target system.

Local Bus Interfaces

7

Communication with other systems in the vicinity of the target is enabled by a few protocols. Most microcontrollers designed for embedded systems support the most common interfaces that control and discipline the access to serial lines. Some of these protocols are so popular that they have become the standard for wired inter-chip communication among microcontrollers, and for controlling electronic devices, such as sensors, actuators, displays, wireless transceivers, and many other peripherals. This chapter describes how these protocols work, specifically focusing on the implementation of the system software, through examples running on the reference platform. In particular, this chapter contains the following sections:

- Introducing serial communication
- UART-based asynchronous serial bus
- SPI bus
- I^2C bus

Introducing serial communication

All the protocols that we analyze in this chapter manage the access to a serial bus, which may consist of one or more wires, transporting the information in the form of electrical signals corresponding to logic levels, zeros and ones, when associated with specific time intervals. The protocols are different in the way they transmit and receive information on the data bus lines. To transmit a byte, the transceiver encodes it as a bit sequence, which is synchronized with a clock. The logic values of the bit are interpreted by the receiver reading its value on a specific front of the clock, depending on the clock's polarity.

Each protocol specifies the polarity of the clock and the bit order required to transmit the data, which can start with either the most or the least significant bit. For example, a system transmitting the ASCII character D over a serial line regulated by raising clock fronts, with most significant bit first, would produce a signal like the following:

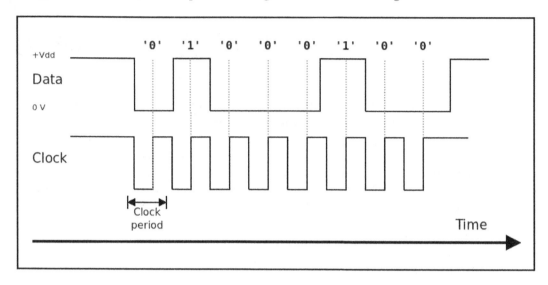

The logic levels of the bus on clock raise fronts are interpreted MSB-first into the byte value of 0x44

Clock and symbol synchronization

In order for the receiving side to understand the message, the clock must be synchronized between the parts. The clock synchronization may be implicit, as in setting the same data rate to read and write on the bus, or achieved by sharing the clock line from one side using an additional line, to explicitly synchronize the transmit data rate. Serial protocols that don't foresee shared clock lines are called asynchronous.

Symbol synchronization should instead be explicit. As we expect to send and receive information in byte form, the beginning of each eight bit sequence should be marked either through special preamble sequences on the data line, or by turning the clock on and off at the right time. The symbol synchronization strategy is defined by each protocol differently.

Bus wiring

The number of lines needed to establish bidirectional communication depends on the specific protocol too. Since one wire can only transport one bit of information in one direction at a time, to achieve full-duplex communication, a transceiver should connect to two different wires for transmitting and receiving data. If the protocol supports half-duplex communication, it should instead provide a reliable mechanism to regulate media access and switch between receiving and transmitting data on the same wire.

Depending on the protocol, devices accessing the bus may either share a similar implementation and act as peers, or have different roles assigned when participating in the communication, for example, if a master device is in charge of synchronizing the clock or regulating the access to the media.

A serial protocol may foresee communication among more than two devices on the same bus. This may be achieved by using extra slave selection wires, one per slave device sharing the same bus, or by assigning logical addresses to each endpoint, and including the destination address for the communication in the preamble of each transmission. Based on these classifications, an overview of the approach taken by the most popular serial protocols implemented in embedded targets is given in the following table:

Protocol	Number of wires	Clock	Symbol synchronization strategy	Bit order	Communication mode
UART-based	Two (data RX/TX)	Asynchronous	Configurable start/stop bit, parity bit	LSB first	One-to-one or one-to-many, single point-to-point communication
SPI	Three (master to slave data, slave to master data, clock)	Shared through CLK	Clock activation	MSB first or LSB first	One-to-many single master, multiple slave, using additional slave-selection lines
I²C	Two (serial data and serial clock)	Shared through SCL	Clock activation, with support for clock stretching	MSB first	One-to-many, master/slave with logic addresses, and dynamic multi-master selection

USB	Two (D+/D- half-duplex differential signal)	Synchronized with a synchronization pattern at the beginning of data transfer	CRC / end of packet	LSB first	One host/multiple devices with device enumeration
CAN bus	Two (CAN-Hi and CAN-Low), differential, half duplex	Asynchronous	Start bit, CRC, and end sequence	MSB first	One-to-many multi-master with address-based master arbitration
Dallas 1-Wire	One data wire	Synchronized with the front of the signal	Slave selection before each byte CRC	LSB first	Master/slave with fixed master, slave discovery with 64-bit addresses

The protocols that are detailed in this chapter are only the first three, as they are the most widely used in communicating with embedded peripherals.

Programming the peripherals

Multiple peripherals implementing the protocols described so far are usually integrated in microcontrollers, which means that the associated serial bus can be directly connected to specific pins of the microcontrollers. The peripherals can be enabled through clock gating, and controlled by accessing configuration registries mapped in the peripheral region in the memory space. The pins connected to serial buses must also be configured to implement the corresponding alternate function, and the interrupt lines involved should be configured to be handled in the vector table.

Some microcontrollers, including our reference platform, support **Direct Memory Access (DMA)** to speed up memory operations between the peripheral and the physical RAM. In many cases, this feature is useful to help process the communication data in a shorter time frame, to improve the responsiveness of the system. The DMA controller can be programmed to initiate a transfer operation and trigger and interrupt when it completes.

The interface to control the features relative to each protocol is specific to the functionalities exposed by the peripheral. In the next sections, the interfaces exposed by UART, SPI, and I²C peripherals are analyzed, and code samples tailored on the reference platform are provided, as examples of one of the possible implementations for similar device drivers.

UART-based asynchronous serial bus

Historically used for many different purposes, thanks to the simplicity of its asynchronous nature, UART dates back to the origins of computing, and it is still a very popular circuit used in many contexts. Personal computers up to the early 2000s included at least one RS-232 serial port, realized with a UART controller and the transceivers allowing to operate at higher voltages. Nowadays, USB has replaced serial communication on personal computers, but host computers can still access TTL serial buses using USB-UART peripherals. Microcontrollers have one or more pairs of pins that can be associated with an internal UART controller, and connected to a serial bus to configure a bidirectional, asynchronous, full-duplex communication channel toward a device connected to the same bus.

Protocol description

As previously mentioned, asynchronous serial communications rely on implicit synchronization of the bit rate between the transmitter and the receiver in order to guarantee that the data is correctly processed on the receiving end of the communication. If the peripheral clock is fast enough to keep the device running at a high frequency, asynchronous serial communication may be pushed up to several megabits per second.

The symbol synchronization strategy is based on the identification of the beginning of the transmission of every single byte on the wire. When no device is transmitting, the bus is in an idle state. To initiate the transmission, the transceiver pulls the TX line down to the low logic level, for a time that is at least half of the bit sampling period depending on the bit rate. The bits composing the byte being transferred are then translated into logical 0 or 1, which are held on the TX line for the time corresponding to each bit, according to the bit rate. After this start condition can be easily recognized by the receiver, the bits composing the symbol follow in a specific order, from the least significant bit up to the most significant one. The number of data bits composing the symbol is also configurable. The default data length of eight bits allows for converting each symbol into a byte. At the end of the data, an optional parity bit can be configured to count the number of active bits, as a very simplistic form of a redundant check. The parity bit, if present, can be configured to indicate whether the number of 1s in the symbol is odd or even. While returning to the idle state, one or two stop bits must be used to indicate the end of the symbol. A stop bit is transmitted by pulling the signal high for the entire duration of a bit transmissions, marking the end of the current symbol, and forcing the receiver to initiate receiving the next one. One stop bit is the most-used default; the 1.5- and 2-stop bit settings provide a longer inter-symbol idling interval that has been useful in the past to communicate with slower, less responsive hardware but is rarely used today.

The two endpoints must be aware of these settings before initiating the communication. Serial controllers do not normally support dynamic detection of the symbol rate or of any of the settings from the device connected to the other end, and, for this reason, the only way to successfully attempt any serial communication is to program both devices on the bus using the same well-known settings. As a recap, these settings are:

- The bit rate, expressed in bits per second
- The number of data bits in each symbol (typically eight)
- The meaning of parity bit, if present (O is odd, E is even, and N is not present)

Additionally, the sender must be configured to send a number of stop bits at the end of each transmission. This group of settings is often abbreviated into something such as 115200-8-N-1 or 38400-8-O-2 to indicate, respectively, a 115.2 Kbps serial line with no parity and one stop bit, and a 38400 line with odd parity and two stop bits.

Programming the controller

Development boards usually provide multiple UARTs, and our reference STM32F407 is not an exception. According to the manual, UART3 can be associated to the pins PD8 (TX) and PD9 (RX), which we will use in this example. This is the code needed to turn on the clock for the GPIO group D, and set the 8 and 9 pins in alternate mode, with an alternate function of 7:

```
#define AHB1_CLOCK_ER (*(volatile uint32_t *)(0x40023830))
#define GPIOD_AHB1_CLOCK_ER (1 << 3)
#define GPIOD_BASE 0x40020c00
#define GPIOD_MODE (*(volatile uint32_t *)(GPIOD_BASE + 0x00))
#define GPIOD_AFL (*(volatile uint32_t *)(GPIOD_BASE + 0x20))
#define GPIOD_AFH (*(volatile uint32_t *)(GPIOD_BASE + 0x24))
#define GPIO_MODE_AF (2)
#define UART3_PIN_AF (7)
#define UART3_RX_PIN (9)
#define UART3_TX_PIN (8)
static void uart3_pins_setup(void)
{
    uint32_t reg;
    AHB1_CLOCK_ER |= GPIOD_AHB1_CLOCK_ER;

    reg = GPIOD_MODE & ~ (0x03 << (UART3_RX_PIN * 2));
    GPIOD_MODE = reg | (2 << (UART3_RX_PIN * 2));
    reg = GPIOD_MODE & ~ (0x03 << (UART3_TX_PIN * 2));
    GPIOD_MODE = reg | (2 << (UART3_TX_PIN * 2));
```

```
        reg = GPIOD_AFH & ~(0xf << ((UART3_TX_PIN - 8) * 4));
        GPIOD_AFH = reg | (UART3_PIN_AF << ((UART3_TX_PIN - 8) * 4));
        reg = GPIOD_AFH & ~(0xf << ((UART3_RX_PIN - 8) * 4));
        GPIOD_AFH = reg | (UART3_PIN_AF << ((UART3_RX_PIN - 8) * 4));
    }
```

The device has its own clock-gating configuration bit in the `APB1_CLOCK_ER` register, at position 18:

```
#define APB1_CLOCK_ER (*(volatile uint32_t *)(0x40023840))
#define UART3_APB1_CLOCK_ER_VAL (1 << 18)
```

Each UART controller can be accessed using registers mapped in the peripheral region, with fixed offsets from the UART controller base address:

- **Status register UART_SR**: A read-only register containing status flags, offset equal to 0
- **Data register UART_DR**: Read/write data register, offset equal to 4
- **Bit rate register, UART_BRR**: To set the clock divisor to obtain the desired bit rate, offset equal to 8
- **Configuration registers UART_CRx**: One or more `UART_CRx` at offset 12, to set the serial port parameters, enable interrupts and DMA, and enable and disable the transceiver

In this example, we define shortcut macros to access the following registers for UART3:

```
#define UART3 (0x40004800)
#define UART3_SR (*(volatile uint32_t *)(UART3))
#define UART3_DR (*(volatile uint32_t *)(UART3 + 0x04))
#define UART3_BRR (*(volatile uint32_t *)(UART3 + 0x08))
#define UART3_CR1 (*(volatile uint32_t *)(UART3 + 0x0c))
#define UART3_CR2 (*(volatile uint32_t *)(UART3 + 0x10))
```

And we define the positions in the corresponding bit fields:

```
#define UART_CR1_UART_ENABLE (1 << 13)
#define UART_CR1_SYMBOL_LEN (1 << 12)
#define UART_CR1_PARITY_ENABLED (1 << 10)
#define UART_CR1_PARITY_ODD (1 << 9)
#define UART_CR1_TX_ENABLE (1 << 3)
#define UART_CR1_RX_ENABLE (1 << 2)
#define UART_CR2_STOPBITS (3 << 12)
#define UART_SR_TX_EMPTY (1 << 7)
```

The `uart3_pins_setup` helper function can be called at the beginning of the initialization function, to set up the pin. The function accepts arguments to set bit rate, parity, and stop bits on the `UART3` port:

```
int uart3_setup(uint32_t bitrate, uint8_t data,
char parity, uint8_t stop)
{
    uart3_pins_setup();
```

The device is turned on:

```
APB1_CLOCK_ER |= UART3_APB1_CLOCK_ER_VAL;
```

In the `CR1` configuration register, the bit to enable the transmitter is set:

```
UART3_CR1 |= UART_CR1_TX_ENABLE;
```

`UART_BRR` is set to contain the divisor between the clock speed and the desired bit rate:

```
UART3_BRR = CLOCK_SPEED / bitrate;
```

Our function also accepts a character to indicate the desired parity. The options are O or E for odd or even. Any other character will keep the parity disabled:

```
switch (parity) {
    case 'O':
        UART3_CR1 |= UART_CR1_PARITY_ODD;
        /* fall through to enable parity */
    case 'E':
        UART3_CR1 |= UART_CR1_PARITY_ENABLED;
    break;
    default:
        UART3_CR1 &= ~(UART_CR1_PARITY_ENABLED |
        UART_CR1_PARITY_ODD);
}
```

The number of stop bits is set according to the parameter. The configuration is stored using two bits of the register, with the value 0 meaning one stop bit, and value 2 meaning two:

```
reg = UART3_CR2 & ~UART_CR2_STOPBITS;
if (stop > 1)
    UART3_CR2 = reg | (2 << 12);
```

The configuration is now complete. The UART can be turned on to initiate transmissions:

```
UART3_CR1 |= UART_CR1_UART_ENABLE;
return 0;
}
```

Serial data can now be transmitted on PD8 simply by copying one byte at a time on the UART_DR register.

Hello world!

One of the most useful functions when developing an embedded system is to convert one of the available UARTs into a logging port, where debug messages and other information produced during the execution can be read on the host computer using a serial-to-USB converter:

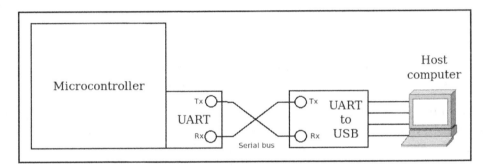

The host is connected to the serial port of the target platform using a converter

The UART logic includes FIFO buffers in both directions. The transmit FIFO is fed by writing on the UART_DR register. To actually output data on the UART TX line in polling mode, we choose to check that the FIFO is empty before writing each character, to ensure that no more that one character is put in the FIFO at a time. When the FIFO is empty, the bit associated with the TX_FIFO_EMPTY flag in UART3_SR is set to 1 by the device. The following function shows how to transmit an entire string of characters passed as an argument, waiting for the FIFO to empty after every byte:

```
void uart3_write(const char *text)
{
    const char *p = text;
    int i;
    volatile uint32_t reg;
    while(*p) {
```

```
        do {
            reg = UART3_SR;
        } while ((reg & UART_SR_TX_EMPTY) == 0);
        UART3_DR = *p;
        p++;
    }
}
```

In the main program, it is possible to call this function with a pre-formatted, NULL-terminated string:

```
#include "system.h"
#include "uart.h"
void main(void) {
    flash_set_waitstates();
    clock_config();
    uart3_setup(115200, 8, 'N', 1);
    uart3_write("Hello World!\r\n");
    while(1)
        WFI();
}
```

If the host is connected to the other endpoint of the serial bus, as a result, we can visualize the Hello World! message using a serial terminal program, such as Minicom, on the host.

By capturing the output of the PD8 pin, used as UART_TX on the target, and setting the right option for the serial decoding, we have a better idea of how the serial flow is parsed on a receiving side. The logic analyzer can show how the data bits are sampled, after every start condition, and reveal the ASCII character associated with the byte on the wire.

Screenshot of the logic analyzer tool, showing the first five bytes sent by the example to the host, using UART3

Newlib printf

Writing pre-formatted strings is not the most ideal API to access a serial port to provide debug messages. Application developers would most certainly prefer if the system exposed a standard C `printf` function. When the toolchain includes an implementation of a standard C library, it usually gives you the possibility to connect the standard output of the main program to a serial interface. Luckily enough, the toolchain in use for the reference platform allows us to link to `newlib` functions. Similar to what we did in Chapter 5, *Memory Management*, using the `malloc` and `free` functions from `newlib`, we provide a backend function called `_write()`, which gets the output redirected from the string formatted by all the calls to `printf()`. The `_write` function implemented here will receive all the strings pre-formatted by `printf()`:

```
int _write(void *r, uint8_t *text, int len)
{
    char *p = (char *)text;
    int i;
    volatile uint32_t reg;
    text[len - 1] = 0;
    while(*p) {
        do {
            reg = UART3_SR;
        } while ((reg & UART_SR_TX_EMPTY) == 0);
        UART3_DR = *p;
        p++;
    }
    return len;
}
```

So, in this case, linking with `newlib` allows us to use `printf` to produce messages, including its variance-argument parsing, like in this example `main()` function:

```
#include <stdio.h>
#include "system.h"
#include "uart.h"

void main(void) {
char name[] = "World";
flash_set_waitstates();
clock_config();
uart3_setup(115200, 8, 'N', 1);

printf("Hello %s!\r\n", name);
    while(1)
```

```
        WFI();
    }
```

This second example will produce the same output as the first one, but this time using the printf function from newlib.

Receiving data

To enable the receiver on the same UART, the initialization function should also turn on the receiver using the corresponding switch in the UART_CR1 register:

```
    UART3_CR1 |= UART_CR1_TX_ENABLE | UART_CR1_RX_ENABLE;
```

This ensures that the receiving side of the transceiver is enabled too. To read data in polling mode, blocking until a character is received, we can use the following function, which will return the value of the byte read:

```
    char uart3_read(void)
    {
        char c;
        volatile uint32_t reg;
        do {
            reg = UART3_SR;
        } while ((reg & UART_SR_RX_NOTEMPTY) == 0);
        c = (char)(UART3_DR & 0xff);
        return c;
    }
```

This way we can, for example, echo back to the console each character received from the host:

```
    void main(void) {
        char c[2];
        flash_set_waitstates();
        clock_config();
        uart3_setup(115200, 8, 'N', 1);
        uart3_write("Hello World!\r\n");
        while(1) {
            c[0] = uart3_read();
            c[1] = 0;
            uart3_write(c);
            uart3_write("\r\n");
        }
    }
```

Interrupt-based input/output

The examples in this section are based on polling the status of UART by continuously checking the flags of UART_SR. The write operation contains a busy loop that can spin for several milliseconds, depending on the length of the string. Even worse, the read function presented earlier spins within a busy loop until there is data to read from the peripheral, which means that the whole system is hanging until new data is received. In a single-thread embedded system, returning to the main loop with the shortest latency possible is important to keep the system responsive.

The correct way to perform UART communication without blocking is by using the interrupt line associated with UART to trigger actions based on the event received. UART can be configured to raise the interrupt signal upon multiple types of events. As we have seen in the previous examples, to regulate input and output operations, we are interested in particular in two specific events, namely:

- TX FIFO empty event, allowing for more data to be transmitted
- RX FIFO not-empty event, signaling the presence of new received data

The interrupt for these two events can be enabled by setting the corresponding bits in UART_CR1. We define two helper functions with the purpose of turning interrupts on and off, independently:

```c
#define UART_CR1_TXEIE (1 << 7)
#define UART_CR1_RXNEIE (1 << 5)

static void uart3_tx_interrupt_onoff(int enable)
{
    if (enable)
        UART3_CR1 |= UART_CR1_TXEIE;
    else
        UART3_CR1 &= ~UART_CR1_TXEIE;
}

static void uart3_rx_interrupt_onoff(int enable)
{
    if (enable)
        UART3_CR1 |= UART_CR1_RXNEIE;
    else
        UART3_CR1 &= ~UART_CR1_RXNEIE;
}
```

A service routine can be associated with the interrupt events, then check the flags in UART_SR to identify the cause of the interrupt:

```
void isr_uart3(void)
{
    volatile uint32_t reg;
    reg = UART3_SR;
    if (reg & UART_SR_RX_NOTEMPTY) {
        /* Receive a new byte */
    }

    if ((reg & UART_SR_TX_EMPTY)
    {
        /* resume pending transmission */
    }
}
```

The implementation of the interrupt routine depends on the specific system design. An RTOS may decide to multiplex access to the serial port to multiple threads, and wake up threads waiting to access the resource. In a single-thread application, it is possible to add intermediate system buffers to provide non-blocking calls, which return immediately after copying the data from the receiving buffer, or to the transmitting one. The interrupt service routine fills the receiving buffer with new data from the bus, and transmits the data from the pending buffer. Using appropriate structures, such as circular buffers to implement system input and output queues, ensures that the use of the memory assigned is optimized.

SPI bus

The **serial peripheral interface** bus, most commonly known as **SPI**, provides a different approach, based on master/slave communication. As the name suggests, the interface was initially designed to control peripherals. This reflects on the design, as all the communication is always initiated by the master on the bus. Thanks to the full-duplex pin configuration and the synchronized clock, it may be much faster than asynchronous communication, due to the better robustness to clock skews between the systems sharing the bus. SPI is widely used as a communication protocol for a number of different devices, due to its simple logic and the flexibility given by the fact that the slave does not have to be preconfigured to communicate at a predefined speed that matches the one on the master. Multiple peripherals can share the same bus, as long as media access strategies are defined. A common way for a master to control one peripheral at a time is by using separate GPIO lines to control the slave selection, although this does require an additional wire toward each slave.

Protocol description

The configuration of the SPI transceiver is very flexible. Usually a transceiver on a microcontroller is able to act as master as well as slave. A number of predefined settings must be known in advance and shared between the master and all the slaves on the same bus:

- The clock polarity, indicating whether the clock tick corresponds to a raising or a falling edge of the clock
- The clock phase, indicating whether the clock idle position is high or low
- The length of the data packet, any value between 4 and 16 bits
- The bit order, indicating whether the data is transmitted starting from the most significant bit or the least significant bit

Since the clock is synchronous and imposed by the master at all times, SPI does not have a predefined frequency of operation, although using too high a speed might not work with all peripherals and microcontrollers.

SPI communication toward a slave is disabled until the master initiates a transaction. At the beginning of each transaction, the master selects the slave by activating its slave-select line:

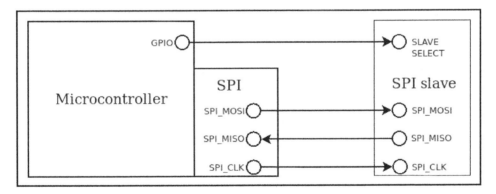

An additional signal may be used to select a specific slave on the bus

To initiate the communication, the master must activate the clock, and may send a command sequence to the slave on the MOSI line. When the clock is detected, the slave can immediately start transferring bytes in the opposite direction, using the MISO line.

Even if the master has finished transmitting, it must comply with the protocol implemented by the slave, and permit it to reply by keeping the clock alive for the duration of the transaction. The slave is given a predefined number of byte slots to communicate with the master.

In order to keep the clock alive even when there is no data to transfer to the slave, the master can keep sending *dummy* bytes through MOSI, which are ignored by the slave. In the meantime, the slave is allowed to send data through the MISO line, as long as the master ensures that the clock keeps running. Unlike UART, in the master-slave communication model implemented in SPI, the slaves can never spontaneously initiate SPI communication, as the master is the only device on the bus allowed to transmit a clock. Each SPI transaction is self-contained, and at the end, the slave is deselected by turning off the corresponding slave-select signal.

Programming the transceiver

On the reference board, an accelerometer is connected as slave to the SPI1 bus, so we can examine how to implement the master side of the communication on the microcontroller by configuring the transceiver and executing a bidirectional transaction toward the peripheral.

The SPI1 bus has its configuration registers mapped in the peripherals region:

```
#define SPI1 (0x40013000)

#define SPI1_CR1 (*(volatile uint32_t *)(SPI1))
#define SPI1_CR2 (*(volatile uint32_t *)(SPI1 + 0x04))
#define SPI1_SR  (*(volatile uint32_t *)(SPI1 + 0x08))
#define SPI1_DR  (*(volatile uint32_t *)(SPI1 + 0x0c))
```

The peripheral exposes a total of four registers:

- Two bit-field configuration registers
- One status register
- One bidirectional data register

It is clear that the interface is similar to that of the UART transceiver, as the configuration of the communication parameters goes through the SPI_CRx registers, the status of the FIFO can be monitored by looking at SPI_SR, and SPI_DR can be used to read and write data to the serial bus.

The value for the configuration register CR1 contains the following:

- The clock phase, zero or one, in bit 0
- The clock polarity in bit 1
- The SPI master mode flag in bit 2
- The bit rate scaling factor in bits 3-5
- The SPI enable flag in bit 6
- Other configuration parameters, such as the word length, LSB first, and other flags that will not be used in this example, as the default will be kept for these parameters

The CR2 configuration register contains the flags to enable the interrupt events and the DMA transfers, as well as the **Slave Select Output Enable (SSOE)** flag, which is relevant for this example.

The SPI1_SR status register is similar to the UART status register in the previous section, as it contains flags to determine whether the transmit FIFO is empty, and when the receive FIFO is not empty, to regulate the phases of the transfer.

The bits corresponding to the flags that are used in this example are defined as follows:

```
#define SPI_CR1_MASTER (1 << 2)
#define SPI_CR1_SPI_EN (1 << 6)
#define SPI_CR2_SSOE (1 << 2)
#define SPI_SR_RX_NOTEMPTY (1 << 0)
#define SPI_SR_TX_EMPTY (1 << 1)
```

The RCC controls the clock and reset lines toward the SPI1 transceiver connected to the APB2 bus:

```
#define APB2_CLOCK_ER (*(volatile uint32_t *)(0x40023844))
#define APB2_CLOCK_RST (*(volatile uint32_t *)(0x40023824))
#define SPI1_APB2_CLOCK_ER_VAL (1 << 12)
```

The transceiver can be reset by sending a reset pulse from the RCC:

```
static void spi1_reset(void)
{
    APB2_CLOCK_RST |= SPI1_APB2_CLOCK_ER_VAL;
    APB2_CLOCK_RST &= ~SPI1_APB2_CLOCK_ER_VAL;
}
```

The PA5, PA6, and PA7 pins can be associated with the `SPI1` transceiver by setting the appropriate alternate function:

```
#define SPI1_PIN_AF 5
#define SPI1_CLOCK_PIN 5
#define SPI1_MOSI_PIN 6
#define SPI1_MISO_PIN 7


static void spi1_pins_setup(void)
{
    uint32_t reg;
    AHB1_CLOCK_ER |= GPIOA_AHB1_CLOCK_ER;
    reg = GPIOA_MODE & ~(0x03 << (SPI1_CLOCK_PIN * 2));
    reg &= ~(0x03 << (SPI1_MOSI_PIN));
    reg &= ~(0x03 << (SPI1_MISO_PIN));
    reg |= (2 << (SPI1_CLOCK_PIN * 2));
    reg |= (2 << (SPI1_MOSI_PIN * 2)) | (2 << (SPI1_MISO_PIN * 2))
    GPIOA_MODE = reg;
    reg = GPIOA_AFL & ~(0xf << ((SPI1_CLOCK_PIN) * 4));
    reg &= ~(0xf << ((SPI1_MOSI_PIN) * 4));
    reg &= ~(0xf << ((SPI1_MISO_PIN) * 4));
    reg |= SPI1_PIN_AF << ((SPI1_CLOCK_PIN) * 4);
    reg |= SPI1_PIN_AF << ((SPI1_MOSI_PIN) * 4);
    reg |= SPI1_PIN_AF << ((SPI1_MISO_PIN) * 4);
    GPIOA_AFL = reg;
}
```

The additional pin connected to the chip select of the accelerometer is PE3, which is configured as output, with a pull-up internal resistor. The logic of this pin is active-low, so that a logical zero will turn the chip on:

```
#define SLAVE_PIN 3
static void slave_pin_setup(void)
{
    uint32_t reg;
    AHB1_CLOCK_ER |= GPIOE_AHB1_CLOCK_ER;
    reg = GPIOE_MODE & ~(0x03 << (SLAVE_PIN * 2));
    GPIOE_MODE = reg | (1 << (SLAVE_PIN * 2));
    reg = GPIOE_PUPD & ~(0x03 << (SLAVE_PIN * 2));
    GPIOE_PUPD = reg | (0x01 << (SLAVE_PIN * 2));
    reg = GPIOE_OSPD & ~(0x03 << (SLAVE_PIN * 2));
    GPIOE_OSPD = reg | (0x03 << (SLAVE_PIN * 2));
}
```

The initialization of the transceiver begins with the configuration of the four pins involved. The clock gate is then activated, and the transceiver receives a reset through a pulse through the RCC:

```
void spi1_setup(int polarity, int phase)
{
    spi1_pins_setup();
    slave_pin_setup();
    APB2_CLOCK_ER |= SPI1_APB2_CLOCK_ER_VAL;
    spi1_reset();
```

The default parameters are left untouched: MSB first, eight bit word length. The bit rate scaling factor of this controller is expressed in powers of two, starting with 2 corresponding to bit field value 0, and doubling at each increment. A generic driver should calculate the correct scaling factor, according to the desired clock rate and the peripheral clock frequency. In this simple case, we enforce a hardcoded scaling factor of 64, corresponding to the value 5.

SPI1_CR1 is then set as:

```
    SPI1_CR1 = SPI_CR1_MASTER | (5 << 3) |
    (polarity << 1) | (phase << 0);
```

Finally, we set the bit corresponding to the SSOE flag in SPI1_CR2, and the transceiver is enabled:

```
    SPI1_CR2 |= SPI_CR2_SSOE;
    SPI1_CR1 |= SPI_CR1_SPI_EN;
}
```

Read and write operations can now begin, as both master and slave SPI controllers are ready to perform the transactions.

SPI transactions

The read and write functions represent the two different phases of the SPI transaction. Most SPI slave devices are capable of communicating using a full-duplex mechanism, so that bytes are exchanged in both directions while the clock is active. During each interval, a byte is transmitted in both directions, using the MISO and MOSI lines independently.

A common strategy, implemented by many slaves, consists of accessing registers for read and write operations in the slave devices, by using well-known command handles that are documented in the device's datasheet.

The STM32F407-Discovery board has an accelerometer connected to the SPI1 bus, which responds to predefined commands accessing specific registers in the device memory for reading or writing. In these cases, the read and write operations are performed sequentially: during the first interval the master transmits the command handle, while the device has nothing to transmit, then the actual bytes are transmitted in either direction in subsequent intervals.

The example operation described here consists of reading the WHOAMI register in the accelerometer, using the 0x8F command handle. The peripheral should respond with one byte containing the 0x3B value, which correctly identifies the device and proves that the SPI communication is working correctly. However, during the transmission of the command byte, the device has nothing to transmit yet, so the result of the first read operation can be discarded. Similarly, after sending the command, the master has nothing else to communicate to the slave, so it outputs a 0xFF value on the MOSI line, while at the same time reading the byte transmitted by the slave through the MISO line.

The steps to perform to successfully perform a one-byte read on this specific device are:

1. Turn on the slave by pulling down the slave-select signal
2. Send a byte containing the code for the one-byte read operation
3. Send one dummy byte while the slave transfers the reply using the clock
4. Read back the value transferred from the slave, during the second interval
5. Turn off the slave by pulling the slave-select signal back up

To do so, we define blocking read and write functions as follows:

```
uint8_t spi1_read(void)
{
    volatile uint32_t reg;
    do {
        reg = SPI1_SR;
    } while ((reg & SPI_SR_RX_NOTEMPTY) == 0);
    return (uint8_t)SPI1_DR;
}

void spi1_write(const char byte)
{
    int i;
    volatile uint32_t reg;
    SPI1_DR = byte;
    do {
        reg = SPI1_SR;
    } while ((reg & SPI_SR_TX_EMPTY) == 0);
}
```

The read operation waits until the RX_NOTEMPTY flag is enabled on SPI1_SR before transferring the contents of the data register. The transmit function instead transfers the value of the byte to transmit onto the data register, and then polls for the end of the operation by waiting for the TX_EMPTY flag.

The two operations can now be concatenated. The master has to explicitly send two data bytes in total, so our main application can query the accelerometer identification register by doing:

```
slave_on();
spi1_write(0x8F);
b = spi1_read();
spi1_write(0xFF);
b = spi1_read();
slave_off();
```

This is what happens on the bus:

- During the first write, the command 0x8F is sent to MOSI.
- The value read using the first spi1_read is the dummy bit that the slave has put into MISO while listening for the incoming command. The value obtained has no meaning in this particular case, therefore it is discarded.
- The second write puts the dummy bit on the MOSI, as the master does not have anything else to transmit. This forces the clock generation for the second byte, which is needed by the slave to reply to the command.
- The second read processes the reply transferred using MISO during the write of the dummy byte from the master. The value obtained in this second transaction is a valid reply from the slave, according to the description of the command in the documentation.

Looking at the serial transaction with the logic analyzer, we can clearly distinguish the two phases, and the alternate relevant content, first on MOSI to transmit the command, then on MISO to receive the reply:

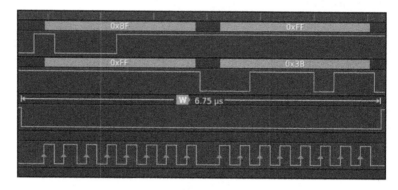

A bidirectional SPI transaction, containing a request from the master and a reply from the slave. From top to bottom: SPI1_MISO, SPI1_MOSI, SLAVE_SELECT, SPI1_CLOCK.

Once again, using blocking operations with a busy loop is a very bad practice. The reason why it is shown here is to explain the primitive operations needed to successfully complete bidirectional SPI transactions. In a real embedded system, it is always recommended to use interrupt-based transfers to ensure that the CPU is not busy-looping while waiting for the transfer to complete. SPI controllers provide interrupt signals to indicate the state of the FIFO buffers of the controller, in order to synchronize the SPI transaction with the actions required upon data transfers on either direction.

Interrupt-based SPI transfers

The interface to enable the interrupt for the SPI transceiver is in fact very similar to that of UART seen in the previous section. In order for non-blocking transactions to be correctly implemented, they have to be split between their read and write phases to allow events to trigger the associated actions.

Setting these two bits in the SPI1_CR2 register will enable the interrupt trigger upon an empty transmit FIFO and a non-empty receive FIFO, respectively:

```
#define SPI_CR2_TXEIE (1 << 7)
#define SPI_CR2_RXNEIE (1 << 6)
```

The associated service routine, included in the interrupt vector, can still peek from the values in SPI1_SR to advance the transaction to the next phase:

```
void isr_spi1(void)
{
    volatile uint32_t reg;
    reg = SPI1_SR;
    if (reg & SPI_SR_RX_NOTEMPTY) {
        /* End of transmission: new data available on MISO*/
    }

    if ((reg & SPI_SR_TX_EMPTY)
    {
        /* End of transmission: the TX FIFO is empty*/
    }
}
```

Once again, the implementation of the top half of the interrupt is left to the reader, as it depends on the API that the system is required to implement, the nature of the transactions, and their impact on the responsiveness of the system. Short, high-speed SPI transactions, however, may be short and scattered in time so that even implementing blocking operations has a smaller influence on the system latency.

I²C bus

The third serial communication protocol analyzed in this chapter is I2C. From the communication strategy point of view, this protocol shares some similarities with SPI. However, the default bit rate for I²C communication is much lower, as the protocol privileges lower-power consumption over throughput.

The same two-wire bus can accommodate multiple participants, both master and slaves, and there is no need for extra signals to physically select the slave of the transaction, as slaves have fixed logic addresses assigned:

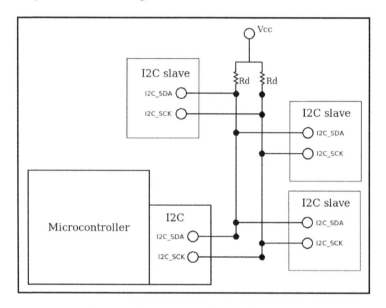

I²C bus with three slaves and external pull-up resistors

One wire transports the clock generated by the master, and the other is used as a full-duplex, bidirectional synchronous data path. This is possible thanks to the unique mechanism of arbitration of the channel, which relies on the electronic design of the transceivers, and may deal with the presence of multiple masters on the same bus in a very clean way.

The two signals must be connected to the high-level voltage of the bus (typically 3.3V) using pull-up resistors. The controllers never drive the signal high, and instead they let it float to its default value imposed by the pull-ups while transmitting 1s. As a consequence, logic level zero is always dominant; if any of the devices connected to the bus enforce a zero by pulling the line down, all the devices will read the line as low, no matter how many other senders are keeping the logic level 1 on the bus. This allows the bus to be controlled at the same time by multiple transceivers, and transmit operations can be coordinated by initiating new transactions only when the bus becomes available. In this section, we provide an introduction to the protocol, in order to introduce the software tools used to manage the I²C controller peripherals. More information on the I²C bus communication and the related documentation can be found at https://www.i2c-bus.org/.

Protocol description

The synchronization between master and slave is achieved by recognizable **START condition** and **STOP condition**, which determine the beginning and the end of a transaction. The bus is initially idle, with both signals at the high logic state when all the participants are idling.

A **START condition** describes the beginning of the transmission, and it is the only case when **SDA** is pulled low before **SCL** by the master. The special condition communicates to slaves and other masters on the bus that a transaction is initiated. A **STOP condition** can be identified by the **SDA** transaction from low to high level, while the **SCL** remains high. After a **STOP condition**, the bus is idle again, and initiating communication is only possible if a new **START condition** is transmitted.

A master sends a **START condition**, by pulling **SDA** and **SCL** low, in this order. A frame is composed by nine clock periods. After the raising edge of each clock pulse, the level of **SDA** is not changed, until the clock is low again. This allows us to transmit one frame of eight bytes in the first eight clock raise fronts. During the last clock pulse, the master does not drive the **SDA** line, which is then held high by the pull-up resistor. Any receiver that wants to acknowledge the reception of the frame can drive the signal low. This condition on the ninth clock pulse is known as **ACK**. If no receiving device acknowledges the frame, **SDA** remains high, and the sender understands that the frame did not reach the intended destination:

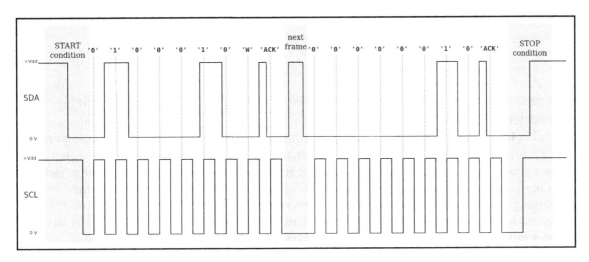

A single-byte I²C transaction on the bus, with the correct START condition and STOP condition, and the ACK flag being set by the receiver

A transaction consists of two or more frames, and is always initiated by a device operating in master mode. The first frame of each transaction is called the **address frame**, and contains the address and the mode for the next operation. All the subsequent frames in the transaction are data frames, containing one byte each. The master decides how many frames compose the transaction and the direction of the data transfer by keeping the transaction active for the desired amount of frames before enforcing a **STOP condition**.

Slave devices have fixed seven bit addresses where they can be contacted using the bus. A slave that notices a start condition on the bus must listen for the address frame and compare it with its address. If the address matches, the address frame must be acknowledged by pulling the SDA line low during the ninth clock pulse within the transmission of the frame.

Data is always transferred with leading **Most Significant Bit (MSB)**, and the format for the address frame is the following:

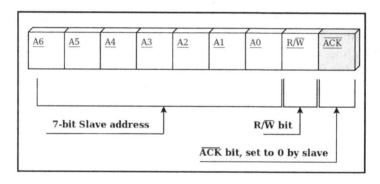

Format of the address frame containing a destination seven bit address and the $R/\overline{W}$ flag

The preceding diagram shows the format used by the address frame. The $R/\overline{W}$ bit is set by the master to indicate the direction of the transaction. $R/\overline{W}$ reads as read, not write, meaning that a value 0 indicates a write operation, and a value 1 indicates a read operation. Depending on the value of this bit, the data bytes following the transactions are either flowing toward the slave (write operation) or from the selected slave to the master (read). In a read operation, the direction of the ACK bit is also inverted for the data frames following the selection of the slave, and the master is supposed to acknowledge each frame received within the transaction. The master can decide to abort the transmission at any time by not pulling down the ACK bit on the last frame, and enforcing a STOP condition afterward.

The transaction continues after the transfer of the address frame, and the data can be transferred using subsequent data frames, each containing one byte, that can be acknowledged by the receiver. If the value of the $R/\overline{W}$ bit in the address frame is set to 0, the master intends to initiate a write operation. Once the slave has acknowledged the address frame by recognizing itself as the destination, it is ready to receive data, and acknowledges data frames, until the master sends the STOP condition.

The I²C protocol specifies that if a START condition is repeated at the end of a transaction, instead of sending the STOP condition, a new transaction can be started right away without setting the bus to its idling state. A repeated START condition ensures that two or more transactions can be performed on the same bus without interruptions, for example, preventing another master from starting a communication in between them.

A less popular format foresees 10-bit addresses for the slaves. 10-bit addresses are an extension of the standard, introduced at a later time, that provide compatibility with seven bit addressable devices on the same bus. The address is selected using two consecutive frames, and the first five bits, A6-A2, in the first frame are set to 11110 to indicate the selection of a 10-bit address, as per protocol specification, addresses starting with 0000 or 1111 are reserved and must not be used by slaves. In the 10-bit format, the most significant two bits are contained in A1 and A0 of the first frame, while the second frame contains the remaining eight bits. The $R/\overline{W}$ bit keeps its position in the first frame. This addressing mechanism is not very common, as only a few slave devices support it.

Clock stretching

We have observed that the master is the only one driving the SCL signal during I²C transactions. This is always true, except when the slave is not yet ready to transmit the requested data from the master. In this particular case, the slave may decide to delay the transaction by keeping the clock line pulled low, which results in the transaction being put on hold. The master recognizes its inability to oscillate the clock, as releasing the **SCL** to a floating state does not result in a change to a high logic level on the bus. The master will keep trying to release **SCL** to its natural high position until the requested data is finally available on the slave, which eventually releases the hold on the line.

The transmission can now resume after being kept on hold for an indefinite amount of time, and the master is still expected to produce the nine clock pulses to conclude the transmission. Because no more frames are expected within this transaction, the master does not pull the **ACK** bit low in the end, and sends the **STOP condition** instead to correctly complete the transaction:

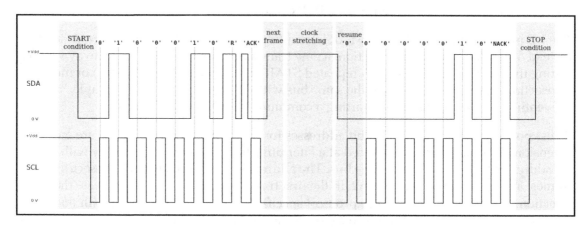

I²C read transaction, with the reply frame delayed by the slave using the clock-stretching technique

Even though not all devices support clock stretching, this mechanism is useful to complete transactions when the requested data is slightly late. Clock stretching is a very unique feature of I²C, making it a very versatile protocol to communicate with sensors and other input peripherals. Clock stretching is very important to communicate with slower devices that cannot provide the values to complete the transaction in time. It is advisable that this feature is correctly supported by a master device that is designed to communicate with generic I²C slaves. On the slave side, to enforce clock stretching, the device must provide a hardware configuration that allows us to keep the **SCL** line to its logical low value until it is ready again. This means that the **SCL** line must be bidirectional in this particular case, and the slave should be designed to access it to enforce a pull-down to keep the transaction alive while preparing the transfer of the next frame.

Multi-master

I²C offers a deterministic mechanism to detect and react to the presence of multiple masters on the bus, which is again based on the electrical property of the SDA line.

Before initiating any communication, the master ensures that the bus is available by sensing the SDA and SCL lines. The way the START condition is designed can already rule out most of the conflicts. Concurrent start conditions can be interrupted whenever the SDA line is sensed low in the initial grace time in between the two edges. This mechanism alone does not prevent two I²C masters to access the channel at the same time, because conflicts are still possible due to the propagation time of the signal across the wire.

Two master devices that initiate a transaction at the same time continuously compare the status of the line, after each bit has been transmitted. In the case of two masters perfectly synchronized in two different transmissions, the first bit with a different value on the two sources will only be noticed by the master transmitting a 1, because the expected value is not reflected by the actual line status. That master aborts the transaction immediately, and the transmitter can detect the error as a conflict on the network, which in this context means that the arbitration was lost in favor of another master. Meanwhile, the other master will not notice anything, and neither will the slaves, because the transaction will continue despite the silently contended bus line.

Programming the controller

Microcontrollers provide a number of I²C controllers on board that can be bound to specific pins using alternate functions. On our reference board, to enable the I2C1 bus, we activate the clock gating, and start the initialization procedure by accessing the control, data, and status register mapped in the peripherals memory region:

```
#define APB1_CLOCK_ER (*(volatile uint32_t *)(0x40023840))
#define APB1_CLOCK_RST (*(volatile uint32_t *)(0x40023820))
#define I2C1_APB1_CLOCK_ER_VAL (1 << 21)
```

The I2C1 controller on STM32F407 is associated with pins PB6 and PB9 when they are configured with the AF4 alternate function:

```
#define I2C1_PIN_AF 4
#define I2C1_SCL 6
#define I2C1_SDA 9
#define GPIO_MODE_AF (2)


static void i2c1_pins_setup(void)
{
    uint32_t reg;
    AHB1_CLOCK_ER |= GPIOB_AHB1_CLOCK_ER;
    /* Set mode = AF */
    reg = GPIOB_MODE & ~(0x03 << (I2C1_SCL * 2));
```

```
    reg &= ~(0x03 << (I2C1_SDA * 2));
    GPIOB_MODE = reg | (2 << (I2C1_SCL * 2)) | (2 << (I2C_SDA * 2));

    /* Alternate function: */
    reg = GPIOB_AFL & ~(0xf << ((I2C1_SCL) * 4));
    GPIOB_AFL = reg | (I2C1_PIN_AF << ((I2C1_SCL - 8) * 4));
    reg = GPIOB_AFH & ~(0xf << ((I2C1_SDA - 8) * 4));
    GPIOB_AFH = reg | (I2C1_PIN_AF << ((I2C1_SDA - 8) * 4));
}
```

The initialization function accesses the configuration registers of the I^2C controller, mapped in the peripheral region. After the pin configuration and the RCC startup sequence, the transceiver speed is calibrated by using the frequency of the APB1 bus clock, in MHz. When the clocks are calibrated, the transceiver is enabled by setting a bit in the CR1 register. The parameters used here configure the master bus clock to run at 400 kHz. While the default setting for the protocol foresees a clock of 100 kHz, the 400 kHz option was added later on, and it is now supported by many devices:

```
#define I2C1 (0x40005400)
#define APB1_SPEED_IN_MHZ (42)
#define I2C1_CR1 (*(volatile uint32_t *)(I2C1))
#define I2C1_CR2 (*(volatile uint32_t *)(I2C1 + 0x04))
#define I2C1_OAR1 (*(volatile uint32_t *)(I2C1 + 0x08))
#define I2C1_OAR2 (*(volatile uint32_t *)(I2C1 + 0x0c))
#define I2C1_DR (*(volatile uint32_t *)(I2C1 + 0x10))
#define I2C1_SR1 (*(volatile uint32_t *)(I2C1 + 0x14))
#define I2C1_SR2 (*(volatile uint32_t *)(I2C1 + 0x18))
#define I2C1_CCR (*(volatile uint32_t *)(I2C1 + 0x1c))
#define I2C1_TRISE (*(volatile uint32_t *)(I2C1 + 0x20))
#define I2C_CR2_FREQ_MASK (0x3ff)
#define I2C_CCR_MASK (0xfff)
#define I2C_TRISE_MASK (0x3f)
#define I2C_CR1_ENABLE (1 << 0)

void i2c1_setup(void)
{
    uint32_t reg;
    i2c1_pins_setup();
    APB1_CLOCK_ER |= I2C1_APB1_CLOCK_ER_VAL;
    I2C1_CR1 &= ~I2C_CR1_ENABLE;
    i2c1_reset();
    reg = I2C1_CR2 & ~(I2C_CR2_FREQ_MASK);
    I2C1_CR2 = reg | APB1_SPEED_IN_MHZ;

    reg = I2C1_CCR & ~(I2C_CCR_MASK);
    I2C1_CCR = reg | (APB1_SPEED_IN_MHZ * 5);
```

```
    reg = I2C1_TRISE & ~(I2C_TRISE_MASK);
    I2C1_TRISE = reg | APB1_SPEED_IN_MHZ + 1;
    I2C1_CR1 |= I2C_CR1_ENABLE;
}
```

From this moment on, the controller is ready to be configured and used, either in master or slave mode. Data can be read and written using I2C1_DR, in the same way as SPI and UART. The main difference here is that, as master I^{2}C device, the START condition and STOP condition must be manually triggered by setting the corresponding values in the I2C1_CR1 register. Functions such as the following are intended for this purpose:

```
static void i2c1_send_start(void)
{
    volatile uint32_t sr1;
    I2C1_CR1 |= I2C_CR1_START;
    do {
        sr1 = I2C1_SR1;
    } while ((sr1 & I2C_SR1_START) == 0);
}

static void i2c1_send_stop(void)
{
    I2C1_CR1 |= I2C_CR1_STOP;
}
```

At the end of each condition, the bus must be tested for possible errors or abnormal events. The combination of the flags in I2C1_CR1 and I2C1_CR2 must reflect the expected status for the transaction to continue, or it must be gracefully aborted in the case of timeouts or unrecoverable errors.

Due to the complexity given by the high number of events possible during the setup of the transaction, it is necessary to implement a complete state machine that keeps track of the phases of the transmission to use the transceiver in master mode.

As a demonstration of basic interactions with the transceiver, we can write a sequential interaction with the bus, but a real-life scenario would require us to keep track of the state of each transaction and react to the many scenarios possible within the combination of the flags contained in I2C1_SR1 and I2C1_SR2. This sequence initiates a transaction toward an I^{2}C slave with an address of 0x42, and if the slave responds it sends two bytes, with values 0x00 and 0x01, respectively. The only purpose of this sequence is to show the interaction with the transceiver, and it does not recover from any of the possible errors. At the beginning of the transaction, we zero the flags related to ACK or the STOP condition, and we enable the transceiver using the lowest bit in CR1:

```
void i2c1_test_sequence(void)
```

```
{
    volatile uint32_t sr1, sr2;
    const uint8_t address = 0x42;
    I2C1_CR1 &= ~(I2C_CR1_ENABLE | I2C_CR1_STOP | I2C_CR1_ACK);
    I2C1_CR1 |= I2C_CR1_ENABLE;
```

To ensure that no other master is occupying the bus, the procedure hangs until the busy flag is cleared in the transceiver:

```
do {
    sr2 = I2C1_SR2;
} while ((sr2 & I2C_SR2_BUSY) != 0);;
```

A START condition is sent, using the function defined earlier, which will also wait until the same START condition appears on the bus:

```
i2c1_send_start();
```

The destination address is set on the highest 7 bit of the byte we are about to transmit. The lowest bit is off as well, indicating a write operation. To proceed after a correct address selection that has been acknowledged by the receiving slave, two flags must be set in I2C1_SR2, indicating that the master mode has been selected and the bus is still taken:

```
I2C1_DR = (address << 1);
do {
    sr2 = I2C1_SR2;
} while ((sr2 & (I2C_SR2_BUSY | I2C_SR2_MASTER)) != (I2C_SR2_BUSY |
   I2C_SR2_MASTER));;
```

The data communication with the slave has now been initiated, and the two data bytes can be transmitted. The TX FIFO EMPTY event indicates when each byte has been transferred within a frame in the transaction:

```
I2C1_DR = (0x00);
do {
    sr1 = I2C1_SR1;
} while ((sr1 & I2C_SR1_TX_EMPTY) != 0);;


I2C1_DR = (0x01);
do {
    sr1 = I2C1_SR1;
} while ((sr1 & I2C_SR1_TX_EMPTY) != 0);;
```

Finally, the STOP condition is set, and the transaction is over:

```
        i2c1_send_stop();
    }
```

Interrupt handling

The event interface of the I^{2}C controller on the reference target is complex enough to provide two separate interrupt handlers for each transceiver. The suggested implementation for a generic I^{2}C master includes proper interrupt setup, and the definition of all the combinations between states and events. The I^{2}C controller can be configured to associate interrupts with all the relevant events happening on the bus, allowing for the fine-tuning of specific corner cases, and a more-or-less complete implementation of the I^{2}C protocol.

Summary

This chapter has given us the necessary information to start programming system support for the most popular local-bus communication interfaces available on embedded targets. Accessing peripherals and other microcontrollers in the same geographical location is one of the typical requirements of embedded systems interacting with sensors, actuators, and other devices in proximity of the target.

There already exist several implementations providing a higher level of abstraction to the transceivers analyzed here. This chapter, however, purposely focused on studying the behavior of the components from the closest possible point of view, to better understand the interface provided by the hardware manufacturer, and possibly provide the tools to design new ways of accessing the interfaces, tailored or optimized for a specific platform or scenario, while also understanding the choices behind some of the the protocol design characteristics.

In the next chapter, we'll provide a description of the mechanisms used to reduce the power consumption on embedded systems, by studying low-power and ultra-low-power features present in modern embedded devices.

Low-Power Optimizations

8

Energy efficiency has always been one of the leading factors in the microcontroller market. Since the early 2000s, signal-processing 16-bit RISC microcontrollers, such as the MSP430, have been designed for extremely low-power usage and are still leading the path of ultra-low-power optimization architectures in embedded systems.

In the last few years, more advanced 32-bit RISC microcontrollers, rich of features and capable of running real-time operating systems, have scaled down in size and power consumption, and set foot in the low-power and ultra-low-power domains. Battery-powered systems, and devices relying on energy harvesting techniques are becoming more and more common in many industries. Low-power wireless communication is now offered by a number of connected platforms, so an increasing number of IoT systems are including low-power and ultra-low-power characteristics in their design.

Depending on the architecture, microcontrollers offer different strategies to reduce power consumption while running, and to implement low-power states that consume very little energy when activated.

Reducing the energy demand of an embedded system is often a tricky process. In fact, all the devices on the board may consume power if not deactivated properly. Generating high-frequency clocks is one of the most expensive operations, so CPU and bus clocks should only be enabled when in use.

Researching the ideal strategy to save energy depends on the compromises that can be made between performance and energy saving. Microcontrollers designed for ultra-low-power applications are capable of slowing down the CPU frequency, and even reach different variations of a hibernation state, where all the clocks are stopped, and the external peripherals are turned off for maximum power savings.

With the appropriate energy profiling techniques, and by implementing ultra-low-power strategies, battery-powered devices can run for several years before replacement. Using alternative power sources, such as solar panels, heat-converting devices, or other forms of energy harvesting from the surrounding environment, a well-profiled embedded system may run indefinitely as long as the external conditions allow it.

Advanced microprocessors running at very high speeds are generally not designed to implement effective power consumption optimizations, which is what makes smaller, low-power microcontrollers such as the Cortex-M so popular in all those embedded systems where a small power footprint is one of the requirements.

In this chapter, we highlight a few practices to approach the design of low-power and ultra-low-power embedded systems. Low-power extensions of the Cortex-M microcontroller are demonstrated as examples of a real-life implementation for low-power optimizations on real targets. The chapter is divided into three sections:

- System configuration
- Measuring power
- Designing low-power embedded applications

System configuration

A system that includes power consumption constraints in its specifications must be designed to meet the requirements in all its aspects, including hardware, software, and mechanical design. The selection of components and peripherals must take into account their energy profiles. External peripherals are often the most power-demanding components, and thus their power source must be interrupted by the microcontroller when they are not being used.

Hardware design

In low-power embedded systems, the hardware design must include the possibility to power on/off peripherals using a GPIO pin. This is better done using a line that is normally low, so that it can be pulled down using passive components when the GPIO is not driven by the microcontroller. MOSFETs are often used to control the power supplied to external peripherals, using a GPIO signal to control the gate voltage.

Even when peripherals are turned off by interrupting their power source line, smaller currents may leak through other signals connected to them, such as a serial bus or other control signals. The hardware design must be able to detect and identify these leakages in early prototyping stages in order to minimize the energy lost this way.

Additionally, if the power-saving strategy includes the possibility to put the microprocessor in a deep-sleep operation mode, input signals' logic must be tailored to provide the correct wake-up events to resume the normal operation. Signals that might not be driven while in sleep mode must maintain a known logic value enforced through passive components.

Clock management

Internal peripherals and interfaces that are not in use must also stay off. If the platform supports it, clock gating is generally the mechanism used to selectively control the clock source for each peripheral and interface on the system. Each clock line enabled in the system clock gating configuration increases the power usage. Furthermore, the higher the scaling factor applied to generate the CPU clock from a slow oscillator, the higher the energy required by the PLL. The PLL is one of the most power-demanding components of the system, and the power consumed by the CPU is also directly proportional to its clock frequency. Many CPUs are designed to run with a reduced clock speed, offering a range of possible trade-offs between performance and energy saving. Accordingly, the PLL can generally be reconfigured at runtime to adapt to different profiles. However, every change of the system clock requires a reconfiguration of all the clock dividers for all timers and peripherals currently in use.

On the reference platform, we can reconfigure the CPU frequency at runtime to save a significant amount of power whenever the system does not require computing performance. To do this, the function in `system.c`, used to set the system clock in all the examples so far, has been modified to allow the selection of two different running frequencies. In performance mode, the system runs at its maximum frequency of 168 MHz. If the `powersave` flag argument is non-zero, the clocks are configured to run at 48 MHz instead, for a more energy-saving scenario:

```
void clock_pll_on(int powersave)
{
    uint32_t reg32, plln, pllm, pllq,
    pllp, pllr, hpre, ppre1, ppre2,
    flash_waitstates;

    if (powersave) {
        cpu_freq = 48000000;
```

```
        pllm = 8;
        plln = 96;
        pllp = 2;
        pllq = 2;
        pllr = 0;
        hpre = RCC_PRESCALER_DIV_NONE;
        ppre1 = RCC_PRESCALER_DIV_4;
        ppre2 = RCC_PRESCALER_DIV_2;
        flash_waitstates = 5;
    } else {
        cpu_freq = 168000000;
        pllm = 8;
        plln = 336;
        pllp = 2;
        pllq = 7;
        pllr = 0;
        hpre = RCC_PRESCALER_DIV_NONE;
        ppre1 = RCC_PRESCALER_DIV_4;
        ppre2 = RCC_PRESCALER_DIV_2;
        flash_waitstates = 3;
    }
```

Setting the number of wait states for flash operation has also been moved here, because, according to the documentation of the STM32F407, at 48 MHz the flash only requires three wait states:

```
    flash_set_waitstates(flash_waitstates);
```

The procedure for setting the system clock is the usual. First the HSI is enabled, then selected as the temporary clock source. Afterwards, the 8 MHz external oscillator is enabled, and it is ready to feed the PLL:

```
RCC_CR |= RCC_CR_HSION;
DMB();
while ((RCC_CR & RCC_CR_HSIRDY) == 0) {};

reg32 = RCC_CFGR;
reg32 &= ~((1 << 1) | (1 << 0));
RCC_CFGR = (reg32 | RCC_CFGR_SW_HSI);
DMB();

RCC_CR |= RCC_CR_HSEON;
DMB();
while ((RCC_CR & RCC_CR_HSERDY) == 0)
;
```

The parameters for the clock divisors and multipliers for the chosen mode are set in the PLL configuration register, and the PLL is enabled:

```
    reg32 = RCC_CFGR;
    reg32 &= ~(0xF0);
    RCC_CFGR = (reg32 | (hpre << 4));
    DMB();
    reg32 = RCC_CFGR;
    reg32 &= ~(0x1C00);
    RCC_CFGR = (reg32 | (ppre1 << 10));
    DMB();
    reg32 = RCC_CFGR;
    reg32 &= ~(0x07 << 13);
    RCC_CFGR = (reg32 | (ppre2 << 13));
    DMB();

    reg32 = RCC_PLLCFGR;
    reg32 &= ~(PLL_FULL_MASK);
    RCC_PLLCFGR = reg32 | RCC_PLLCFGR_PLLSRC | pllm |
    (plln << 6) | (((pllp >> 1) - 1) << 16) | (pllq << 24);
}
```

Changing the CPU and system clocks means that all the peripherals that use the clocks must be reconfigured. If a timer is running, or any device using the clocks as reference is in use by the application, the pre-scaler register that is used for providing the timing reference must be adapted accordingly upon clock speed updates.

Running the system at a lower speed offers other benefits, such as the possibility to decrease the number of wait states required to access the flash memory, and to enable extra low-power features that are only available when the system is not running at full speed.

An embedded platform usually includes low-frequency clock generators, in the kHz range, that may be used as sources for time keeping devices such as watchdog and **real-time clock** (**RTC**). External or internal oscillators can be active during low-power operating modes, and used to implement wake-up strategies.

Voltage control

Microcontrollers have a relatively wide range of operating voltages. Supplying lower voltages, however, makes it impossible to run the CPU at full speed, and flash memory may require additional wait states due to the physical characteristics of the hardware. Nevertheless, lower-voltage-tolerant logic may improve the overall economy of the system in some cases.

Internal regulators are often configurable to produce a lower voltage for the core signals, to reach a compromise between power consumption and performance, when the CPU is not running at its maximum frequency.

An important aspect that is often neglected is the power consumed by the Schmitt triggers in the digital input logic. When GPIOs are configured as digital input, but not forced to a known logic state through external passive components, they might be floating around the average value, due to the electromagnetic fields in the environment. This causes the triggering of the input signal, resulting in a little energy being lost at every change in the logic state.

Low-power operating modes

Microcontrollers can execute in different power modes, switching from full performance to complete hibernation. A proper understanding of the microcontroller low-power modes is fundamental to design systems with improved energy profiles. Each architecture provides specific power configurations, where CPU or other buses and peripherals are disabled, as well as appropriate mechanisms to be used by the system software to enter and exit low-power modes.

In an ARM-based microcontroller, the terminology used for the different low-power modes can be summarized as follows:

- **Normal operation mode**: Active components are selected through clock gating, and the clock is running at the desired frequency.
- **Sleep mode**: The CPU clock is temporarily suspended, but all the peripherals keep functioning as in normal mode. As long as the CPU is not executing, there is a noticeable, even if marginal, amount of power saved in this mode. Execution can be resumed after receiving an interrupt request. This mode is also referred to as *wait mode* by some chip manufacturers.
- **Stop mode**: The CPU clock and the bus clocks are disabled. All the peripherals powered by the microcontroller are off. The internal RAM and the CPU registers retain the stored values, because the main voltage regulator stays on. The power consumption drops consistently, but it is still possible to wake up and resume the execution through an external interrupt or event. This mode is often also less appropriately called deep-sleep mode, although it is in fact one of the two deep-sleep modes available.

- **Standby mode**: All the voltage regulators are off, and the content of RAM and register is lost. A small amount of power, in the range of a few microwatts, can be required to keep the backup circuitry alive during the standby phase. Wake up is then only possible under a few specific conditions, such as an externally powered RTC, or a hardware-predefined wake-up event pin. When the system wakes up from standby, the normal boot procedure is followed, and the execution resumes from the reset service routine.

The ARMv7 microcode provides two instructions to enter low-power operating modes, namely:

- **Wait for interrupt (WFI)**
- **Wait for event (WFE)**

These instructions can be invoked at any time while in normal running mode. `WFI` will put the system in a low-power mode until the next interrupt request is received, while `WFE` is slightly different. Only a few events in the system, including the external interrupts, can be configured to generate an event. Normal interrupt requests will not put the system back in normal running mode if it is in a sleep or stop mode that has been entered using `WFE`.

The low-power mode that is entered upon invocation depends on the settings stored in the **System Control Register (SCR)**, which on Cortex-M is located in the system configuration region, at address `0xE000ED10`. The SCR provides only three meaningful one-bit flag fields:

- `SLEEPONEXIT` (bit 1): When enabled, the system will go to low-power mode at the end of the execution of the next interrupt handler.
- `SLEEPDEEP` (bit 2): Determines which mode is entered upon the invocation of `WFI` or `WFE`, or when returning from an interrupt with `SLEEPONEXIT` active. If this bit is cleared, sleep mode is selected. When low-power mode is entered with this bit active, the system will be put on stop or standby mode, depending on the configuration of the power management registers.
- `SEVONPEND` (bit 4): When this bit is active, any interrupt pending during a low-power mode will cause a wake-up event, regardless of whether the sleep mode or the stop mode was entered using a `WFI` or a `WFE` instruction.

Deep-sleep configuration

To select between stop and standby mode, and to set up a number of parameters related to the deep-sleep modes, our reference platform provides a power controller, mapped in the internal peripherals region, at address 0x40007000. The controller consists of two registers:

- PWR_CR (control register) at offset 0
- PWR_SCR (status and control register) at offset 4

The relevant parameters that can be configured in these two registers are the following:

- **Regulator Voltage-scaling Output Selection (VOS)**, set through PWR_CR bit 14. When active, saves extra power in normal running mode, by configuring the internal regulator to produce a slightly lower voltage for the CPU core logic. This feature is only available if the target is not running at maximum frequency.
- **Flash power down in deep-sleep (FPDS)** mode, set through PWR_CR bit 9. If active while going to one of the deep-sleep modes, the flash will be turned completely off while the system is sleeping. This results in a moderate amount of power saved, but also impacts on the wake-up time.
- **Power down in deep sleep (PDDS)**, set through PWR_CR, bit 1. This bit determines which mode is entered when the CPU goes to deep sleep. If cleared, stop mode is selected. If set, the system enters standby.
- **Low-power deep sleep (LPDS)**, set through PWR_CR bit 0. This bit has only an effect in stop mode. If enabled, it slightly reduces the energy used while in deep sleep, by enabling the *under-drive* mode in the internal voltage regulator. The current is supplied to the core logic in a reduced leakage mode, which still allows you to preserve the content of memory and registers. This feature is only available if the system is not running at full speed.
- **Enable wake-up pin (EWUP)**, set through PWR_CSR bit 4. This flag determines whether the wake-up pin can be used as a normal GPIO, or if it is reserved to detect a wake-up signal during standby. The pin associated to this function in the reference platform is PA0.

A **wake-up flag (WUF)** is automatically set by the hardware when exiting a sleep or a deep-sleep mode, and can be read through PWR_CSR bit 0. Writing 1 into PWR_CR bit 2 clears the wake-up flag (CWUF flag).

On the STM32F407 microcontroller, we can access the registers related to the low-power modes and configuration using the following macros:

```
#define SCB_SCR (*(volatile uint32_t *)(0xE000ED10))
#define SCB_SCR_SEVONPEND (1 << 4)
#define SCB_SCR_SLEEPDEEP (1 << 2)
#define SCB_SCR_SLEEPONEXIT (1 << 1)

#define POW_BASE (0x40007000)
#define POW_CR (*(volatile uint32_t *)(POW_BASE + 0x00))
#define POW_SCR (*(volatile uint32_t *)(POW_BASE + 0x04))

#define POW_CR_VOS (1 << 14)
#define POW_CR_FPDS (1 << 9)
#define POW_CR_CWUF (1 << 2)
#define POW_CR_PDDS (1 << 1)
#define POW_CR_LPDS (1 << 0)
#define POW_SCR_WUF (1 << 0)
#define POW_SCR_EWUP (1 << 4)
```

For the activation of the low-power modes, and for the generation of spontaneous events, we define macros containing single inline assembly instructions as follows:

```
#define WFI() asm volatile ("wfi")
#define WFE() asm volatile ("wfe")
```

If sleep mode is entered through WFI, the system suspends the execution until the next interrupt. Entering sleep mode with WFE instead ensures that only selected *events* can wake up the system again. Events of different types that occur on the system can be enabled to wake up the WFE.

When WFE is entered, all interrupts active in the NVIC will still count as events, thereby waking up the WFE call. Interrupts can be temporarily filtered out by disabling the corresponding IRQ line in the NVIC. If an interrupt is filtered this way, using NVIC, it remains in pending state and it is handled as soon as the system goes back to normal running mode.

Stop mode

Sleep mode is entered by default every time that the WFI or WFE instructions are invoked, as long as SCB_SCR_SLEEPDEEP remains off. Other low-power modes can be enabled by enabling the SLEEPDEEP flag. To enter one of the available deep-sleep modes, the SCB_SCR and the POW registers must be configured before calling WFI or WFE. Depending on the configuration, the system enters one of the two deep-sleep modes, stop or standby.

In the following example, a continuous 1 Hz timer is toggling the LED 10 times before switching to deep-sleep mode, using WFE. The main loop stays in sleep mode in between timer interrupts, using WFI:

```c
void main(void) {
    int sleep = 0;
    pll_on(0);
    button_setup();
    led_setup();
    timer_init(CPU_FREQ, 1, 1000);
    while(1) {
        if (timer_elapsed) {
            WFE(); /* consume timer event */
            led_toggle();
            timer_elapsed = 0;
        }
        if (tim2_ticks > 10) {
            sleep = 1;
            tim2_ticks = 0;
        }
        if (sleep) {
            enter_lowpower_mode();
            WFE();
            sleep = 0;
            exit_lowpower_mode();
        } else
            WFI();
    }
}
```

The interrupt service routine for the timer is increasing the tim2_ticks counter by 1, and setting the timer_elapsed flag, which will make the main loop toggle the LED and consume the event generated by the timer:

```c
void isr_tim2(void) {
    nvic_irq_clear(NVIC_TIM2_IRQN);
    TIM2_SR &= ~TIM_SR_UIF;
    tim2_ticks++;
```

```
        timer_elapsed++;
    }
```

The `enter_lowpower_mode` procedure is responsible for setting the values in the system control block and in the power control registers, depending on the desired low-power mode, and configuring all the optimizations accordingly.

The procedure `enter_lowpower_mode` performs the following actions:

- Turn off the LED
- Set the values in `SCB_SCR` and power register to configure the low-power mode that will be entered upon `WFE`
- Select the single extra power optimizations

And it is implemented as follows:

```
void enter_lowpower_mode(void)
{
    uint32_t scr = 0;
    led_off();
    scr = SCB_SCR;
    scr &= ~SCB_SCR_SEVONPEND;
    scr |= SCB_SCR_SLEEPDEEP;
    scr &= ~SCB_SCR_SLEEPONEXIT;
    SCB_SCR = scr;
    POW_CR |= POW_CR_CWUF | POW_CR_FPDS | POW_CR_LPDS;
}
```

In this case, the stop mode is configured to reduce power consumption as much as possible, by activating the low-power voltage regulator settings (through `POW_CR_LPDS`) and by turning off the flash (through `POW_CR_FPDS`).

The low-power mode is now entered through a `WFE()` call. In order to be able to wake up the system, we configure an EXTI event, which is associated to the press of the user button on the board. To do so, we configure `EXTI0` to be sensitive to raised edges, as pin PA0 changes its logical value from 0 to 1 on button press.

As we are not particularly interested in the interrupt itself, we ensure that the flag to generate an interrupt request is turned off in EXTI. The event controller will ensure that an event is generated instead, because the flag relative to the input pin is enforced in the register `EXTI_EMR`.

The initial configuration for the user button event looks like the following:

```
void button_setup(void)
{
    uint32_t reg;
    AHB1_CLOCK_ER |= GPIOA_AHB1_CLOCK_ER;
    APB2_CLOCK_ER |= SYSCFG_APB2_CLOCK_ER;
    GPIOA_MODE &= ~ (0x03 << (BUTTON_PIN * 2));
    EXTI_CR0 &= ~EXTI_CR_EXTI0_MASK;
    EXTI_IMR &= ~0x7FFFFF;
    reg = EXTI_EMR & ~0x7FFFFF;
    EXTI_EMR = reg | (1 << BUTTON_PIN);
    reg =  EXTI_RTSR & ~0x7FFFFF;
    EXTI_RTSR = reg | (1 << BUTTON_PIN);
    EXTI_FTSR &= ~0x7FFFFF;
}
```

No interrupts are configured for the button, as the event alone is sufficient to wake up the board during stop mode.

Upon entering stop mode, the PLL will be disabled, and HSI will be automatically selected as the clock source when the system is back in normal running mode. In order to restore the clock configuration, there are a few steps to implement as soon as the stop mode is exited:

- SCB_SCR_SLEEPDEEP flag is cleared, so that the next invocation of WFI/WFE does not trigger another switch to stop mode.
- The POW_CR register is accessed to clear the wake-up flag set by the hardware at the end of the stop mode.
- The PLL is configured again, as the clock is restored.
- The LED is turned on.
- The TIM2 interrupt is enabled again for the timer to restore its functionality in normal running mode:

```
void exit_lowpower_mode(void)
{
    SCB_SCR &= ~SCB_SCR_SLEEPDEEP;
    POW_CR |= POW_CR_CWUF | POW_CR_CSBF;
    clock_pll_on(0);
    timer_init(cpu_freq, 1, 1000);
    led_on();
}
```

Deep-sleep mode reduces the power consumption consistently, and it is the ideal situation whenever the system must maintain the currently running status but can be frozen for a longer period.

Standby mode

In standby mode, the system can go into ultra-low-power mode, consuming only a few microamperes, while waiting to be reinitialized by an external event. Entering standby mode requires you to set the flag SCB_SCR_PDDS prior to invoking WFI or WFE. While the system is in standby, all the voltage regulators are off, with the exception of the low-speed oscillators, which are used to clock the independent watchdog timer and the real-time clock.

The procedure to enter standby mode is slightly different from the one used to enter stop mode. The SCB_SCR_PDDS flag is set to select standby mode as a deep-sleep variant. The flag SCB_SCR_LPDS is not activated in this case, because we know it has no effect in standby mode:

```
void enter_lowpower_mode(void)
{
    uint32_t scr = 0;
    led_off();
    scr = SCB_SCR;
    scr &= ~SCB_SCR_SEVONPEND;
    scr |= SCB_SCR_SLEEPDEEP;
    scr &= ~SCB_SCR_SLEEPONEXIT;
    SCB_SCR = scr;
    POW_CR |= POW_CR_CWUF | POW_CR_FPDS | POW_CR_PDDS;
    POW_SCR |= POW_CR_CSBF;
}
```

In this case, it is useless to set up the EXTI event for the button press, as the GPIO controllers will be disabled while the microcontroller is in standby mode. The easiest way to exit this state is configuring the real-time clock to generate a wake-up event after a fixed amount of time. In fact, during the standby phase, only a few peripherals will be kept alive, and they are all grouped in a special section of the clock configuration, namely the backup domain. The backup domain consists of the real-time clock and a small portion of the clock tree, containing the internal and external low-speed oscillators. The write access to the registers related to the backup domain is controlled by the flag disable protection of the backup domain, or POW_CR_DPB, located in the POW_CR register at bit 8. Additionally, the RTC configuration registers, mapped in the peripherals area starting at address 0x40002870, are protected from accidental writing due to electromagnetic interference, meaning that a special value sequence must be written to the write protection register before accessing the other registers. The RTC integrated on the reference platform is complex and has a lot of features, such as keeping track of date and time, and setting custom alarms and regular timestamp events. For this example, we want to use only the wake-up event, so most of the RTC registers are not documented here.

The restricted set of registers we access for RTC are:

- Control register (RTC_CR) which exposes the configuration of the various functionalities provided by the RTC. In the example, we use the values related to the wake-up trigger, enabling the interrupt with the wake-up timer interrupt enable flag RTC_CR_WUTIE, and enabling the wake-up timer counter using the RTC_CR_WUTE.
- Initialization and status register (RTC_ISR), in this example used to check the write status of the setup register for the wake-up timer through the special flag RTC_ISR_WUTWF during the timer setup.
- Wake-up timer register (RTC_WUTR), used to set the interval before the next wake-up event.
- Write protection register (RTC_WPR), used to transmit the unlock sequence before writing to other registers in the region.

The preprocessor macros that map these registers and the meaningful fields are:

```
#define RTC_BASE (0x40002800)
#define RTC_CR (*(volatile uint32_t *)(RTC_BASE + 0x08))
#define RTC_ISR (*(volatile uint32_t *)(RTC_BASE + 0x0c))
#define RTC_WUTR (*(volatile uint32_t *)(RTC_BASE + 0x14))
#define RTC_WPR (*(volatile uint32_t *)(RTC_BASE + 0x24))

#define RTC_CR_WUP (0x03 << 21)
#define RTC_CR_WUTIE (1 << 14)
#define RTC_CR_WUTE (1 << 10)

#define RTC_ISR_WUTF  (1 << 10)
#define RTC_ISR_WUTWF (1 << 2)
```

The procedure to initialize the RTC to generate a wake-up event includes the following steps:

1. Turn on the clock gating for the power configuration registers, if not already on, to enable the POW_CR_DPB flag, in order to initiate the setup of the RTC:

```
void rtc_init(void) {
    APB1_CLOCK_ER |= PWR_APB1_CLOCK_ER_VAL;
    POW_CR |= POW_CR_DPB;
```

2. Enable the RTC using the bit 15 in the backup domain register configuration within the RCC:

```
RCC_BACKUP |= RCC_BACKUP_RTCEN;
```

3. Enable a backup clock source, selecting from the **Low-Speed Internal (LSI)** oscillator or a **Low-Speed External (LSE)** oscillator, if available.

4. In this example, we use the LSI because the LSE is not present on the reference platform. However, external oscillators are more accurate and should always be preferred, when available, for reliable timekeeping. After the clock has been enabled, the procedure waits until it becomes ready, by polling a bit in the status register:

```
RCC_CSR |= RCC_CSR_LSION;
while (!(RCC_CSR & RCC_CSR_LSIRDY))
    ;
```

5. Select the LSI as the source for the RTC:

```
RCC_BACKUP |= (RCC_BACKUP_RTCSEL_LSI <<
RCC_BACKUP_RTCSEL_SHIFT);
```

6. Enable the interrupt and event generation for EXTI line 22, associating an event to the raised edge:

```
EXTI_IMR |= (1 << 22);
EXTI_EMR |= (1 << 22);
EXTI_RTSR |= (1 << 22);
```

7. Unlock the writing to the RTC registers by writing the unlock sequence to RTC_WPR:

```
RTC_WPR = 0xCA;
RTC_WPR = 0x53;
```

8. Disable the RTC, so it is permitted to write to the configuration registers. Wait until the write operation is possible, by polling RTC_ISR_WUTWF:

```
RTC_CR &= ~RTC_CR_WUTE;
DMB();
while (!(RTC_ISR & RTC_ISR_WUTWF))
    ;
```

9. Set the value for the interval before the next wake-up event. The LSI frequency is 32,768 Hz, and the default divider for the wake-up interval register is set to 16, so each unit in the RTC_WUTR represents one 2048 of a second. To set an interval of 5 seconds, we use:

```
RTC_WUTR = (2048 * 5) - 1;
```

10. Enable the wake-up event:

```
RTC_CR |= RTC_CR_WUP;
```

11. Clear the wake-up flag that might have been set when returning from standby mode:

```
RTC_ISR &= ~RTC_ISR_WUTF;
```

12. To complete the sequence, we write an invalid byte to RTC_WPR. This way, the write protection on the RCC register is turned on again:

```
RTC_WPR = 0xb0;
    }
```

13. To enable the RTC, right before entering standby mode the following procedure ensures that the timer is active and counting, and the event generation for the wake-up event is active:

```
void rtc_start(void)
{
    RTC_WPR = 0xCA;
    RTC_WPR = 0x53;
    RTC_CR |= RTC_CR_WUTIE |RTC_CR_WUTE;
    while (((RTC_ISR) & (RTC_ISR_WUTWF)))
        ;
    RTC_WPR = 0xb0;
}
```

If the procedure just shown is called before entering standby, the system will be up again when the wake-up event occurs, but it does not resume the execution from where it suspended, as it happens in the other low-power modes. Instead, it starts over from the reset interrupt handler, at the beginning of the interrupt vector. For this reason, this example does not need an implementation for exit_lowpower_mode, and the WFE that switches the system to standby will never return to the same context of execution. Eventually, the main function for the standby example looks like the following:

```
void main(void) {
    int sleep = 0;
    clock_pll_on(0);
    led_setup();
    rtc_init();
    timer_init(cpu_freq, 1, 1000);
    while(1) {
        if (timer_elapsed) {
            WFE(); /* Consume timer event */
```

```
        led_toggle();
        timer_elapsed = 0;
    }
    if (tim2_ticks > 10) {
        sleep = 1;
        tim2_ticks = 0;
    }

    if (sleep) {
        enter_lowpower_mode();
        rtc_start();
        WFE(); /* Never returns */
    }
    else
        WFI();
    }
}
```

Wake-up intervals

An important aspect to consider while designing a low-power strategy is the wake-up time intervals, or, in other words, how long the system takes to resume the execution after switching to a low-power mode. A system with real-time requirements may leave some room for compromises between power usage and reactivity, but it is important to understand the impact of the wake-up operations from the different low-power modes, in order to predict the latency of operations in the worst-case scenario. Wake-up times are very much conditioned by the hardware design of the microcontroller, and largely dependent on the architecture.

On our reference platform, while waking up from sleep mode takes a small number of CPU cycles, the situation changes for deep-sleep modes. Waking up from stop mode takes several microseconds. Further optimizations that have been activated while in stop mode, such as changing voltage regulators or turning off the flash memory, consistently impact on the amount of time spent restoring the values to return to normal running. Resetting after standby mode produces even longer wake-up intervals, in the order of milliseconds, as the system should completely reboot after a wake-up event, and the start-up code execution time adds up to the fraction of milliseconds needed by the CPU to wake up.

When designing a low-power system, these wake-up times must be taken into account and properly measured, especially when the system has to deal with real-time constraints. The optimal low-power mode that fits the application timing and energy profile requirements must be chosen taking into account the overhead produced by leaving the low-power modes, if the system wakes up often enough for these intervals to become non-negligible.

Measuring power

The current in use by the target can be measured at any time by connecting an ammeter in series with the device. This mechanism, however, does not show all the oscillations of the values during a time interval, which is why it is often useful to sample the values of the parasitic voltage at the ends of a shunt resistor, using an oscilloscope.

A shunt resistor is placed in series with the target device, on either side of the power source. Its typical value is relatively small, in the range of a few ohms, to ensure that the parasit voltage stays low, but is still measurable by the oscilloscope:

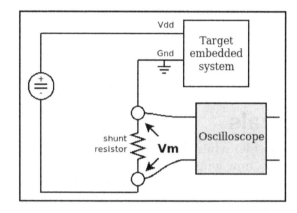

Measuring current using an oscilloscope to sample the voltage applied to the shunt resistor

Due to the properties of a series circuit, the current running through the shunt is the same as the one used by the target system, so the voltage on the ends of the shunt resistor varies accordingly.

Development boards

In order to see the effects of the power optimizations, we must exclude the electronics that are not related to the system. Our reference board, for example, the STM32F407-Discovery, has an additional microcontroller that is used to provide a debug interface towards the host, and it is powered using the same USB connector. However, development kits often offer a way to measure the current excluding the unrelated hardware, allowing to properly evaluate the low-power features of the microcontroller, excluding the development-related circuitry on board.

On our reference board, the jumper JP1 can be used to open the circuit between the power supply and the microcontroller circuitry. Replacing the jumper with an ammeter connected to the two pins, we can measure the current used by the actual system. In the same way, it is possible to apply a shunt resistor to monitor the current, using the oscilloscope to sample the voltage on the shunt.

A lab equipped with a reliable energy metering is a good starting point to evaluate low-power implementations, and to assist in the prototype and design phase of the energy optimizations.

Designing low-power embedded applications

In this section, a few design patterns are proposed to achieve a better energy profile on the target device, by evaluating the power demand of all the components and the states of the system we are about to design. Once we know how to measure the values in the target, and the details about the low-power mode in the selected architecture and microprocessor family, the application can be programmed keeping other parameters in mind, such as the energy efficiency of the software we are writing.

Replacing busy loops with sleep mode

The reason busy loops are very popular among hobbyists is that they are so easy to implement. Suppose that the system needs to wait for a digital input to switch to a low-logic state, and this input is mapped to a certain GPIO. This can be easily done with the following one-liner:

```
while((GPIOX_IDR & (1 << INPUT_PINX)) != 0)
    ;
```

While this is perfectly working as expected, it will force the CPU in a loop of fetch-decode-execute, and jumping around the same few instructions until the condition becomes `false`. As we have seen, the power used by the microcontroller depends mostly on how fast the CPU is running. A lower frequency corresponds to a smaller amount of power used per instruction. Executing instructions in an infinite loop without switching to low-power mode sets the power demand from the CPU at its highest value for a measurable amount of time, in this case, all the time needed for the logic input to change state.

Actively polling a value is the only way to go if interrupts are not enabled. The examples contained in this book tend to guide towards a proper interrupt-handling approach. The proper way to handle the wait for the logic switch foresees instead the activation of an interrupt line related to the next operation. In the case of a GPIO line, we can use external interrupt triggers to wake up the main loop when the condition is met, and switch to a low-power mode, instead of looping, while waiting for the event.

In many other cases, the temptation of implementing loops like the previous one could be avoided by investigating another way to access the peripheral that is currently holding the system from the next execution step. Modern serial and network controllers are equipped with interrupt signals, and when those are not available for the hardware we are accessing, there is always another way to sense an event through an external interrupt line. When a device can really exclusively function in polling mode, as a last resort, the polling frequency can be reduced by associating the action to a timer interrupt, which would allow polling a few times per second, or even once in a while, using intervals that are more in line with the actual peripheral speed. Executing timed operations allows the CPU to sleep in between, and to switch to a low-power mode, reducing the average energy that the CPU would have used while busy-looping.

The exception to this rule, seen many times in this chapter, is waiting for a ready flag after activating a system component. The following code activates the internal low-speed oscillator, and it is used in the standby mode example before entering the low-speed mode. The CSR register is polled until the low-speed oscillator is actually running:

```
RCC_CSR |= RCC_CSR_LSION;
while (!(RCC_CSR & RCC_CSR_LSIRDY))
    ;
```

Operations like this, performed on the integrated peripherals in the microcontroller silicon, have a well-known latency of a few CPU clocks, and thus do not impact the real-time constraints, as the maximum latency for similar internal actions is often mentioned in the microcontroller documentation. The situation changes whenever the polling occurs on a less predictable register, whose state and reaction times may depend on external factors, and long busy loops may occur in the system.

Deep sleep during longer inactivity periods

As we know, standby allows the system to be frozen with the minimum possible power consumption, in the ultra-low-power range. The use of standby is advised when the design has very strict ultra-low-power requirements, when the following conditions are met:

- A viable wake-up strategy exists and it is compatible with the current hardware design
- The system can restore the execution without relying on its previous state, as the content of RAM and CPU registers is lost and the system restarts from the reset service routine at wake-up

Usually, longer periods of inactivity, where for instance the RTC can be used to program a wake-up alarm at a given time, are more fit for using the standby mode. This applies to cases such as reading sensors and enabling actuators at programmed intervals during the day, keeping track of the time and a few status variables.

In most other cases, the stop mode still allows for enough power saving, and provides a shorter wake-up interval. Another major advantage of stop mode is the increased flexibility for the wake-up strategy options. In fact, any interrupt-based or configurable event can be used to wake up the system from its low-power deep-sleep mode, so it is more fit for these states where there is still some asynchronous interactivity with the peripherals and interfaces surrounding the microcontroller.

Choosing the clock speed

Is all the computing power offered by the platform actually needed all the time?

Microcontrollers' processing performance nowadays is comparable to that of personal computers of 20 years ago, which were already capable of fast operations and even processing real-time multimedia content. Embedded applications do not always require the CPU to run at full frequency. Especially when accessing peripherals, rather than crunching numbers, it does not matter how fast we clock the CPU and the bus. Both normal running mode and sleep mode require much less energy when the selected frequency is scaled down every single time CPU performance is not actually the bottleneck of the execution pipe.

Many microcontrollers are designed to scale down the operating frequency for the CPU and the internal buses, which in general also allows the system to be fed with lower voltages. As we have seen, changing clocks can be done at runtime to implement different performance/power compromises. However, this implies that all the devices using a clock as reference must be reconfigured, so the change has a cost in terms of execution time and should not be abused. A convenient way to add frequency changes to the system design is to separate the two or more CPU frequency scaling options into custom power states, and switch to the required state by fading between performance and power usage.

Power state transitions

Consider a system connected to a sensor, producing and transmitting data through a network interface. The sensor is activated, then the system has to wait until it becomes ready, which is known to take several seconds. The sensor is then read multiple times in a row, then turned off. The data is processed, encrypted and transmitted using a network device. The system remains idle for the next few hours before repeating the same operation. A first rough modeling of the state machine is the following:

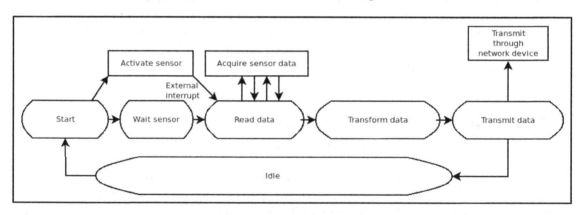

State machine for a hypothetical sensor-reading system

The long idle interval foreseen in between two consecutive cycles suggests that it is perhaps a good idea to put the system in standby for most of the time, and program an RTC alarm for the system to autonomously wake up in time for the next acquisition.

Other, less obvious optimizations are possible for the other states as well. While acquiring data from the sensor, the full computing power of the CPU is possibly never used, as the system is mostly busy communicating with the sensor, or waiting, possibly in sleep mode, until the next value is received. In this case, we can provide a power-saving running mode, which ensures that the system runs at a reduced frequency so, when alternating between running and sleeping mode, both are affected by a smaller energy footprint. The only phases where performances are required are while the data is processed, transformed and sent over the network device. A faster system in this case would be optimized to run faster and elaborate data in a shorter time frame. A stop phase can be foreseen right after the sensor activation, if the sensor is able to send an interrupt to wake up the system when it is ready to begin the acquisition of the data. Once each phase has been associated with its optimized low-power mode and selected operating frequency, we can add notations to our design documentation, to remind us how the low-power optimization will be implemented, in the form of state transition, to achieve the best combination of performance, energy economy and low latency:

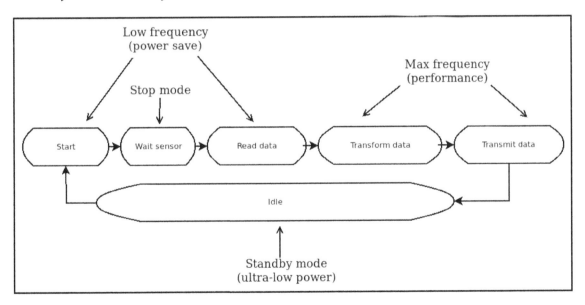

Power usage optimization for each running and idling state

Summary

Modern embedded systems open multiple possibilities for low-power and even ultra low-power designs. By understanding the several options available on the target, implementing low-power modes and further types of energy-saving techniques is the key to building durable and reliable battery-powered and/or energy-harvesting devices.

In the next chapter, we switch focus to introducing connected devices, and to describing the impact of dealing with network protocols and interfaces on the embedded system architecture.

Distributed Systems and IoT Architecture

By accessing communication peripherals, such as network controllers and radio interfaces, microcontrollers are able to establish data communication with nearby devices and even with remote servers through the internet.

A set of embedded targets connected together and interacting with each other can be seen as a self-contained distributed system. Homogeneous machine-to-machine communication can be implemented using non-standard, and even proprietary, protocols.

Depending on the set of standard protocols it implements, an embedded system may be able to successfully communicate with heterogeneous, remote systems. Implementing standard protocols that are standardized and/or widely supported introduces the possibility to interact with gateways in the same geographic area, and with remote cloud servers across the internet.

The connectivity range of small embedded devices may include remote coordination using information technology systems. The encounter between the two worlds has changed the modern interpretation of distributed systems: low-power, inexpensive devices can now be part of services with solid roots in IT, which in turn can extend their branches into localized and specialized sensors and actuators, creating what has been known as the **Internet of Things**, or **IoT** for short.

This technological step, considered revolutionary by many, is capable of changing the way we access technology, and the human-to-machine interaction processes, forever. Unfortunately, the security aspects of IoT communication are too often neglected, leading to unpleasant incidents, which may compromise the confidentiality and the integrity of the data transmitted, and permit attackers to take control of remote devices.

This chapter analyzes the telecommunication technologies and protocols that are possible to integrate in embedded targets through their implementation, using them to better understand the design from the point of view of the whole embedded system, up to the integration within IoT networks.

The networking model is described starting from the physical layer, and the possible technologies to establish wireless or wired links, up to tailored embedded applications that can establish secure communication with cloud services, using standard communication protocols, and more; in particular:

- Network interfaces
- The Internet Protocols
- Transport Layer Security
- Application protocols

Network interfaces

Embedded devices often integrate one or more communication interfaces. Many microcontrollers integrate the **Media Access Control (MAC)** portion of an Ethernet interface, so connecting a **physical layer transceiver (PHY)** would enable LAN access. Some devices are coupled with radio transceivers operating at fixed frequency ranges and implementing one or more protocols to communicate over wireless links. Frequently used frequencies for wireless communication are the 2.4 GHz band, in use by Bluetooth and 802.11 Wi-Fi, and some specific ISM ranges of frequency below 1 GHz, which depend on the local regulations. Usable sub-GHz frequencies include the 868 MHz ISM band in the European Union and the 915 MHz ISM band in the USA. Transceivers are usually designed to access the physical layer according to specific link protocols, regulating the shared access to the physical media among two or more devices. While two interfaces accessing the same media can have different configurations, the MAC model implemented must follow the same specifications on all the endpoints in order to establish point-to-point communication. Part of the MAC layer may be implemented in the device itself, which in turn can use a parallel or a serial interface to transfer data to and from the microcontroller.

Hardware manufacturers may distribute the device drivers to access the link layer. When the full source code is made available, it is easier for a developer to customize the media access, integrate the device-communication features, and tailor the communication to any protocol stack supported by the media. However, many device drivers are only partially open source, sometimes limiting the possibilities for integration with open standards. Moreover, integrating third-party proprietary code in an embedded system impacts the project maintenance and often requires workarounds to known issues or to enable features not foreseen by the manufacturer, and definitely impacts the security model of the system.

The implementation of device drivers in embedded systems, for either wired and wireless network interfaces, includes integrating the relevant access control mechanism in the communication logic, and dealing with specific channel features. Some characteristics of the link may affect the design of higher-level communication, thus impacting the architecture of the entire distributed system. Alongside a reliable interaction with the MAC mechanisms, aspects such as bit rate, latency, and maximum packet size must be addressed and evaluated in the design phase to evaluate the resources required based on the goals of the system.

Media Access Control

The most important components to establish successful communication links over any physical media is grouped in the MAC logic, whose implementation is often a shared responsibility between software and hardware. Different technologies have evolved to define standards to access the links that are used nowadays for machine-to-machine communication, while only a few are able to scale within the context of a geographically distributed IoT system without intermediate gateways performing protocol conversions.

Some of the standards are directly derived from the IT world, and consist of adaptations of existing TCP/IP technologies capable of scaling down to fit within the limited resources available on embedded systems. Other standards have developed entirely in the context of small embedded devices, and the interaction with the classic IT infrastructure is achieved through the modeling of TCP/IP protocols on top of low-power wireless technologies. In both cases, the research for a convergence is dictated by the need for a broader integration of small, inexpensive, self-powered devices in IoT services.

There is no such thing as a definitive one-size-fits-all solution to define the network access for embedded systems. The differences among requirements across the embedded industry have encouraged the development of tailored MAC protocols and technologies, both standardized and proprietary, each of them tailored to respond to the need for specific features, or for a range of embedded systems.

In this section, some of the most successful MAC technologies for machine-to-machine communication are described, taking into consideration the aspects related to the adoption of the technology and the modes of integration.

Ethernet

Even though it may sound a little impractical for contexts where the size of the whole system is comparable to an RJ-45 connector, Ethernet is still the most reliable and the fastest channel of communication available to integrate in embedded systems.

Many Cortex-M microcontrollers are equipped with one Ethernet MAC controller, which must be integrated with an external PHY. Other link-layer protocols implement the same mechanism for link-layer addressing, consisting of a 14-byte preamble, attached to each packet transmitted, indicating the source and destination link addresses and the type of payload contained in the packet being transported. The addresses are rewritten every time a packet is routed toward an Ethernet-like interface by the TCP/IP stack, so that they match the next link that the packet must cross in its journey toward its final destination.

Device drivers can activate filters to discard all the traffic that does not involve the host, which would otherwise impact the amount of background data communication unnecessarily being processed by the TCP/IP stack.

Wi-Fi

Among all the possibilities in the wireless universe, 802.11 Wi-Fi is chosen for its high-speed, low-latency channel, and for the widest possible compatibility in a topology including personal computers and mobile devices. However, the power requirement of a Wi-Fi transceiver can sometimes be difficult to afford for low-power devices. The complexity of protocols and mechanisms to regulate media access requires a consistent amount of controlling software, which is often distributed in binary form, and thus impossible to debug and maintain without the support of the manufacturers.

Wi-Fi provides large bandwidth and reasonably low latency, and may implement authentication and encryption at the data-link level.

While it is technically possible to realize a local mesh network configuring the Wi-Fi transceivers to operate in an ad hoc mode, embedded systems equipped with 802.11 technology are mostly used to connect to existing infrastructures to interact with other portable devices and to access the internet.

Several embedded low-cost platforms are available on the market, equipped with a TCP/IP stack and a built-in RTOS, which can be used as a standalone platform or integrated in complete systems to access Wireless LAN, either as a station, or providing an access point.

Low-Rate Wireless Personal Area Networks (LR-WPAN)

Sensors mesh networks make large use of wireless technology to establish communication in a local geographical area. The 802.15.4 standard regulates the access to 2.4 GHz and sub-GHz frequencies to provide limited-range local area networks with a typical maximum bit rate of 250 Kbps, which can be accessed using low-cost, low-power transceivers. The media access is not based on an infrastructure, and supports contention resolution and collision detection at the MAC level, using a beaconing system. Each node can be addressed using two bytes, and the special address 0xFFFF is reserved for broadcast traffic, to reach all the nodes in visibility. The maximum payload size for 802.15.4 frames is fixed to 127 bytes, and thus it is not possible to encapsulate full-size IP packets routed from an Ethernet or a wireless LAN link. Network protocol implementations that are capable of communicating through 802.15.4 interfaces either are application-specific, don't support Internet Protocol networking, or offer fragmentation and compression mechanisms to transmit and receive each packet across multiple wireless frames.

While not specifically designed for the IoT, and not directly compatible with classic IP infrastructures, there are multiple choices available to build networks on top of 802.15.4. In fact, while the standard specifies the MAC protocol for exchanging frames among nodes that are in visibility, multiple link-layer technologies, standard and non-standard, have been developed to define networks on top of 802.15.4.

LR-WPAN industrial link-layer extensions

Thanks to the flexibility of the transceivers, and the capability of transmitting and receiving 802.15.4 raw frames, it is relatively easy to implement networking protocols for LR-WPANs.

In the pre-IoT era, the process automation industry had been the first to adopt the 802.15.4 technology, and for a long time had been searching for a standard protocol stack to enable compatibility among devices from different manufacturers. The Zigbee protocol stack has tried to find its way to become a de-facto, industry-imposed standard for 802.15.4 networking, with noticeable success, considering the proprietary, closed-source, and the royalties applicable to its commercial use. In a parallel effort, the **International Society of Automation (ISA)** has created a proposal for the open standard ISA100.11a, which aims to define the guidelines for building networks based on 802.15.4 links, to be used in industrial automation processes. Another industrial automation protocol, originally developed by a consortium of enterprises and then approved by the **International Electrotechnical Commission (IEC)** as standard for industrial automation, is WirelessHART.

Technologies such as Zigbee, ISA100.1, and WirelessHART define the entire protocol stack above 802.15.4, including network definition and transport mechanisms, providing custom address mechanism and communication models, exporting an API that can be used to integrate applications. From the perspective of the design of the distributed system, enabling internet connectivity for devices in a custom network, not implementing the internet protocol stack, requires one or more devices to act as gateway, rerouting and transforming each packet for the custom LR-WPAN protocol stack. The transformation procedure, however, violates the end-to-end semantic of TCP/IP communication, impacting various aspects of the communication, including end-to-end security.

6LoWPAN

6LoWPAN, described in RFC 4944, is the IETF-standardized 802.15.4 link protocol that is able to transport IPv6 packets, and it is the established standard for IP-compatible LR-WPANs. 6LoWPAN makes it possible for embedded systems to access the internet using 802.15.4 interfaces, as long as the nodes implement TCP/IP networking, and the link layer provides mechanisms to transmit and receive full-size IP packets using short LR-WPAN frames. The content of the packet is fragmented and transmitted into consecutive transport units, and optionally the network and transport headers are compressed to reduce the transmission overhead.

There is currently no IPv4 counterpart of the 6LoWPAN standard; however IETF is evaluating proposals adopting a similar approach, in order to enable legacy IPv4 connectivity for embedded nodes.

6LoWPAN is part of several network stack implementations, and it is included in a recent attempt to create an industrial alliance, the Thread group, whose goal is to promote a fully IPv6, low-power mesh network technology based on open-standard protocols and designed for the IoT. Multiple free and open source TCP/IP stacks and embedded operating systems support 6LoWPAN and can access 802.15.4 transceivers to provide the necessary link infrastructure to build IP networks based on the functionalities and the protocol implemented.

Mesh networking can optionally be added to the link layer, to provide a transparent bridge mechanism called mesh-under, where all the frames are repeated by the link layer to the remote corners of the mesh until their destination is reached.

Because 6LoWPAN provides the infrastructure for building the network topology, mesh networking can be approached in a different way, using application-level protocols to update the routing tables at IP level. These mechanisms, known as route-over mesh networking, are based on standardized dynamic routing mechanisms, and may also be used to extend the mesh network across different physical links.

Bluetooth

Another machine-to-machine connectivity technology in constant evolution is Bluetooth. Its physical layer is based on 2.4 GHz communication to establish host/device communication, or providing the infrastructure for PAN supporting multiple protocols, including TCP/IP communication. Thanks to its longtime success and the consequent wide adoption in the market of personal computers and portable devices, Bluetooth connectivity has started to gain popularity in the universe of embedded microcontrollers, mostly due to the recent evolution of the standard in the direction of lower power consumption.

Initially designed as a wireless replacement of serial communication for devices at a close range, the *classic* Bluetooth technology has evolved to support integrated dedicated channels, including TCP/IP-capable network interfaces and dedicated audio and video streaming links.

A low-power variant of the protocol stack, introduced with version 4 of the standard definition, has been designed with the purpose of limiting energy consumption for embedded sensor nodes, and introduces a new set of services. A sensor device may export a **Generic Attribute Profile (GATT)** that can be accessed by a client (usually a host machine) to establish communication with a device. When the transceiver on the target is inactive, it consumes a small amount of power, while it is still possible to discover its attribute and initiate a GATT transfer from a client. Bluetooth is mostly used nowadays for short-range communication, to access sensor nodes from personal computers and portable devices, to exchange multimedia content with remote audio devices such as speakers, headsets, hands-free automotive voice interfaces, and in several healthcare applications, thanks to some profiles being specifically designed for this purpose.

Mobile networks

Connecting remote devices with no fixed infrastructure available in their surroundings has been made possible using the same technology that portable devices use to access the internet, over mobile networks, such as GSM/GPRS, 3G, and LTE. The increasing complexity, costs, and energy requirements characterizing the devices accessing broadband mobile connectivity have increased the impact of integrating this sort of network communication in microcontroller-based embedded devices. Mobile networks support TCP/IP protocols natively and provide direct connectivity to the internet, or in some cases, to restricted networks provided by the access infrastructure.

Although still popular in some specific markets, such as automotive and railway, broadband network access profiles are usually overkill to transfer a small amount of information from remote sensor devices, while simpler modems to access older, narrow-bandwidth technologies are slowly disappearing from the market.

While the mobile network technologies evolve, focusing on the requirements of the mobile phone market, embedded device architects are in search of new technologies that better match the needs of distributed IoT systems. New technologies better meet the embedded market goals and evolution toward low-power, cost-effective, long-distance communication.

Low-power Wide Area Networks (LPWANs)

LWPANs are a family of emerging technologies that fill the market gap for cost-effective, low-power, long-distance, narrow-band communication. As for LR-WPAN, different industrial alliances have been formed in the attempt to conquer the market, and in some cases, establish a standard protocol stack for universal LPWAN networks. This process has led to a healthy competition on features, costs, and power-saving features.

LPWAN technologies are usually based on sub-GHz physical channels, but using different radio settings, allowing for an increased range. Devices can communicate with each other over the air, and in some cases use an infrastructure to increase coverage, even across thousands of kilometers, when in visibility of a base station.

The most noticeable emerging technologies in this field include:

- **LoRa/LoRaWAN**: Based on patented wireless radio access mechanisms, and a fully proprietary protocol stack, this technology provides long-distance communication with a relatively high bit rate, compared to similar technologies. While it offers several interesting features, such as local node-to-node communication in the absence of an infrastructure, the closed-protocol approach makes this approach less appealing for the embedded market, and less likely to keep its place in the LPWAN competition in the long run, in favor of more open standards.
- **Sigfox**: This ultra-narrow-band radio technology requires an infrastructure to operate, and offers a very low bit rate on very long ranges. Regulated infrastructure access allows for a limited number of bytes that can be transferred from/to a node every day, and the payload of the messages is fixed to 12 bytes. While the physical layer implementation is proprietary, the protocol stack is distributed in source code form. Radio regulations in some countries are still an open point, though, and may impact the development of this technology worldwide, despite its large success in the European market.
- **Weightless**: Another technology based on ultra-narrow-band, Weightless is a fully open standard for LPWAN operating in the sub-GHz range. Similar to Sigfox in terms of range and performance, it provides an improved security model as an alternative to the classic pre-shared keys deploying mechanisms, allowing for over-the-air security key negotiation mechanisms.

- **DASH7**: The youngest of the technologies described here is based on fully open a fully open design. The source code for the entire lightweight protocol stack is provided by the Dash7 alliance, which allows for an easier integration of the technology in embedded systems. The protocol stack is designed to provide flexibility while designing distributed systems, due to the multiple choices in defining the network topology.

LPWAN protocols are not directly compatible with IP, and require one of the nodes on the network to generate TCP/IP traffic based on the long-range communication data acquired from the nodes. The sporadic, low-bit rate characteristics of the network traffic make these technologies operate in their own field, and require nodes capable of rerouting data from the nodes when the architecture of the distributed systems foresees accessing remote nodes on the internet.

Selecting the appropriate network interfaces

Depending on the use cases, each embedded system may benefit from the communication facilities offered by the technologies described in this section. Due to the high specialization of some embedded devices, a design tailored to specific use cases may even go beyond this classification and use technologies that are designed for one specific use case. Wireless communication is impossible in some cases, due to emission regulations in some environments, and when the media is not capable of transporting radio waves reliably, such as underwater or through the human body.

Submarines may communicate by specific transceivers, using sound waves to represent the data. Special technologies have been researched to improve communication for wearable devices, such as NXP MiGLO, which uses the **near-field magnetic induction (NFMI)** mechanism, increasing the range and efficiency of body networks when compared to wireless radio. Other widespread technologies are available for wired communication as well. Power line communication allows the reusing of existing wires to refit older devices and bring local network connectivity, extending Ethernet or serial interfaces bus using high frequency modulation that does not impact on the original purpose of the wires used.

As it turns out, embedded devices are offered a broad range of possibilities when it comes to connectivity. The optimal choice always depends on the specific use case and the resources available on the system to implement protocols and standards required to reach the other endpoints of the communication. When selecting a communication technology, there might be several aspects to take into account:

- Range of communication
- Bit rate required for data transfer

- Total cost of ownership (transceiver price, integration effort, service costs)
- Media-specific limitations, such as latency introduced by the transceiver
- Impact of the RF interference on the hardware design requirements
- Maximum transfer unit
- Power consumption, energy footprint
- Protocols/standards supported for compatibility with third-party systems
- Compliance to internet protocols for integration in IoT systems
- Topology flexibility, dynamic routing, mesh network feasibility
- Security model
- Resources required to implement drivers and protocols for a specific technology
- Use of open standards to avoid lock-in for long-lived projects

Each and every technology for connected devices offers a different take on how these aspects are addressed in its intrinsic design, also depending on whether the technology has been borrowed from a different context, such as Ethernet or GSM/LTE, or has been designed with low-power embedded systems in mind, as in RL-WPAN and LWPAN protocols.

Selecting the appropriate communication channels when designing distributed systems is an operation that requires strict collaboration between hardware and software design, to truly understand the challenges posed by the additional complexity of creating connected devices, especially in the low-power domain.

The next section focuses on how the implementation of IPs can be adapted to scale down to embedded devices, in all those cases where the IP-to-the-host approach has been selected, and the TCP/IP stack can be extended and configured to meet the requirements of an IoT-distributed system. Cases where non-IP protocols are translated by a border gateway to integrate non-standard communication in IoT systems are not covered, as both the TCP/IP endpoints lie outside the scope of the embedded development in the distributed system.

The Internet Protocols

Standardized at the beginning of the 1980s, the Internet Protocol stack, mostly referred to nowadays as TCP/IP, is a family of network, transport, and application protocols providing standard communication over a wide range of technologies and interfaces.

As we have observed, the embedded industry is specialized enough to operate at the edge of the standards, but a new research trend is taking TCP/IP communication back to its original place as the established standard for network communication, due to the increasing influence of the existing IT infrastructure in distributed systems including small, low-power, cost-effective embedded systems. Creating custom non-IP protocol stacks is, in almost all cases, not worth the effort spent to reinvent state-of-the-art technology, which has been the subject of extensive research for many decades, and has been the main building block for the internet as we know it today, integrating billions of heterogeneous devices.

Designing an embedded system with TCP/IP capabilities is no longer a pioneering task, as several open source implementations exist, and they can be easily integrated into small embedded systems, as long as they are able to access physical communication channels providing data transfer capabilities between two or more endpoints.

TCP/IP implementations

A modern TCP/IP stack is perhaps the most fundamental part of a distributed embedded system. The reliability of the communications depends on how accurately the standard protocols are implemented, and the security of the services running on the device may be compromised by defects hidden in the TCP/IP stack implementation, its interface drivers, and the glue code to provide socket abstractions.

The most popular open source TCP/IP library for embedded devices is the **lightweight IP** stack, best known as **lwIP**. Integrated with many real-time OSes and even distributed in a bundle by hardware manufacturers, lwIP provides the IPv4 and IPv6 network, UDP and TCP socket communication, DNS and DHCP client, and a rich bundle of application-layer protocols that can be integrated in an embedded system using just a few tens of kilobytes of memory. Despite being tailored for small microcontrollers, the resources required by a fully featured stack, such as lwIP, are out of range for some smaller devices, including most sensor processing targets with ultra-low power characteristics.

Micro IP, mostly referred to as **uIP**, is a minimalistic TCP/IP implementation based on the unusual but brilliant intuition of processing one single buffer at a time. Not having to allocate multiple buffers in memory keeps the amount of RAM needed for TCP/IP communication as limited as possible, and reduces the complexity of the implementation of TCP and other protocols, and, as a result of this, the code size of the entire stack. uIP is not designed to scale up to a higher bit rate or for implementing advanced features, but it is sometimes the best compromise to connect nodes with very limited resources, mostly to low-bit rate LR-WPAN networks.

picoTCP is a free software TCP/IP stack with a more recent history. It shares similar resources footprints and features lists with lwIP, but has a different modular design and a stronger focus on IoT protocols, providing dynamic routing, IP filtering, and NAT capabilities. With native support for 6LoWPAN over 802.15.4 devices, picoTCP can be used to build mesh networks, using either the mesh-under capabilities in 6LoWPAN, or a more classic route-over approach, using dynamic routing protocols, such as OLSR and AODV, provided in the modules.

Other implementations exist for both open source and proprietary TCP/IP stacks, which can be integrated in both bare-metal applications and embedded operating systems, often providing similar APIs for integrating interface drivers and interacting with the system to provide socket communication to higher-level applications. An embedded TCP/IP stack is connected to network devices through a device driver, providing a function to send frames to the network, and capable of delivering the received packets using an entry point function, which the TCP/IP stack uses to take the packet in charge. The packets that are currently being handled by the TCP/IP stack may require asynchronous operations, so the application, or the OS, must ensure that the stack loop function is called periodically, so it is able to process the packets in the buffers. Finally, a socket interface is provided by the transport layer for the application to create and use the socket to communicate with remote endpoints.

Network device drivers

In order to integrate a driver for a network interface, the TCP/IP stack exposes an interface to its lowest layers, sending and receiving buffers containing frames or packets. If the device supports the link-layer Ethernet address, TCP/IP stacks must connect an additional component to deal with Ethernet frames, and activate the neighbor discovery protocols to learn the MAC address of the receiving device before initiating any IP communication.

lwIP provides a `netif` structure, describing a network interface, which must be allocated by the driver code, but is then initialized automatically by the stack using the `netif_add` function:

```
struct *netif netif_add(struct netif *mynetif, struct ip_addr *ipaddr,
    struct ip_addr *netmask,
    struct ip_addr *gw, void *state,
    err_t (* init)(struct netif *netif),
    err_t (* input)(struct pbuf *p, struct netif *netif)
);
```

The `ipaddr`, `netmask`, and `gw` arguments can be used to set an initial IPv4 configuration for the link created through this interface. lwIP supports one IPv4 address and three IPv6 addresses per interface, but all of them can be reconfigured at a later stage by accessing the relative fields in the `netif` structure. IP can be configured to use a static IP address, or a mechanism to automatically assign the IP, such as DHCP or automatic link-local addresses.

The state variable is a user-defined pointer that can create an association between the net device and a private field that can be accessed using the `netif | state` pointer in the driver code.

The function pointer provided as the `init` argument is called during the initialization of the stack, with the same `netif` pointer, and it must be used by the driver to initialize the remaining fields for the `netif` device.

The function pointer provided through the input argument describes the internal action that the stack has to perform when it receives a packet from the network. If the device communicates using Ethernet frames, the `ethernet_input` function should be supplied to indicate that additional processing for the Ethernet frame would be required before parsing the frame content, and that the network supports neighbor discovery protocols to associate IP addresses to MAC addresses before transmitting the data. If the driver is handling naked IP packets instead, the receiving function to associate is `ip_input`.

The device driver initialization is finalized in the `init` function, which must also assign a value to other important fields in the `netif` structure:

- `hw_addr`: Containing the MAC address for the Ethernet device, if supported.
- `mtu`: The maximum transfer unit size allowed by this interface.
- `name/num`: For device identification on the system.
- `output`: Function pointer called by the stack to append a custom link header to the IP packet ready for transmission. For Ethernet devices, this should point to `etharp_output` to trigger neighbor discovery mechanisms.
- `link_output`: Function pointer called by the stack when a buffer is ready to be transmitted.

After the link has been marked as `up` by calling `netif_up`, the device driver can call the input function upon the reception of new packets, and the stack itself will call the `output/link_output` functions to interact with the driver.

picoTCP exports a similar interface to implement device drivers, but it supports multiple addresses per interface, so the IP configuration is separate from the device drivers. Each device has a list of associated IPv4 and IPv6 links, each with its own IP configuration, to implement multi-homed services. A device driver structure in picoTCP must begin with a physical entry of the `pico_device` structure as its first field. This way, both structures point to the same address and the device can maintain its own private fields at the end of the `pico_device` structure. To initialize the device, the structure is allocated in the driver, and the `pico_device_init` is called:

```
int pico_device_init(struct pico_device *dev, const char *name, const
uint8_t *mac);
```

The three arguments required are the pre-allocated device structure, a name used for identification within the system, and the Ethernet MAC address, if present. If the MAC is null, the stack bypasses the Ethernet protocol, and all the traffic handled by the driver is naked IP packets with no link-layer extensions. The driver must implement the `send` function that is used by the stack to deliver the frames or packets to be transmitted by the interface, and input is managed through the `pico_stack_recv` function:

```
int32_t pico_stack_recv(struct pico_device *dev, uint8_t *buffer, uint32_t
len);
```

The device is passed again as an argument so that the stack recognizes automatically whether the interface is receiving an Ethernet frame or a raw IP packet with no headers, and reacts accordingly. IP addresses can be configured using `pico_ipv4_link_add` and `pico_ipv6_link_add`, and the routing table accessed through its API to add gateways and static routes to specific networks.

Running the TCP/IP stack

To integrate a network stack, the system must generally provide a few commodities, such as timekeeping and heap-memory management. All the system features required by the stack are associated at compile time using a system-specific configuration header, which associates functions and global values accordingly.

Depending on the characteristics of the physical channels and the throughput to achieve, a TCP/IP stack may become very demanding in terms of heap memory used, allocating space for new incoming buffers until the upper layers are able to process them. Assigning separate memory pools to TCP/IP stack operations might help in some designs to keep the memory usage of the stack under control by placing thresholds and hard limits without impacting the functionality of the other components on the system.

Most libraries implement their own internal timers using a monotonic counter, provided by the system and increased independently by another component in the system. The time tracking value can be increased using the SysTick interrupt, providing an acceptable accuracy for the stack to organize timed operations for the protocols. For lwIP, it is sufficient to export a global variable called `lwip_sys_now`, which contains the time elapsed from boot, expressed in milliseconds. picoTCP needs to export a macro or an inline function called `PICO_TIME_MS` returning the same value. Both stacks expect that the main loop of the application provides recurring entry points, by calling a function in the core API, required to manage the internal states of the system protocols.

To check whether any of the pending timers have expired, the system calls `sys_check_timeouts` in lwIP, or `pico_stack_tick` in picoTCP, from the main event loop, or from a dedicated thread when running within an OS. The interval in between consecutive calls may impact timer accuracy, and in general should not be longer than a few milliseconds to ensure that the network stack is responsive to timed events.

Network interfaces must also be polled for input from the network, either continuously, or through an appropriate interrupt handling implemented in the system. When new data is available, the device drivers allocate new buffers and initiate the processing, by calling the input functions of the data link or the network layer.

A typical bare-metal application using lwIP begins by performing all the initialization steps for the stack and the device driver. The structure for the network interface is allocated in the main function stack, and initialized with a static IPv4 configuration. The following code assumes that the device driver exports a function called `driver_netdev_create`, which populates the interface-specific fields and callbacks:

```
void main(void)
{
    struct netif netif;
    struct ip_addr ipaddr, gateway, netmask;
    IP4_ADDR(&ipaddr, 192,168,0,2);
    IP4_ADDR(&gw, 192,168,0,1);
    IP4_ADDR(&netmask, 255,255,255,0);

    lwip_init();
    netif_add(&netif, &ipaddr, &netmask, &gw, NULL,
    driver_netdev_create, ethernet_input);
    netif_set_default(&netif);
```

The network interface is then activated in the TCP/IP stack:

```
    netif_set_up(&netif);
```

Before entering the main loop, the application initializes the communication by creating and configuring the sockets, and associating the callbacks:

```
application_init_sockets();
```

The main loop relies on the driver to export a function called `driver_netdev_poll` in this case, which is the function where the driver calls `ethernet_input` whenever a new frame is received. Finally, `sys_check_timeouts` is called so lwIP can keep track of the pending timers:

```
while (1) {
    /* poll netif, pass packet to lwIP */
    driver_netdev_poll(&netif);
    sys_check_timeouts();
    WFI();
}
}
```

A similar procedure is expected from bare-metal applications running picoTCP. The initialization of the device driver is independent from the stack, and the driver is expected to call `pico_device_init` on a struct `pico_device` contained in the custom `driver_device` type as the mandatory first member. The only function exported by the driver is `driver_netdev_create`, which also associates its specific network-polling function pointer, which will be called by `pico_stack_tick`. The stack expects a callback to `pico_stack_recv` whenever the poll function of the driver has new incoming packets to process:

```
void main(void)
{
    struct driver_device dev;
    struct ip4 addr, netmask, gw, zero;
    pico_string_to_ipv4("192.168.0.2", &ipaddr.addr);
    pico_string_to_ipv4("255.255.255.0", &netmask.addr);
    pico_string_to_ipv4("192.168.0.1", &gw.addr);
    any.addr = 0;

    pico_stack_init();
    driver_netdev_create(&dev);
```

The IPv4 address configuration is performed by accessing the API of the IPv4 module. Applications may associate one or more IP address configurations by calling `pico_ipv4_link_add` and specifying the address and netmask. A route in the IP protocol is created automatically to reach all the neighbors in the subnet through the interface:

```
pico_ipv4_link_add(&dev, ipaddr, netmask);
```

To add a default route, the gateway is associated to the `0.0.0.0` address (indicating any host) with the `1` metric. The default gateway can be later overridden by defining more specific routes for other subnetworks:

```
pico_ipv4_route_add(any, any, gw, 1, NULL);
```

As in the previous example, the application can now initialize its sockets, and associate callbacks that will be called by the stack when needed:

```
application_init_sockets();
```

This simple main loop calls `pico_stack_tick` repeatedly, which will poll all the associated network interfaces in round robin, and perform all the pending actions in all protocol modules:

```
while (1)
    pico_stack_tick();
    WFI();
}
```

All the TCP/IP actions are associated to socket callbacks, which are called whenever the application is expected to react to network and timeout events, and timeouts are set up automatically by the stack when required to manage the internal states of the single protocols. The interface that is provided to access the socket communication in the absence of an operating system is based on custom callbacks, depending on the stack implementation.

Socket communication

Sockets are the standard way to access transport-layer communication from network applications. The Berkeley socket model, later standardized by POSIX, includes a naming standard for functions and components, and the behavior in a UNIX operating system. If the TCP/IP stack is integrated in the operating system, the scheduler can provide a mechanism to suspend the caller while waiting for a specific input, and the socket call API can be implemented to match POSIX specifications. In a bare-metal event-based application, however, the synchronization with the sockets is done using callbacks, as previously mentioned, in order to follow the event-based model of the main loop.

The interface provided by lwIP for bare-metal socket communication, also called the raw socket API, consists of custom calls, each specifying a callback whenever an event is expected from the stack. When the specific event occurs, lwIP will call the callback from the main loop function.

The description of a TCP socket in lwIP is contained in a TCP-specific protocol control-block structure, `tcp_pcb`. To allocate a new control block for the listening TCP socket, the following function is used:

```
struct tcp_pcb *tcp_new(void);
```

To accept a TCP connection, a bare-metal lwIP TCP server would first call:

```
err_t tcp_bind(struct tcp_pcb *pcb, ip_addr_t *ipaddr, u16_t port);
err_t tcp_listen(struct tcp_pcb *pcb);
```

These non-blocking functions bind the socket to a local address and put it into a listening state.

At this point, a POSIX application would call the blocking `accept` function, which would wait indefinitely for the next incoming connection on the socket. A lwIP bare-metal application instead calls:

```
void tcp_accept(struct tcp_pcb *pcb, err_t (* accept)(void *arg,
                struct tcp_pcb *newpcb,
                err_t err)
);
```

This simply indicates that the server is ready to accept new connections, and wants to be called back to the address of the `accept` function call that has been passed as a parameter when a new incoming connection is established.

Using the same mechanism, to receive the next data segment, the application calls:

```
void tcp_recv(struct tcp_pcb *pcb, err_t (* recv)(void *arg,
              struct tcp_pcb *tpcb,
              struct pbuf *p, err_t err)
);
```

This indicates to the TCP/IP stack that the application is ready to receive the next segment over the TCP connection, and the operation can be performed when a new buffer is available because the stack calls the actual `recv` function that has been specified as the argument when `tcp_recv` has been called.

Similarly, picoTCP associates one callback with each socket object. The callback is a common point to react to any socket-related events, such as a new incoming TCP connection, new data to be read on the socket buffer, or the end of the previous write operation.

The callback is specified when the socket is created:

```
struct pico_socket *pico_socket_open(uint16_t net, uint16_t proto,
                void (*wakeup)(uint16_t ev, struct pico_socket *s)
);
```

The preceding function creates a new socket object for use in the specified network and transport protocol context, the `net` and `proto` arguments respectively, and reacts to all socket events by calling the `wakeup` function that is provided by the application. Using this mechanism, picoTCP successfully detects half-closed socket connections, and other events that are not specifically related to the current operation in progress but may occur due to a state change in the socket communication model.

A TCP socket server can be configured on the newly created socket using these functions:

```
int pico_socket_bind(struct pico_socket *s, void *local_addr,
                uint16_t *port);
int pico_socket_listen(struct pico_socket *s, int backlog);
```

At this point, the application has to wait for the incoming connections without calling `accept`. An event is generated, which calls the `wakeup` function, whenever a new incoming connection is established, and the application can finally call `accept` to generate the new socket object, corresponding to the incoming connection:

```
struct pico_socket *pico_socket_accept(struct pico_socket *s,
                                    void *orig,
                                    uint16_t *local_port);
```

The first argument passed to the picoTCP `wakeup` callback is a bitmask indicating the event types that occurred on the socket. Events may be:

- `EV_RD`: Indicating that there is data to read on the incoming data buffer.
- `EV_CONN`: Indicating that a new connection has been established, after calling `connect`, or while waiting in listening state, before calling `accept`.
- `EV_CLOSE`: Triggered when the other side of the connection sent a `FIN` TCP segment, indicating that it has finished its transmission. The socket is in the `CLOSE_WAIT` state, meaning that the application may still send data before terminating the connection.
- `EV_FIN`: Indicating that the socket has been closed, and it is not usable anymore after returning from `syscall`.
- `EV_ERR`: An error occurred.

The callback interface provided by the TCP/IP stacks may be a little obscure to use at the beginning, but it is a very efficient way to achieve higher throughput when correctly implemented in the application.

Both the TCP/IP stacks we analyzed are capable of providing more standardized APIs only in combination with an operating system, by running the TCP/IP library main loop in a separate thread, and providing access to the sockets using system calls.

Socket communication is only one of the APIs exposed by the TCP/IP stacks. Other protocols implemented by the stack provide their own function signatures; they are described in both libraries' manuals.

Mesh networks and dynamic routing

As previously mentioned, a link-layer protocol may be able to implement mesh-under mechanisms, which hide the complexity of the topology for the upper layers. A different approach is applied when the link-layer protocol does not implement this feature, or whenever the mesh solution may be extended across different network interfaces, and thus must implement a standard protocol that is interface-agnostic. Each link connects two devices in direct visibility, which in turn coordinates to detect the optimal network path to reach a remote node, based on the detected topology. Intermediate nodes along the path are configured to route the traffic toward the destination, based on the information available on the current topology:

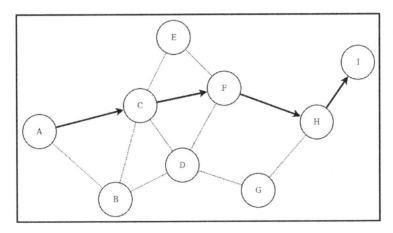

Example of a mesh network topology. Node A chooses node C to route packets towards I, after detecting the optimal 4-hops route

In some scenarios, the topology is not fixed but evolves when nodes in the path become unavailable, or change their location, altering their direct visibility with adjacent nodes. Mesh networks with non-static topology are referred to as **MANETs, mobile ad-hoc networks**. Dynamic routing mechanisms designed for MANETs must be able to react to topology changes and update their routes accordingly, as the network is in continuous evolution.

Route-over mesh mechanisms are implemented within the TCP/IP stack, because they must be able to reconfigure the IP routing table at runtime, and access socket communication. Mesh networks based on dynamic IP routing rely on different protocols, which can be divided into two categories:

- **Proactive dynamic-routing protocols**: Each network node sends a broadcast message to announce its presence on the network, and other nodes can detect a neighbor's presence by reading the messages, and communicating the neighbor list to the neighbors. The mesh network is ready to use at all times, and requires a fixed reconfiguration time on topology changes.
- **Reactive dynamic-routing protocols**: Nodes can be idling when there is no data to exchange, then the path is configured by querying every neighbor, asking for a route to the destination. The message is then repeated, increasing a counter to keep track of the hops, until it reaches the destination, at which point, using the reply, the network can define the path requested by the sender. These mechanisms imply that dynamic routes are formed on demand, so the first messages of the communication can suffer an additional delay; on the other hand, it requires less power and may react faster to topology changes.

The most widely used protocols in the former group are:

- **Optimized Link-State Routing (OLSR)**, standardized by IETF in RFC3626 and RFC7181
- **Better Approach To Mobile Ad-hoc Networking (B.A.T.M.A.N.)**
- Babel (IETF RFC6126)
- **Destination Sequence Distance Vector (DSDV)**

The reactive, on-demand routing protocols standardized by IETF are:

- **Ad-hoc, On-demand, Distance Vector (AODV)**, RFC3561
- Dynamic Source Routing (RFC4728)

The choice of a routing protocol depends once again on the requirement of the mesh network that must be built. Reactive, on-demand protocols are the best fit in networks with sporadic data and battery-powered nodes, where a longer reaction time from the routing protocol is acceptable. Always-on embedded systems may instead benefit from proactive routing mechanisms, which ensure that the routing tables are always updated to the last known state of the network, and each node knows the best route toward each possible destination at all times, but at the same time requires regular updates to travel across the network in the form of broadcast packets, constantly refreshing the status of the network nodes and their neighbors.

picoTCP, which has been designed to provide advanced routing technologies for IoT devices, supports one mesh-under mechanism, in the 6LoWPAN link layer, and two route-over protocols, namely OLSR (reactive) and AODV (proactive), giving a broader choice to integrate TCP/IP communication in mobile, ad hoc networks. To enable OLSR, for example, it is sufficient to compile the stack with support for OLSR, and the OLSR daemon service will automatically be enabled and run within the main TCP/IP stack loop. All the devices that must participate in the definition of the mesh network must be added by calling `pico_olsr_add`:

```
pico_olsr_add(struct pico_device *dev);
```

AODV networking can be enabled in a similar way, and the interfaces are added through the `pico_aodv_add` function:

```
pico_aodv_add(struct pico_devices *dev);
```

In both cases, the services will run in a transparent way for the user, and alter the routing table every time a new node is detected on the network, in the case of OLSR, or every time that we request communication to a remote node, and an on-demand route is created to reach it. Nodes that are not in direct visibility specify a first-hop gateway that guarantees that the destination node can be reached, using the routing metric as an indication of the number of hops, so that when a new, shorter destination is found, the route is replaced and the communication can continue, ideally with no disruptions caused by the route being replaced.

Routing protocols, such as OLSR, can consider other parameters rather than the number of hops when calculating the best path to a given destination in the mesh network. It is possible, for instance, to integrate information about the wireless link quality, such as the signal-to-noise ratio, or the indication of the received signal strength, when calculating the best path. This allows us to select routes based on multiple parameters, and always select the best option available in terms of wireless signal.

Route-over mesh network strategies do not foresee mechanisms to forward broadcast packets, which must be repeated by the link-layer protocol in order to reach all the nodes in the network. However, it is known that implementing such a mechanism can easily trigger a ping-pong effect where a single packet is bounced across two or more nodes, so broadcast-forwarding mechanisms implemented in the link layer must avoid retransmitting the same frame twice, by keeping track of the last few frames forwarded this way.

Transport Layer Security

Link-layer protocols often provide some basic security mechanisms to guarantee authentication of the client connecting to a specific network, and encrypt data by using symmetric keys such as AES. In most cases, authentication at the link layer is sufficient to guarantee a basic level of security. Nevertheless, pre-shared, well-known keys often used in LR-WPAN network stacks may be vulnerable to multiple kinds of attacks, and using a pre-shared key would give an attacker the opportunity to decipher any traffic that has been previously captured on the same link.

A device that takes part in an IoT-distributed system is required to implement a higher grade of security, especially in embedded devices not protecting the memory in any way, where any backdoor means that attackers can take control of the device, and retrieve all the sensitive information, such as private keys used for authentication and encryption in the communication with remote systems.

Transport Layer Security, or **TLS** for short, is a set of cryptography protocols aimed to provide secure communication over standard TCP/IP sockets. The responsibilities of this component are mostly focused around three key requirements for secure communication in distributed systems:

- **Confidentiality** of communication between the parts involved, by the use of symmetric cryptography. TLS defines cryptographic techniques aimed to generate one-time symmetric keys, which lose their validity at the end of the session they were generated for.
- **Authentication** of the parts involved in the communication, using public-key cryptography to sign and verify a challenge payload. Due to the properties of asymmetric keys, only the part that owns the secret, private key is able to sign a payload, while anyone can verify the authenticity of the signature by checking the signature with the public key counterpart of the key that signed the message.
- **Integrity** of the communication, using secured authentication codes that do not verify when the message has been modified along its path.

A few open source implementations of the required protocol suite to enable standard cryptography algorithms and strategies for secure socket communications are available for the embedded market. Closed-source, proprietary implementations should be avoided in this context as much as possible, because security issues are much harder to track down in a closed system, and the source of the implementation has to be blindly trusted.

One of the most interesting implementations is provided by the free and open source software library wolfSSL, implementing the latest standards included in TLS v1.3 and designed for performance and reliability on small embedded systems, including support for hardware accelerators and random number generators for many embedded platforms designed for system security.

wolfSSL implements both cryptographic primitives and SSL algorithms, which can be easily integrated in bare-metal network applications, or in any embedded operating system providing a socket communication API. Cryptography primitives are optimized for embedded devices, and use assembly code for the most performance-critical operations for best performance.

The adoption of a TLS library with support for bleeding-edge cryptography algorithms allows for perfect integration with security measures implemented in the classic IT infrastructure components of the IoT network. On the cloud side, services meant to be accessed by remote embedded systems should allow the selection of ciphers based on elliptic curves, as the classic RSA-based public key encryption requires larger keys and complex calculations to reach the same level of security. New standards for public-key-based encryption, such as Curve22519, are included in the TLS 1.3 specifications to provide more efficient key handling for systems with fewer resources, while keeping the same security level of older algorithms. Selecting a cipher set for TLS communication among heterogeneous systems must take into account the computation times of the operations performed on the target, such as encryption, session key generation, payload signing, and verification.

Securing socket communication

Being designed for embedded devices, wolfSSL has built-in support for many embedded operating systems, to adapt to the specific memory configurations and socket interfaces provided by different systems, and can also be integrated in a bare-metal system with a compatible TCP/IP stack. In either case, the application must be designed to access the SSL layer to communicate with the remote system, while the library is responsible for providing the abstraction for the secure communication channel with the remote system.

To integrate SSL/TLS sessions on top of an existing bare-metal TCP/IP implementation, wolfSSL can be configured to work in non-blocking mode, polling the system for new packets received on the socket, which must be processed by the SSL layer.

The application initiates a TCP connection as usual, either by connecting to a remote socket in the client mode, or by accepting new connections from a local listening socket. After the connection is established, wolfSSL assigns a context to it when the application calls `wolfSSL_accept` or `wolfSSL_connect`, in server mode or in client mode respectively, to initiate the TLS handshake with the remote system. Data communication is then available using the `wolfSSL_read` and `wolfSSL_write` functions, instead of the normal socket read/write functions exported by the TCP/IP stack, so the stream can be processed by the additional SSL built by the TLS library on top.

The library is first initialized before accessing any API, using `wolfSSL_Init`. After, new TLS contexts can be created and associated with existing sockets, by setting the callbacks that wolfSSL can use to query the system for incoming data, or delivering the processed data through the socket connection:

```
wolfSSL_Init();
wolfSSL_CTX *ctx;
ctx = wolfSSL_CTX_new(wolfTLSv1_2_server_method());
wolfSSL_SetIORecv(ctx, wolfssl_recv_cb);
wolfSSL_SetIOSend(ctx, wolfssl_send_cb);
```

The two callbacks are implemented in the system to access socket communication in the TCP/IP stack, by using the TCP socket API. Supposing that a TCP implementation exports read and write functions as `tcp_socket_write` and `tcp_socket_read` in a bare-metal context, no action is taken they return 0. The `wolfssl_send_cb` callback can be:

```
int wolfssl_send_cb(WOLFSSL* ssl, char *buf, int sz, void *sk_ctx)
{
    tcp_ip_socket *sk = (tcp_ip_socket *)sk_ctx;
    int ret = tcp_socket_write(sk, buf, sz);
    if (ret > 0)
        return ret;
    else
        return WANT_WRITE;
}
```

And the corresponding read callback will be:

```
int wolfssl_recv_cb(WOLFSSL *ssl, char *buf, int sz, void *sk_ctx)
{
    tcp_ip_socket *sk = (tcp_ip_socket *)sk_ctx;
    int ret = tcp_socket_read(sk, buf, sz);
```

```
    if (ret > 0)
        return ret;
    else
        return WANT_WRITE;
}
```

The `wolfSSL_CTX` object, used to initialize SSL for every connection, must be associated with a set of certificates and keys prior to initiating any communication. In a more complex system, certificates and keys are stored in the filesystem, and can be accessed when wolfSSL has been integrated to use file operations. In embedded systems, where filesystems are often not supported, certificates and keys can be stored in memory instead, and loaded into the context using pointers to their locations in memory:

```
wolfSSL_CTX_use_certificate_buffer(ctx, certificate, len,
SSL_FILETYPE_ASN1);
wolfSSL_CTX_use_PrivateKey_buffer(ctx, key, len,SSL_FILETYPE_ASN1 );
```

The socket context that is passed to the callbacks is set after the underlying TCP connection is established. For a server, this can be done contextually to the `accept` function, while a client can associate the socket to the specific SSL context after the `connect` function has returned successfully. Accepting an SSL connection on the server side requires the application to call `wolfSSL_accept`, so that the SSL handshake can be finalized before any actual data transfers. The SSL accept procedure should follow the socket accept call, after the pointer to the TCP/IP socket object is associated as context in the SSL object, and will be used as the `sk_ctx` argument for the callbacks related to this socket:

```
tcp_ip_socket new_sk = accept(listen_sk, origin);
wolfSSL ssl = wolfSSL_new(ctx);

if (new_sk) {
    wolfSSL_SetIOReadCtx(ssl, new);
    wolfSSL_SetIOWriteCtx(ssl, new);
```

`wolfSSL_accept` is called after setting the socket context, because the accept mechanism may already need to call the underlying stack to progress through its states:

```
    int ret = wolfSSL_accept(ssl);
```

If the SSL handshake is successful, `wolfSSL_accept` returns the `SSL_SUCCESS` special value, so the secure socket is now ready for communication through the `wolfSSL_read` and `wolfSSL_write` functions. When running in a bare-metal application, `wolfSSL_read` and `wolfSSL_write` must be used in non-blocking mode, by setting this flag at runtime on the SSL session object:

```
    wolfSSL_set_using_nonblock(ssl, 1);
```

Using non-blocking I/O for wolfSSL functions ensures that the event-driven main loop model can be kept, because calling library functions never stalls the system. More complex integration is required to coordinate blocking I/O when integrating wolfSSL in a multi-threading system, but the library already contains bindings for several real-time embedded OSes.

Application protocols

In order to be able to communicate with remote devices and cloud servers in a distributed scenario, embedded systems must implement standard protocols that are compatible with the existing infrastructure. In general, two different approaches are taken when designing remote services:

- Web-based services
- Message protocols

The former is mainly the classic, client-server, REST-based communication that is popular in web services accessed through personal computers or portable devices. Web services require no adaptation in particular on the cloud side to support embedded systems, except for the choice of an embedded-friendly cipher set as described in the *Securing socket communication* section. However, the request-reply communication model introduces some restrictions on the design of distributed applications. The HTTP protocol can be upgraded by common agreement on the two HTTP endpoints, and support WebSocket, which is a protocol providing the abstraction of a symmetric, bidirectional channel on top of the HTTP services.

Message protocols are a different approach that better reflect the functions of a sensor-/actuator-embedded system, where information is exchanged by using short binary messages, which can be relayed by intermediate agents, and gathered or distributed from server nodes. Message protocols are the preferred choice when the network includes smaller nodes, because of the simpler presentation of the data, as opposed to web services, mostly based on human-readable strings and adding a much larger overhead to the transport size and memory footprint of the targets having to handle the ASCII strings.

In both cases, TLS should be supported at infrastructure- and device-level, for end-to-end encryption and reliable device identification. Plaintext authentication and pre-shared key encryption are obsolete techniques and thus should not be part of the security strategy of modern distributed systems.

Message protocols

Message-based communication protocols are not a novelty in computer networking software, but have found a particularly good match with IoT-distributed systems, especially in those scenarios where a one-to-many message-based model allows us to reach many devices at a time and establish bidirectional communication, or multiple devices from different locations can communicate with each other using an external server that acts as a communication broker. The lack of standardization in this area has led to several different models, each one with its own API and network protocol definition.

Some open standards in particular, however, have been designed to implement secure distributed messaging systems specifically tailored for a system with reduced resources and networks with limited bandwidth, by including specifications that are reasonably feasible to implement within a small code footprint. This is the case of the **Message-Queuing Telemetry Transport (MQTT)** protocol. Thanks to its publisher-subscriber model and the possibility to interconnect embedded devices at different physical locations over TCP/IP, MQTT has become widely used and is supported by several cloud architectures.

The protocol relies on TCP for establishing connections to a central broker, which dispatches messages from publishers to subscribers. Publishers push data for a certain topic, described by a URI, and subscribers can filter the topics they want to follow upon connection, so that the broker selectively forwards only the messages matching the filters.

A few implementations for the client library exist for small embedded devices too, although many of them lack support for security mechanisms. The protocol supports a plaintext password-authentication mechanism, which is not a valid security measure, and should never be used on top of clear TCP/IP communication, because passwords can be easily intercepted along the path.

According to the standard, instead of the socket-based TCP communication through IANA-registered TCP port 1883, it is possible to establish an SSL session, which uses TCP port 8883 instead. A secure implementation that uses SSL sessions on top of TCP is provided by wolfSSL, in a separate GPL-licensed library called **wolfMQTT**. This library offers secure MQTT socket connections by default. It is capable of implementing both client and server authentication through certificates and public keys, and provides symmetric-key encryption through the established session.

REST architectural pattern

REST is the acronym for **Representational State Transfer**, a term introduced by Roy Fielding to describe the pattern used by web services to communicate with remote systems using a stateless protocol. In a REST-compliant system, resources are accessed in the form of HTTP requests targeting a specific URI, using the same protocol stack as web pages obtained through a request from a remote browser. In fact, REST requests are extended HTTP requests, representing all data as encoded strings, transported through TCP in a readable HTTP stream.

Adopting this pattern provides a number of architectural benefits on the server side, and allows us to build distributed systems with a very high scalability. Although not very efficient and definitely not designed with embedded systems resources in mind, embedded systems can interact with remote web services exposed by a RESTful system by implementing a REST client.

The Mongoose Web Server Library is a GPL-licensed collection of protocols for embedded devices, with native support for both lwIP and picoTCP. This library provides APIs to build RESTful applications based on local and remote web services, and a few of the most popular message protocols. Because the library is tailored to small embedded systems, it is simple to integrate in a bare-metal event-driven application by calling the periodic function from the main loop. Moreover, Mongoose supports TLS on web services through SSL bindings, which can be used to integrate a third-party secure library such as wolfSSL to run the web services through HTTPS sockets.

Distributed systems – single points of failure

Designing distributed systems also means taking into account link defects, unreachable gateways, and other failures. Embedded devices should not stop working when disconnected from the internet, but rather offer fall-back mechanisms, based on local gateways. Consider, for example, a demotic IoT system for controlling all the heating and cooling units in a house, accessible from portable devices and coordinated remotely using any network access. Temperature sensors, heaters, and coolers are controlled by a mesh network of embedded devices, while the central control is on remote cloud servers. The system can control the actuators remotely, based on user settings and sensor readings. This gives us the possibility of accessing the service even from a remote location, allowing the user to tune the system to set the desired temperature in each room, based on the commands sent from user interfaces, which are processed and relayed by the cloud to reach their destination in the embedded devices. As long as all the components are connected to the internet, the IoT system works as expected.

Nevertheless, in the case of connection failure, users would not be able to control the system or activate any function. Terminating the application service on a local device within the local area network ensures the continuity of the services across failures of the link to the internet and any issues that would prevent the local network from accessing the remote cloud device. If such a mechanism is in place, a system disconnected from the internet would still provide a failover alternative to access sensors and actuators, assuming that all the actors in play are connected to a common LAN. Moreover, having a local system processing and relaying settings and commands reduces the latency of the actions requested, because requests do not have to travel across the internet to be processed and forwarded back to the same network. Designing reliable IoT networks must include a careful assessment of the single points of failure among all the links and devices used to provide services, and this must include the backbone link used to reach services, message brokers, and remote devices that can cause malfunctions or other issues to the entire system.

Summary

This chapter has given us an overview of the design of machine-to-machine distributed systems and IoT services including connected embedded devices, with a focus on security elements that are too often overlooked or underestimated in embedded development. The technology proposed allows full, professional-grade, secure, and fast TCP/IP connectivity on very small targets, and uses state-of-the-art technology, such as the most recent version of the TLS cipher suites. Multiple approaches have been considered for a broader view on the technologies, protocols, and security algorithms available for building distributed embedded systems.

The next chapter will illustrate the multitasking possibilities of modern embedded microcontrollers, by explaining how to write a small scheduler for Cortex-M microprocessors from scratch, and will summarize the key roles of a real-time operating system running on an embedded target.

Parallel Tasks and Scheduling

10

If the complexity of the system increases, and the software has to manage multiple peripherals and events at the same time, it is more convenient to rely on an operating system to coordinate and synchronize all the different operations. Separating the application logic into different threads offers a few important architectural advantages. Each component performs the designed operation within its own running unit, and it may release the CPU while it is suspended, waiting for input or a timeout event.

In this chapter, the mechanisms used to implement a multithreading embedded operating system are observed, through the development of a minimalistic operating system, tailored to the reference platform, and written step by step from scratch, providing a working scheduler to run multiple tasks in parallel.

The scheduler's internals are mostly implemented within system service calls, and its design impacts the system performance and other features, such as different priority levels and time constraints for real-time-dependent tasks. Some of the possible scheduling policies, for different contexts, are explained and implemented in the example code.

Running multiple threads in parallel implies that resources can be shared, and there is the possibility of concurrent access to the same memory. Most microprocessors designed to run multithreading systems provide primitive functions, accessible through specific assembly instructions, to implement locking mechanisms, such as semaphores. The example operating system exposes mutex and semaphore primitives that can be used by the threads to control access to the shared resources.

By introducing memory protection mechanisms, it is possible to provide a separation of the resources based on their addresses, and let the kernels supervise all the operations involving the hardware through a system call interface. Most real-time embedded operating systems prefer a flat model with no segmentation, to keep the kernel code as small as possible and with a minimal API, to optimize the resources available for the applications. The example kernel will show us how to create a system call API to centralize the control of the resources, using physical memory segmentation to protect the resources of the kernel, the system control block, the mapped peripherals' and the other tasks, with the purpose of increasing the level of safety of the system.

This chapter is split into the following sections:

- Task management
- Scheduler implementation
- Synchronization
- System resource separation

Task management

An operating system provides the abstraction of parallel running processes and threads, by alternating the applications to run in parallel. In fact, on systems with a single CPU, there can only be one running thread at a time. While the running thread executes, all the others are waiting in line until the next task switch.

In a cooperative model, switching the task is always a voluntary action requested by the thread implementation. The opposite approach, known as **preemption**, requires that the kernel periodically interrupts tasks at any point of their execution, to temporarily save the status and resume that of the next task in line.

Switching the running task consists of storing the first store of values of the CPU registers in RAM, and restoring those of the next task selected for running. This operation is better known as **context switch**, and is the core of the scheduling system.

The task block

Tasks have their representation in the system in the form of a task block structure. This object contains all the information needed for the scheduler to keep track of the state of the task at all times, and is dependent on the design of the scheduler. Tasks might be defined at compile time and started after the kernel boots, or spawned and terminated while the system is running.

Each task block may contain a pointer to the start function, that defines the beginning of the code executed when the task is spawned, and a set of optional arguments. Memory is assigned for each task to use it as its private stack region. This way, the execution context of each thread and process is separated from all the others, and the values of the registers can be stored in a task-specific memory area when the task is interrupted. The task-specific stack pointer is stored in the task block structure, and it will be used to store the values of the CPU register upon context switches.

Running with separate stacks requires that some memory is reserved in advance, and associated with each task. In the simplest case, all tasks are using a stack of the same size, are created before the scheduler starts, and cannot be terminated. This way, the memory reserved to be associated with private stacks can be contiguous and associated with each new task. The memory region used for the stack areas can be defined in the linker script.

The reference platform has a separate core-coupled memory, mapped at `0x10000000`. Among the many possibilities to arrange the memory sections, we decide to map the start of the stack space, used to associate stack areas to the threads, at the beginning of the CCRAM. The remaining CCRAM space is used as a stack for the kernel, which leaves all the SRAM, excluding the `.data` and `.bss` sections, for heap allocation. The pointers are exported by the linker script with the following `PROVIDE` instructions:

```
PROVIDE(_end_stack = ORIGIN(CCRAM) + LENGTH(CCRAM));
PROVIDE(stack_space = ORIGIN(CCRAM));
PROVIDE(_start_heap = _end);
```

In the kernel source, `stack_space` is declared as external, because it is exported by the linker script. We also declare the amount of space reserved for the execution stack of each task (expressed in number of four-bytes words):

```
extern uint32_t stack_space;
#define STACK_SIZE (256)
```

Every time a new task is created, the next kilobyte in the stack space is assigned as its execution stack, and the initial stack pointer will be set at the highest address in the area, as the execution stack grows backward:

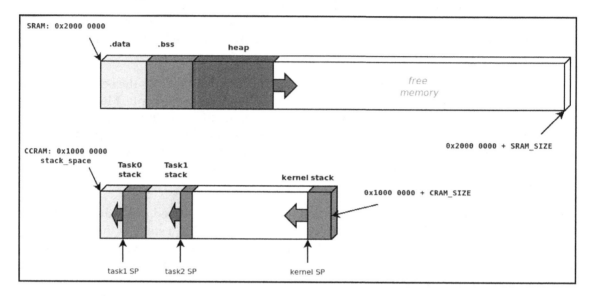

Memory configuration used to provide separate execution stacks to tasks

A simple task block structure can then be declared, as follows:

```
#define TASK_WAITING 0
#define TASK_READY 1
#define TASK_RUNNING 2

#define TASK_NAME_MAXLEN 16;

struct task_block {
    char name[TASK_NAME_MAXLEN];
    int id;
    int state;
    void (*start)(void *arg);
    void *arg;
    uint32_t *sp;
};
```

A global array is defined to contain all the task blocks of the system. We use a global index to keep track of the tasks already created, to use the position in memory relative to the task identifier and the ID of the current running task:

```
#define MAX_TASKS 8
static struct task_block TASKS[MAX_TASKS];
static int n_tasks = 1;
static int running_task_id = 0;
#define kernel TASKS[0]
```

With this model, the task block is pre-allocated in the data section, and the fields are initialized in place, keeping track of the index. The first element of the array is reserved for the task block of the kernel, which is the current running process.

In our example, tasks are created by invoking the `task_create` function, providing a name, an entry point, and its argument. For a static configuration with a predefined number of tasks, this is done in the kernel initialization, but more advanced schedulers may allow us to allocate new control blocks to spawn new processes at runtime, while the scheduler is running:

```
struct task_block *task_create(char *name, void (*start)(void *arg), void
*arg)
{
    struct task_block *t;
    int i;
    if (n_tasks >= MAX_TASKS)
    return NULL;
    t = &TASKS[n_tasks];
    t->id = n_tasks++;
    for (i = 0; i < TASK_NAME_MAXLEN; i++) {
        t->name[i] = name[i];
        if (name[i] == 0)
            break;
    }
    t->state = TASK_READY;
    t->start = start;
    t->arg = arg;
    t->sp = ((&stack_space) + n_tasks * STACK_SIZE);
    task_stack_init(t);
    return t;
}
```

In order to implement the `task_stack_init` function, which initializes the values in the stack for the process to start running, we need to understand how the context switch works, and how new tasks are actually started when the scheduler is running.

Context switch

The context switch procedure consists of getting the values of the CPU register during the execution and saving them at the bottom of the stack of the currently running task. Then, restore the values for the next task, to resume its execution. This operation must happen in the interrupt context, and its internal mechanisms are CPU-specific. On the reference platform, any interrupt handler can replace the current running task and restore another context, but this operation is more often done within interrupt service routines associated with system events. Cortex-M provides two CPU exceptions that are designed to provide the basic support for context switching, because they can be arbitrarily triggered in any context: PendSV and SVCall. The former is the default way for a preemptive kernel to force an interrupt in the immediate future, after setting one bit in a specific register within the system control block, and it is usually associated with the context switch of the next task.

SVCall is the main entry point for the user application to submit a formal request to access a resource that is managed by the kernel. This feature is designed to provide an API to access the kernel safely to request operations from a component or a driver. As the result of the operation may be not immediately available, SVCall can also permit preempting the calling task, in order to provide the abstraction of blocking system calls.

The routines to store and restore the values of the CPU registers to/from memory during the context switch are partially implemented in hardware on the Cortex-M CPU. This means that, when the interrupt is entered, a copy of part of the register is pushed automatically into the stack. The copy of the registers into the stack is called the **stack frame**, and contains the registers **R0** to **R3**, **R12**, **LR**, **PC**, and **xPSR**, in the order shown in the figure:

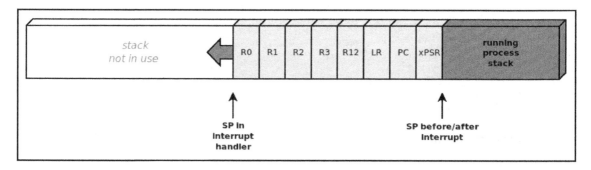

Registers are automatically copied to the stack when entering an interrupt handler

The stack pointer, however, does not include the other half of CPU registers, R4-R11. For this reason, in order to complete the context switch successfully, a system handler that intends to replace the running process must store the extra stack frame containing the value for these registers, and restore the extra stack frame of the next task just before returning from the handler. ARM Thumb-2 assembly provides instructions to push the value of contiguous CPU registers to the stack and pop them back in place. The following two functions are used to push and pop the extra stack frame in the stack:

```
static void __attribute__((naked)) store_context(void)
{
    asm volatile("mrs r0, msp");
    asm volatile("stmdb r0!, {r4-r11}");
    asm volatile("msr msp, r0");
    asm volatile("bx lr");
}

static void __attribute__((naked)) restore_context(void)
{
    asm volatile("mrs r0, msp");
    asm volatile("ldmfd r0!, {r4-r11}");
    asm volatile("msr msp, r0");
    asm volatile("bx lr");
}
```

The reason for the ((naked)) attribute is to prevent GCC from putting prologue and epilogue sequences, consisting of a few assembly instructions each, into the compiled code. The prologue would change the values of some of the registers in the extra stack frame area, which would be restored in the epilogue, and this is conflicting with the purpose of the functions accessing register values using assembly instructions. Due to the missing epilogue, the naked functions return by jumping back to the calling instruction, which is stored in the LR register.

As a result of the assembly push operation, this is how the stack of the process being preempted looks:

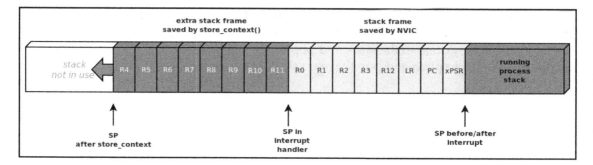

The remaining register values are copied to the stack to complete the context switch

Creating tasks

When the system is running, all the tasks except the one running are in a *wait* state, which means that the full stack frame is saved at the bottom of the stack, and the stack pointer is stored in the control block to be used by the scheduler to resume each process.

A newly created task will wake up for the first time in the middle of the context switch. At that point, the task is expected to have preserved the previous state of its CPU registers, but obviously a new task does not have such a thing. Upon stack creation, a forged stack frame is pushed to the end of the stack, so that when the task resumes, the values stored are copied into the system registers, and the task can resume from its entry point.

The task_create function relies on a stack initialization function, task_stack_init, which pushes the initial values for the system registers to allow the restoring of the task, and moves the stored stack pointer to the beginning of the extra frame, which can be left uninitialized. To easily access the stored register in the stack frame, we declare a stack_frame structure that uses one field per register, and an extra_frame structure, just for completeness:

```
struct stack_frame {
    uint32_t r0, r1, r2, r3, r12, lr, pc, xpsr;
};

struct extra_frame {
    uint32_t r4, r5, r6, r7, r8, r9, r10, r11;
};
```

```
static void task_stack_init(struct task_block *t)
{
    struct stack_frame *tf;
    t->sp -= sizeof(struct stack_frame);
    tf = (struct stack_frame *)(t->sp);
    tf->r0 = (uint32_t) t->arg;
    tf->pc = (uint32_t) t->start;
    tf->lr = (uint32_t) task_terminated;
    tf->xpsr = (1 << 24);
    t->sp -= sizeof(struct extra_frame);
}
```

When the context is restored, the exception handler return procedure automatically restores the context from the stack frame we are forging. The registers for the starting task are initialized as follows:

- The **program counter**, **PC**, contains the address of the start function, where the system will jump to switch to this task for the first time.
- **R0-R3** may contain optional arguments to pass to the start function, according to the ABI of the CPU. In our case, we carry the value of the single argument given for the start function by the caller of `task_create`.
- The **execution program status register**, **xPSR**, must be programmed to have only the mandatory thumb flag set at bit 24.
- The **link register**, **LR**, contains the pointer to the procedure called when the start function returns. In our case, tasks are not allowed to return from the start function, so the `task_terminated` function is just an infinite loop, and it is considered a system error. In other cases, if tasks are allowed to terminate, a function can be set as common exit points for the tasks, to perform the cleanup operations required upon returning from the start function.

Once the initial stack frame has been created, the task can participate in multitasking, and can be picked by the scheduler at any time to resume the execution, from the same state as all the other tasks not running:

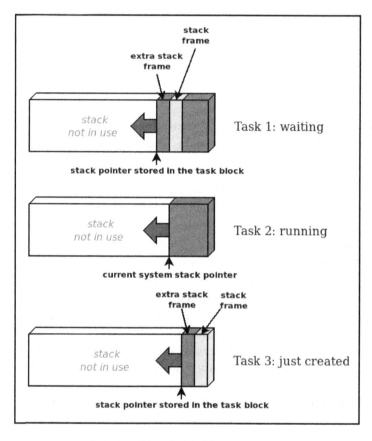

Stack pointers of three tasks during different execution states

Our simple kernel main function can now create processes and prepare the stack, but is not yet actually able to run them until we implement the scheduler internals. Timekeeping is useful in this case, so the SysTick is enabled at startup to keep track of time in the system. The task block of the kernel is initialized, and two new tasks are created:

```
void main(void) {
    clock_pll_on(0);
    systick_enable();
    led_setup();
    kernel.name[0] = 0;
    kernel.id = 0;
```

```
    kernel.state = TASK_RUNNING;
    task_create("test0",task_test0, NULL);
    task_create("test1",task_test1, NULL);
    while(1) {
        schedule();
    }
}
```

The two main tasks are created pointing to different start functions, and a `NULL` argument. Both functions should in fact never return, and can be interrupted and resumed according to the implemented scheduler policy.

To proceed from this point, the scheduler internals need to be implemented to actually start and alternate the execution of the parallel tasks we just defined.

Scheduler implementation

The architecture of the system depends on the way the scheduler is implemented. Tasks can be running in a cooperative model, until they voluntarily decide to yield the CPU to the next task, or the OS can decide to trigger an interrupt to swap the running task behind the scene, applying a specific policy to decide the interval in between task switches and the priority for the selection of the next task. In both cases, the context switch happens within one of the supervisor calls available, set to decide which tasks to schedule next, and to perform the context switch. In this section, the full context switch procedure through the PendSV is added to the example, and then a few of the possible scheduling policies are analyzed and implemented.

Supervisor calls

The core component of the scheduler consists of the exception handler associated with the system interrupt events, such as PendSV and SVCall. On Cortex-M, a PendSV exception can be triggered at any time by the software, setting the PENDSET flag, corresponding to bit 28 of the interrupt control and state register, located in the SCB at address `0xE000ED04`. A simple macro is defined to initiate the context switch by setting the flag:

```
#define SCB_ICSR (*((volatile uint32_t *)0xE000ED04))
#define schedule() SCB_ICSR |= (1 << 28)
```

The call to schedule from the kernel, and all the subsequent calls, would cause a context switch, which can now be implemented in the PendSV handler. To complete a context switch, the handler has to perform the following steps:

1. Store the current stack pointer from the SP register to the task block
2. Push the extra stack frame to the stack, by calling `store_context`
3. Change the state of the current task into `TASK_READY`
4. Select a new task to resume
5. Change the state of the new task into `TASK_RUNNING`
6. Retrieve the new stack pointer from the associated task block
7. Pop the extra stack frame from the stack, by calling `restore_context`
8. Set a special return value for the interrupt handler, to activate the thread mode at the end of the PendSV service routine

The `isr_pendsv` function must be naked, because it accesses the CPU register directly through the `store/restore_context` functions:

```c
void __attribute__((naked)) isr_pendsv(void)
{
    store_context();
    asm volatile("mrs %0, msp" : "=r"(TASKS[running_task_id].sp));
    TASKS[running_task_id].state = TASK_READY;
    running_task_id++;
    if (running_task_id >= n_tasks)
        running_task_id = 0;
    TASKS[running_task_id].state = TASK_RUNNING;
    asm volatile("msr msp, %0"::"r"(TASKS[running_task_id].sp));
    restore_context();
    asm volatile("mov lr, %0" ::"r"(0xFFFFFFF9));
    asm volatile("bx lr");
}
```

The value loaded in the LR before returning is used to indicate that we are returning to the thread mode at the end of this interrupt. Depending on the value of the last three bits, the service routine informs the CPU which stack pointer to use when returning from the interrupt. The `0xFFFFFFF9` value used in this case corresponds to the thread mode using the main stack pointer. Different values will be needed later on, when the example is expanded to support separate stack pointers between the kernel and the process.

The complete context switch is now implemented inside the PendSV service routine, which for now is simply selecting the next task, and wraps around to execute the kernel, with ID 0, after the last task in the array. The service routine is triggered to run in handler mode every time that the schedule macro is called.

Cooperative scheduler

Different policies can be defined to alternate the execution of the tasks in the system. In the simplest case, the main functions of each task voluntarily suspend its execution, by invoking the schedule macro.

In this example implementation, two threads are defined. Both will turn on an LED and hold the CPU in a busy-loop for one second, then turn off the LED, and explicitly call the schedule() function to trigger a context switch:

```
void task_test0(void *arg)
{
    uint32_t now = jiffies;
    blue_led_on();
    while(1) {
        if ((jiffies - now) > 1000) {
            blue_led_off();
            schedule();
            now = jiffies;
            blue_led_on();
        }
    }
}

void task_test1(void *arg)
{
    uint32_t now = jiffies;
    red_led_on();
    while(1) {
        if ((jiffies - now) > 1000) {
            red_led_off();
            schedule();
            now = jiffies;
            red_led_on();
        }
    }
}
```

The little operating system is finally working, and the kernel is scheduling the two tasks in sequence. The task with ID 0 is also being resumed at the beginning of each loop, but in this simple case, the kernel task is only calling the schedule in a loop, immediately resuming the task with ID 1. With this design, the reactivity of the system depends entirely on the implementation of the tasks, as each task can hold the CPU indefinitely, and prevent other tasks from running. The cooperative model is only used in very specific scenarios, where each task is directly responsible of regulating its own CPU cycles and cooperating with the other threads, and may impact on the responsiveness and the fairness of the entire system.

For the sake of simplicity, this implementation does not take into account the wrap-around of the `jiffies` variable. If incremented every millisecond, `jiffies` would in fact overflow its maximum value after about 42 days. A real operating systems, unlike our simplistic example, must implement an appropriate mechanism to compare time variables, not shown here, that can detect that the wrap-around while calculating time differences.

Concurrency and timeslices

A different approach consists of assigning short intervals of the CPU time to each task, and continuously swapping processes at a very short interval. A preemptive scheduler autonomously interrupts the running task to resume the next one without an explicit request from the task itself, and can impose its policy regarding the selection of the next task to run and the duration of the interval where the CPU is assigned to each task, namely its timeslice.

From the task's point of view, the execution can now be continuous and completely independent from the scheduler, which acts behind the scenes to interrupt and resume each task continuously, giving the illusion that all the tasks are actually running at the same time. The threads can be redefined to blink the LEDs at two different intervals:

```
void task_test0(void *arg)
{
    uint32_t now = jiffies;
    blue_led_on();
    while(1) {
        if ((jiffies - now) > 500) {
            blue_led_toggle();
            now = jiffies;
        }
    }
}

void task_test1(void *arg)
```

```
{
    uint32_t now = jiffies;
    red_led_on();
    while(1) {
        if ((jiffies - now) > 125) {
            red_led_toggle();
            now = jiffies;
        }
    }
}
```

To alternate tasks in round-robin, we trigger the PendSV execution from within the SysTick handler, and this results in a task switch happening at regular intervals. The new SysTick handler triggers a context switch every TIMESLICE milliseconds:

```
#define TIMESLICE (20)
void isr_systick(void)
{
    if ((++jiffies % TIMESLICE) == 0)
        schedule();
}
```

In this new configuration, we now have a more complete model, allowing multiple tasks to run independently, and the scheduling to be supervised completely by the kernel.

Blocking tasks

The simple scheduler implemented so far provides only two states for the tasks, TASK_READY and TASK_RUNNING. A third state can be implemented to define a task that does not actually need to be resumed, because it is blocked waiting for an event or a timeout. A task can be waiting for a system event of some type, such as:

- Interrupt events from an input/output device in use by the task
- Communication from another task, such as the TCP/IP stack
- Synchronization mechanisms, such as a mutex or a semaphore, to access a shared resource in the system that is currently unavailable
- Timeout events

To manage the different states, the scheduler may implement two or more lists, to separate the tasks currently running, or ready to run, from those waiting for an event. The scheduler then selects the next task among those in the TASK_READY state, and ignores the ones in the list of the blocked tasks:

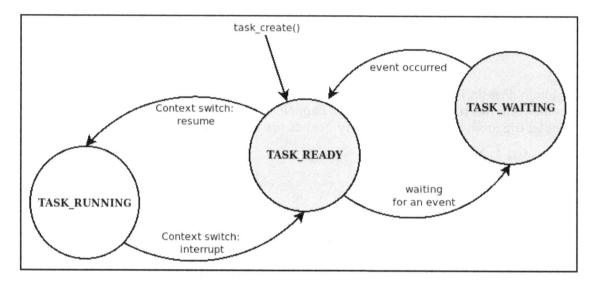

State machine describing the task's execution states

This second version of the scheduler keeps track of the current running task using a global pointer, instead of the index of the array, and organizes the tasks into two lists:

- tasklist_active: Containing the task block for the running task and all the tasks in the TASK_READY state, waiting to be scheduled
- tasklist_waiting: Containing the task block of the tasks currently blocked

The easiest showcase to implement for this new mechanism is a sleep_ms function, which can be used by tasks to temporarily switch to a waiting state and set up a resume point in the future to be scheduled again. Providing this kind of facility allows our tasks to sleep in between LED toggle actions, instead of running a busy-loop, repeatedly checking for the timer expired. These new tasks are not only more efficient, because they do not waste CPU cycles in a busy-loop, but also more readable:

```
void task_test0(void *arg)
{
    blue_led_on();
    while(1) {
```

```
            sleep_ms(500);
            blue_led_toggle();
        }
    }

    void task_test1(void *arg)
    {
        red_led_on();
        while(1) {
            sleep_ms(125);
            red_led_toggle();
        }
    }
```

To arrange the task blocks into lists, a pointer to the next element is added to the structure, and the two lists are populated at runtime. To manage the `sleep_ms` function, a new field is added to keep track of the system time when the task is supposed to be put in the active list to be resumed:

```
    struct task_block {
        char name[TASK_NAME_MAXLEN];
        int id;
        int state;
        void (*start)(void *arg);
        void *arg;
        uint8_t *sp;
        uint32_t wakeup_time;
        struct task_block *next;
    };
```

The lists can be managed with two simple functions to the insert/delete elements:

```
    struct task_block *tasklist_active = NULL;
    struct task_block *tasklist_waiting = NULL;

    static void tasklist_add(struct task_block **list,struct task_block *el)
    {
        el->next = *list;
        *list = el;
    }

    static int tasklist_del(struct task_block **list, struct task_block *delme)
    {
        struct task_block *t = *list;
        struct task_block *p = NULL;
        while (t) {
            if (t == delme) {
```

```
                if (p == NULL)
                    *list = t->next;
                else
                    p->next = t->next;
                return 0;
            }
            p = t;
            t = t->next;
        }
        return -1;
    }
```

Two additional functions are added to move the tasks from the active list to the waiting list and vice versa, which additionally change the state of the task itself:

```
static void task_waiting(struct task_block *t)
{
    if (tasklist_del(&tasklist_active, t) == 0) {
        tasklist_add(&tasklist_waiting, t);
        t->state = TASK_WAITING;
    }
}
static void task_ready(struct task_block *t)
{
    if (tasklist_del(&tasklist_waiting, t) == 0) {
        tasklist_add(&tasklist_active, t);
        t->state = TASK_READY;
    }
}
```

The `sleep_ms` function sets the resume time and moves the task to the waiting state, then activates the scheduler so that the task is preempted:

```
void sleep_ms(int ms)
{
    if (ms < TASK_TIMESLICE)
        return;
    t_cur->wakeup_time = jiffies + ms;
    task_waiting(t_cur);
    schedule();
}
```

The new PendSV handler selects the next task to run from the active list, which is assumed to always contain at least one task, as the kernel main task is never put in the waiting state. The new thread is selected through the `tasklist_next_ready` function, which also ensures that if the current task has been moved from the active list, or is the last in line, the head of the active list is selected for the next timeslice:

```
static inline struct task_block *tasklist_next_ready(struct task_block *t)
{
    if ((t->next == NULL) || (t->next->state != TASK_READY))
        return tasklist_active;
    return t->next;
}
```

This small function is the core of the new scheduler based on the double list, and is invoked in the middle of each context switch to select the next active task in PendSV:

```
void __attribute__((naked)) isr_pendsv(void)
{
    store_context();
    asm volatile("mrs %0, msp" : "=r"(t_cur->sp));
    if (t_cur->state == TASK_RUNNING) {
        t_cur->state = TASK_READY;
    }
    t_cur = tasklist_next_ready(t_cur);
    t_cur->state = TASK_RUNNING;
    asm volatile("msr msp, %0" ::"r"(t_cur->sp));
    restore_context();
    asm volatile("mov lr, %0" ::"r"(0xFFFFFFF9));
    asm volatile("bx lr");
}
```

Finally, in order to check for the wake-up time of each sleeping task, the kernel visits the list of waiting tasks, and moves the task blocks back to the active list whenever the wake-up time has elapsed. The kernel initialization now includes a few extra steps to ensure that the kernel task itself is put in the list of running tasks at boot:

```
void main(void) {
    clock_pll_on(0);
    led_setup();
    button_setup();
    systick_enable();
    kernel.name[0] = 0;
    kernel.id = 0;
    kernel.state = TASK_RUNNING;
    kernel.wakeup_time = 0;
    tasklist_add(&tasklist_active, &kernel);
```

```
task_create("test0",task_test0, NULL);
task_create("test1",task_test1, NULL);
task_create("test2",task_test2, NULL);
while(1) {
    struct task_block *t = tasklist_waiting;
    while (t) {
        if (t->wakeup_time && (t->wakeup_time < jiffies)) {
            t->wakeup_time = 0;
            task_ready(t);
            break;
        }
        t = t->next;
    }
    WFI();
}
}
```

Waiting for resources

Blocking on a given time interval is only one of the possibilities for a task to be temporarily excluded from the active list. The kernel may implement other event and interrupt handlers to bring the tasks back into the scheduler loop, so that the task may block waiting for I/O events from a specific set of resources while in a TASK_WAITING state.

In our example code, a read function can be implemented to retrieve the status of the button from a task, which would block and only return once the button is pressed. Until then, the calling task remains in the waiting list and is never scheduled. A task toggling the green LED every time the button is pressed relies on button_read() as its blocking point:

```
#define BUTTON_DEBOUNCE_TIME 120
void task_test2(void *arg)
{
    uint32_t toggle_time = 0;
    green_led_off();
    while(1) {
        if (button_read()) {
            if ((jiffies - toggle_time) > BUTTON_DEBOUNCE_TIME) {
                green_led_toggle();
                toggle_time = jiffies;
            }
        }
    }
}
```

The `button_read` function keeps track of the calling task, so the `button_task` pointer is used to wake it up when the button is pressed. The task is moved to the waiting list and the read operation is initiated in the driver, and then the task is preempted:

```
struct task_block *button_task = NULL;
int button_read(void)
{
    if (button_task)
        return 0;
    button_task = t_cur;
    task_waiting(t_cur);
    button_start_read();
    schedule();
    return 1;
}
```

In order to notify the scheduler whenever the button is pressed, the driver uses a callback, specified by the kernel during the initialization, and passed as an argument to `button_setup`:

```
static void (*button_callback)(void) = NULL;

void button_setup(void (*callback)(void))
{
    AHB1_CLOCK_ER |= GPIOA_AHB1_CLOCK_ER;
    GPIOA_MODE &= ~ (0x03 << (BUTTON_PIN * 2));
    EXTI_CR0 &= ~EXTI_CR_EXTI0_MASK;
    button_callback = callback;
}
```

The kernel associates the `button_wakeup` function with the driver callback, so that when an event occurs, if a task is awaiting the button press notification, it is moved back to the active tasks list, and resumes as soon as the scheduler selects it to run:

```
void button_wakeup(void)
{
    if (button_task) {
        task_ready(button_task);
        button_task = NULL;
        schedule();
    }
}
```

In the button driver, to initiate the blocking operation, the interrupt is enabled and associated to the rising edge of a signal, corresponding to the button press event:

```
void button_start_read(void)
{
    EXTI_IMR |= (1 << BUTTON_PIN);
    EXTI_EMR |= (1 << BUTTON_PIN);
    EXTI_RTSR |= (1 << BUTTON_PIN);
    nvic_irq_enable(NVIC_EXTI0_IRQN);
}
```

The callback is executed in the interrupt context when the event is detected. The interrupt is disabled until the next call to `button_start_read`:

```
void isr_exti0(void)
{
    nvic_irq_disable(NVIC_EXTI0_IRQN);
    EXTI_PR |= (1 << BUTTON_PIN);
    if (button_callback)
        button_callback();
}
```

Any device driver or system module that relies on interrupt handling to unlock the associated task may use a callback mechanism to interact with the scheduler. Using a similar blocking strategy, read and write operations can be implemented to keep the calling task in the waiting list until the desired event is detected and handled toward a callback in the scheduler code.

Other system components and libraries designed for bare-metal embedded applications may require an additional layer to integrate in the operating system with blocking calls. Embedded TCP/IP stack implementations, such as lwIP and picoTCP, provide a portable RTOS integration layer, including blocking socket calls, implemented by running the loop functions in a dedicated task, which manages the communication with the socket API used in the other tasks. Locking mechanisms, such as mutexes and semaphores, are expected to implement blocking calls, which would suspend the task when the resource requested is unavailable.

The scheduling policy implemented in the example so far is very reactive and gives a perfect level of interaction among tasks, but it does not foresee priority levels, which is necessary to design real-time systems.

Real-time scheduling

One of the key requirements for real-time operating systems is the ability to react to a selected number of events by executing the associated code within a short and predictable amount of time. In order to implement features with strict timing requirements, the operating system must focus on quick interrupt handling and dispatching, rather than other metrics, such as throughput or fairness. Each task might have specific requirements, such as *deadlines*, indicating the exact time when the execution must start or stop, or related to shared resources that might introduce dependencies to other tasks in the system. A system that can execute tasks with a *deterministic* time requirement must be able to meet the deadlines within a measurable, fixed amount of time.

Approaching real-time scheduling is a complex matter. Authoritative literature exists on the topic, so the subject is not extensively explained here. Research has indicated that a number of approaches based on *priorities* assigned to each task, combined with an appropriate strategy used to switch the tasks at runtime, provides a sufficient approximation to provide a generic solution to real-time requirements.

To support hard real-time tasks with deterministic deadlines, an operating system should consider implementing the following characteristics:

- Fast context switch procedure implemented in the scheduler
- Measurable intervals where the system runs with the interrupts disabled
- Short interrupt handlers
- Support for interrupt priorities
- Support for task priorities to minimize the latency of hard real-time tasks

From the point of view of the task scheduling, the latency for real-time tasks is mostly related to the ability of the system to resume the task when an external event occurs.

To guarantee a deterministic delay for a selected group of tasks, RTOSes often implement fixed-priority levels, which are assigned to tasks upon creation, and determine the order of selection of the next task at each execution of the supervisor call of the scheduler.

Time-critical operations should be implemented in tasks with a higher priority. Many scheduler policies have been researched to optimize the reaction time of real-time tasks while keeping the system responsive and allowing issues related to the possible starvation of the tasks with a lower priority. Finding an optimal scheduling policy for a specific scenario can be very hard, and the details for the deterministic calculation of the latency and the jitter of a real-time system are outside the scope of this book.

One of the proposed approaches is very popular among real-time operating systems. It provides immediate context switches for real-time tasks, by selecting the task with the highest priority among those ready for execution, upon every invocation of the scheduler supervisor call. This scheduling policy, known as **static priority-driven preemptive scheduling**, is not optimal in all cases, as the latency of the tasks depends on the number of tasks at the same priority level, and foresees no mechanism to prevent potential starvation of tasks with a lower priority in the case of higher system loads. However, the mechanism is simple enough that it can be easily implemented to demonstrate the impact of priority mechanisms on the latency of real-time tasks.

Another possible approach would consist of reassigning priorities dynamically at runtime, based on the characteristics of the tasks. Real-time schedulers may benefit from a mechanism that ensures that the task with the closest deadline is selected first. This approach, known as **earliest-deadline-first** scheduling, or simply **EDF**, is more efficient in meeting real-time deadlines in a system under a heavier load. The SCHED_DEADLINE scheduler, included in Linux starting from version 3.14, is an implementation of this mechanism, which is less popular in embedded operating systems despite being relatively simple to implement.

This example shows a simplistic implementation of a static priority-driven scheduler. We use four separate lists to store the active tasks, one for each priority level supported on the system. A priority level is assigned to each task upon creation, and the kernel is kept at priority 0, with its main task running only when all the other tasks are sleeping, and whose unique purpose is to check the timers of the sleeping tasks. Tasks can be inserted into the active task list with the corresponding priority level when they become ready, and they are moved to the waiting list when they are blocked. To keep track of the static priority of the task, the priority field is added to the task block:

```
struct task_block {
    char name[TASK_NAME_MAXLEN];
    int id;
    int state;
    void (*start)(void *arg);
    void *arg;
    uint8_t *sp;
    uint32_t wakeup_time;
    uint8_t priority;
    struct task_block *next;
};
```

Two shortcut functions are defined to quickly add and remove the task block from the list of tasks with the same priority:

```
static void tasklist_add_active(struct task_block *el)
{
    tasklist_add(&tasklist_active[el->priority], el);
}


static int tasklist_del_active(struct task_block *el)
{
    return tasklist_del(&tasklist_active[el->priority], el);
}
```

They can then be used in the new version of `task_waiting`/`task_ready` functions, when the task is removed or inserted into the corresponding list of active tasks at the given priority:

```
static void task_waiting(struct task_block *t)
{
    if (tasklist_del_active(t) == 0) {
        tasklist_add(&tasklist_waiting, t);
        t->state = TASK_WAITING;
    }
}

static void task_ready(struct task_block *t)
{
    if (tasklist_del(&tasklist_waiting, t) == 0) {
        tasklist_add_active(t);
        t->state = TASK_READY;
    }
}
```

The three tasks are created on the system, but the one that would block on the button press event is created with a higher priority level:

```
void main(void) {
    clock_pll_on(0);
    led_setup();
    button_setup(button_wakeup);
    systick_enable();
    kernel.name[0] = 0;
    kernel.id = 0;
    kernel.state = TASK_RUNNING;
    kernel.wakeup_time = 0;
    kernel.priority = 0;
```

```
tasklist_add_active(&kernel);
task_create("test0",task_test0, NULL, 1);
task_create("test1",task_test1, NULL, 1);
task_create("test2",task_test2, NULL, 3);

while(1) {
    struct task_block *t = tasklist_waiting;
    while (t) {
        if (t->wakeup_time && (t->wakeup_time < jiffies)) {
            t->wakeup_time = 0;
            task_ready(t);
            break;
        }
        t = t->next;
    }
    WFI();
}
}
```

The function that selects the next task is reworked to find the task with the highest priority among those ready to run. To do so, the priority lists are visited, from the highest to the lowest. If the list with the highest priority is the same as the one of the current tasks, the next task in the same level is selected, if possible, to guarantee a round-robin mechanism in the case of tasks competing for the CPU within the same priority level. In any other case, the first task of the list with the highest priority is selected:

```
static int idx;
static inline struct task_block *
tasklist_next_ready(struct task_block *t)
{
    for (idx = MAX_PRIO - 1; idx >= 0; idx--) {
        if ((idx == t->priority) && (t->next != NULL) &&
        (t->next->state == TASK_READY))
            return t->next;
        if (tasklist_active[idx])
            return tasklist_active[idx];
    }
    return t;
}
```

The major difference between this scheduler and the one with a single priority level on the specific use case of reacting to the button press event in the task with ID equal to 2 is the time interval between the button press event and the reaction from the task itself. Both schedulers implement preemption, by immediately putting the task back to the ready state within the interrupt handler of the button event.

However, in the first case, the task comes back to the carousel of the tasks being scheduled, to compete with the other tasks on the same priority level, which can cause a delay in the reaction of the task that we can estimate to be $N *$ TIMESLICE in the worst-case scenario, where N is the number of processes ready to run at the moment when the interrupt occurs.

With the priority-driven scheduling approach, there is a degree of certainty that the real-time task is the first one to be scheduled after the interrupt occurs, so that the time required from the interrupt to resuming the task is measurable, and in the order of a few microseconds, as the CPU executes a predictable amount of instructions to perform all the actions in between.

Real-time embedded OSes are fundamental to implement life-critical systems, mostly in the transport and medical industries. On the other hand, they rely on simplified models with the purpose of keeping the basic system operations as lightweight as possible, and with the minimum overhead for system call interfaces and system APIs. An opposite approach could consist of increasing the complexity of the kernel to introduce optimizations in terms of throughput, task interaction, memory safety improvements, and other performance indicators, which may be a better fit in those many embedded systems with loose or non-existent real-time requirements. Stricter priority-based scheduling policies improve latency and guarantee real-time responses in well-controlled scenarios, but are less flexible to use in a general-purpose embedded system where other constraints are more compelling than task latency, where a time-based preemption-scheduling approach may provide better results.

Synchronization

In a multithreaded environment where memory, peripherals, and system accesses are shared, a system should provide synchronization mechanisms to allow the tasks to cooperate on the arbitration of the access to system-wide available resources.

Mutexes and semaphores are two of the most commonly used mechanisms of synchronization between parallel threads, as they provide the minimal set to solve most of the concurrency problems. Functions that could block the calling tasks must be able to interact with the scheduler, to move the task in the waiting state whenever the resource is not available, until the lock is released or the semaphore is incremented.

Semaphore

A semaphore is the most common synchronization primitive, which provides a counter with exclusive access, and it is used by two or more threads to cooperate on the arbitration of the usage of a specific shared resource. The API provided to the tasks must guarantee that the object can be used to implement a counter with exclusive access, which in general requires some auxiliary features on the CPU. For this reason, the internal implementation of the synchronization strategies is dependent on the microcode implemented in the target processor.

On Cortex-M3/M4, the implementation of locking mechanisms relies on instructions provided by the CPU to perform exclusive operations. The instruction set of the reference platform provides the following two instructions:

- **Load Register Exclusive (LDREX)**: Loads a value from an address in memory into a CPU register.
- **Store Register Exclusive (STREX)**: Attempts to store the new value contained in the register in an address in memory corresponding to the last LDREX instruction. If the STREX succeeds, the CPU guarantees that writing the value in memory happened exclusively, and that the value has not been modified since the last LDREX call. Between two concurrent LDREX/STREX sections, only one will result in a successful write to the register, and the second STREX instruction fails, returning zero.

The characteristics of these instructions guarantee exclusive access to a counter, which is then used to implement the primitive functions at the base of semaphores and mutexes.

The sem_trywait function attempts to decrement the value of the semaphore. The operation is always allowed, unless the value of the semaphore is 0, which results in an immediate failure. The function returns 0 upon success, and -1 if the semaphore value is zero, and it is impossible to decrement the semaphore value at this time.

The sequence of the events in the sem_trywait is the following:

1. The value of the semaphore variable (an integer accessed with exclusive load and store instructions) is read from the memory pointed by the function argument into the register, R1
2. If the value of R1 is 0, the semaphore cannot be acquired, and the function returns -1

3. The value of R1 is decremented by one
4. The value of R1 is stored in the memory pointed by the function argument, and the result of the STREX operation is put into R2
5. If the operation succeeds, R2 contains 0, the semaphore is acquired and successfully decremented, and the function can return with a success status
6. If the store operation fails (attempted a concurrent access), the procedure is immediately repeated for a second attempt

Here is the assembly routine implementing all of the steps, returning 0 upon success, and −1 when the decrement fails:

```
sem_trywait:
    LDREX  r1,  [r0]
    CMP  r1,  #0
    BEQ  sem_trywait_fail
    SUBS  r1,  #1
    STREX  r2,  r1,  [r0]
    CMP  r2,  #0
    BNE  sem_trywait
    DMB
    MOVS  r0,  #0
    BX  lr
sem_trywait_fail:
    DMB
    MOV  r0,  #-1
    BX  lr
```

The following code is the corresponding function to increase the semaphore, which is similar to the wait routine, except that the counting semaphore is increased instead, and the operation is eventually going to succeed, even if multiple tasks are trying to access the semaphore at the same time. The function returns 0 on success, except if the value before the counter was zero, in which case it returns 1, to remind the caller to notify any listener in a wait state that the value has increased and the associated resource is now available:

```
.global sem_dopost
sem_dopost:
    LDREX  r1,  [r0]
    ADDS  r1,  #1
    STREX  r2,  r1,  [r0]
    CMP  r2,  #0
    BNE  sem_dopost
    CMP  r0,  #1
    DMB
    BGE  sem_signal_up
    MOVS  r0,  #0
```

```
        BX lr
sem_signal_up:
        MOVS r0, #1
        BX lr
```

To integrate the blocking status of the sem_wait function into the scheduler, the semaphore interface exposed by the OS to the tasks wraps the non-blocking sem_trywait call into its blocking version, which blocks the task when the value of the semaphore is zero.

To implement a blocking version of the semaphore interface, the semaphore object may keep track of the tasks accessing the resources and waiting for a post event. In this case, the identifiers of the tasks are stored in an array named listeners:

```
#define MAX_LISTENERS 4
struct semaphore {
    uint32_t value;
    uint8_t listeners[MAX_LISTENERS];
};

typedef struct semaphore semaphore;
```

When a wait operation fails, the task is blocked and it will try again only after a successful post operation from another task. The task identifier is added to the array of listeners for this resource:

```
int sem_wait(semaphore *s)
{
    int i;
    if (s == NULL)
        return -1;
    if (sem_trywait(s) == 0)
        return 0;
    for (i = 0; i < MAX_LISTENERS; i++) {
        if (!s->listeners[i])
        s->listeners[i] = t_cur->id;
        if (s->listeners[i] == t_cur->id)
        break;
    }
    task_waiting(t_cur);
    schedule();
    return sem_wait(s);
}
```

The assembly routine `sem_dopost` returns a positive value if the post operation has triggered an increment from zero to one, which means that the listeners, if present, must be resumed to try to acquire the resource that just became available.

Mutex

Mutex is short for **mutual exclusion**, and is closely related to the semaphore, to the point that it can be implemented using the same assembly routines. A mutex is nothing but a binary semaphore, being initialized with value of 1 to allow the first lock operation.

Due to the property of the semaphore, which would fail any attempt to decrement its counter after its value has reached 0, our quick implementation of the mutex interface renames the semaphore primitives `sem_wait` and `sem_post` to `mutex_lock` and `mutex_unlock`, respectively.

Two tasks can try to decrement an unlocked mutex at the same time, but only one succeeds; the other will fail. In the blocking version of the mutex for the example scheduler, the wrappers for the mutex API built on top of the semaphore functions are the following:

```
typedef semaphore mutex;
#define mutex_init(m) sem_init(m, 1)
#define mutex_trylock(m) sem_trywait(m)
#define mutex_lock(x) sem_wait(x)
#define mutex_unlock(x) sem_post(x)
```

For both semaphores and mutexes, the example operating system written so far offers a complete API for synchronization mechanisms integrated with the scheduler.

Priority inversion

A phenomenon that is often encountered when developing operating systems with preemptive, priority-based schedulers using integrated synchronization mechanisms is the priority inversion. This condition affects the reactivity time of the real-time tasks that share resources with other tasks with a lower priority, and, in some cases, may cause the higher-priority tasks to starve for an unpredictable amount of time. The event occurs when the high-priority task is waiting for a resource to be freed by a lower-priority one, which in the meanwhile may be preempted by other unrelated tasks in the system.

In particular, the sequence of events that might trigger this phenomenon is the following:

1. T1, T2, T3 are three of the running tasks, with priority 1,2,3 respectively
2. T1 acquires a lock using a mutex on resource X
3. T1 is preempted by T3, which has a higher priority
4. T3 tries to access the shared resource X, and blocks on the mutex
5. T1 resumes the execution in the critical section
6. T1 is preempted by T2, which has a higher priority
7. An arbitrary number of tasks with priority greater than 1 can interrupt the execution of T1 before it is able to release the lock and wake up T3

One of the possible mechanisms that can be implemented to avoid this situation is called **priority inheritance**. This mechanism consists of temporarily increasing the priority of a task sharing a resource to the highest priority of all the tasks accessing the resource. This way, a task with a lower priority does not cause scheduling delays for the higher-priority ones, and the real-time requirements are still met.

System resource separation

The example operating system built throughout this chapter already has many interesting features, but it is still characterized by a flat model, with no memory segmentation or privilege separation. Minimalist systems do not provide any mechanisms to separate system resources and regulate the access to the memory space. Instead, tasks in the system are allowed to perform any privileged operation, including reading and altering other tasks' memory, executing operations in the address space of the kernel, and directly access peripherals and CPU registers at runtime.

Different approaches are available on the target platform, aimed at increasing the level of safety on the system by introducing a limited number of modifications to the kernel in order to:

- Implement kernel/process privilege separation
- Integrate memory protection in the scheduler
- Provide a system call interface through the supervisor call to access resources

Privilege levels

The Cortex-M CPU is designed to run code with two different levels of privilege. Privilege separation is important whenever untrusted application code is running on the system, allowing the kernel to keep control of the execution at all times, and prevent system failures due to a misbehaving user thread. The default execution level at boot is privileged, to allow the kernel to boot. Applications can be configured to execute in the user level and use a different stack-pointer register during the context switch operations.

Changing privilege levels is possible only during an exception handler, and it is done using the special exception return value, stored in LR before returning from an exception handler that performed a context switch. The flag that controls the privilege level is the lowest bit of the CONTROL register, which can be changed during context switches before returning from the exception handler, to relegate application threads to run in the user privilege level.

Moreover, most Cortex-M provides two separate stack-pointer CPU registers:

- A **Master Stack Pointer**, **MSP**
- A **Process Stack Poitner**, **PSP**

Following the ARM recommendation, operating systems must use PSP for executing user threads, while MSP is used by interrupt handlers and the kernel. The stack selection depends on the special return value at the end of the exception handler. The scheduler implemented so far has this value hardcoded to 0xFFFFFFF9, which is used to return in thread mode after an interrupt and keeps executing the code at privileged level. Returning the 0xFFFFFFFD value from the interrupt handler tells the CPU to select the PSP as a stack-pointer register when returning to the thread mode.

In order to implement privilege separation properly, the PendSV handler used for switching tasks has to be modified to save and restore the context using the right stack pointer for the task being preempted and the stack being selected. The store_context and restore_context functions used so far are renamed to store_kernel_context and restore_kernel_context, respectively, because the kernel is still using the master stack pointer. Two new functions are added to the store and restore thread contexts from the new context switch routine, which uses the PSP register instead, for storing and restoring the contexts of the threads:

```
static void __attribute__((naked)) store_user_context(void)
{
    asm volatile("mrs r0, psp");
    asm volatile("stmdb r0!, {r4-r11}");
    asm volatile("msr psp, r0");
    asm volatile("bx lr");
```

```
    }

    static void __attribute__((naked)) restore_user_context(void)
    {
        asm volatile("mrs r0, psp");
        asm volatile("ldmfd r0!, {r4-r11}");
        asm volatile("msr psp, r0");
        asm volatile("bx lr");
    }
```

In the safe version of the scheduler, the PendSV service routine selects the correct stack pointer for storing and restoring the context, and calls the associated routines. Depending on the new context, the return value stored in LR is used to select the register used as a new stack pointer, and the privilege level is set in the CONTROL register to switch to the user or privileged level in the upcoming thread mode, using values 1 or 0, respectively:

```
    void __attribute__((naked)) isr_pendsv(void)
    {
        if (t_cur->id == 0) {
            store_kernel_context();
            asm volatile("mrs %0, msp" : "=r"(t_cur->sp));
        } else {
            store_user_context();
            asm volatile("mrs %0, psp" : "=r"(t_cur->sp));
        }
        if (t_cur->state == TASK_RUNNING) {
            t_cur->state = TASK_READY;
        }
        t_cur = tasklist_next_ready(t_cur);
        t_cur->state = TASK_RUNNING;
        if (t_cur->id == 0) {
            asm volatile("msr msp, %0" ::"r"(t_cur->sp));
            restore_kernel_context();
            asm volatile("mov lr, %0" ::"r"(0xFFFFFFF9));
            asm volatile("msr CONTROL, %0" ::"r"(0x00));
        } else {
            asm volatile("msr psp, %0" ::"r"(t_cur->sp));
            restore_user_context();
            asm volatile("mov lr, %0" ::"r"(0xFFFFFFFD));
            asm volatile("msr CONTROL, %0" ::"r"(0x01));
        }
        asm volatile("bx lr");
    }
```

A task running with the privilege mode bit set in the CONTROL register has restricted access to the resources of the system. In particular, it is not possible for threads to access registers in the SCB region, which means that some basic operations, such as enabling and disabling interrupt through the NVIC, are reserved for exclusive use of the kernel. When used in combination with the MPU, privilege separation improves the safety of the system even further, by imposing memory separation at the access level, which can detect and interrupt misbehaving application code.

Memory segmentation

Dynamic memory segmentation strategies can be integrated in the scheduler to ensure that the single tasks do not access memory regions associated with system-critical components and the resources that require the kernel supervision to be accessed from user space.

In Chapter 5, *Memory Management*, we saw how the MPU can be used to delimit contiguous segments of memory and disallow access to specific areas by any of the code running on the systems. In fact, the MPU controller provides a permission mask to change the attributes of the single-memory regions with more granularity. In particular, we can allow access to some areas only if the CPU is running in privileged level, which is an efficient way of preventing user applications from accessing certain areas of the system without the supervision of the kernel. A safe operating system may decide to completely exclude the application tasks from accessing the peripheral region and the system registers, by using kernel-only permission flags for these areas. The value associated with specific permissions in the MPU region attribute register can be defined as follows:

```
#define RASR_KERNEL_RW (1 << 24)
#define RASR_KERNEL_RO (5 << 24)
#define RASR_RDONLY (6 << 24)
#define RASR_NOACCESS (0 << 24)
#define RASR_USER_RW (3 << 24)
#define RASR_USER_RO (2 << 24)
```

The MPU configuration can be enforced at boot by the kernel. In this example, we set the flash region to be globally readable, as region 0, using RASR_RDONLY, and the SRAM region to be globally accessible, as region 1 mapped at address 0x20000000:

```
int mpu_enable(void)
{
    volatile uint32_t type;
    volatile uint32_t start;
    volatile uint32_t attr;
    type = MPU_TYPE;
    if (type == 0)
```

```
        return -1;
    MPU_CTRL = 0;
    start = 0;
    attr = RASR_ENABLED | MPUSIZE_256K | RASR_SCB | RASR_RDONLY;
    mpu_set_region(0, start, attr);

    start = 0x20000000;
    attr = RASR_ENABLED | MPUSIZE_128K | RASR_SCB |
    RASR_USER_RW | RASR_NOEXEC;
    mpu_set_region(1, start, attr);
```

A stricter policy may even restrict the usage of the SRAM by the user tasks in non-privileged mode, but it would require a reorganization of the `.data` and `.bss` regions mapped when the task is started. In this example, we simply demonstrate how to integrate the per-task memory protection policy into the scheduler to prevent access to system resources and protect the stack areas of the other tasks. The CCRAM is the area we want to protect, as it contains the execution stack of the kernel as well as those of the other tasks in the system. To do so, the CCRAM area is marked to be of exclusive access of the kernel as region 2, and later, an exception is created for the selected task during context switch, to permit the access to its own stack space:

```
    start = 0x10000000;
    attr = RASR_ENABLED | MPUSIZE_64K | RASR_SCB |
    RASR_KERNEL_RW | RASR_NOEXEC;
    mpu_set_region(2, start, attr);
```

Peripheral regions and system registers are restricted areas in our system, so they too are marked for exclusive kernel access at runtime. In our safe OS design, tasks that want to access peripherals must use system calls to perform supervised privileged operations:

```
    start = 0x40000000;
    attr = RASR_ENABLED | MPUSIZE_1G | RASR_SB |
    RASR_KERNEL_RW | RASR_NOEXEC;
    mpu_set_region(4, start, attr);
    start = 0xE0000000;
    attr = RASR_ENABLED | MPUSIZE_256M | RASR_SB |
    RASR_KERNEL_RW | RASR_NOEXEC;
    mpu_set_region(5, start, attr);
    SHCSR |= MEMFAULT_ENABLE;
    MPU_CTRL = 1;
    return 0;
}
```

During the context switch, just before returning from the `isr_pendsv` service routine, the scheduler can invoke the function exported by our custom MPU module to temporarily permit the access to the stack area of the task selected to run next in the non-privileged mode:

```
void mpu_task_stack_permit(void *start)
{
    uint32_t attr = RASR_ENABLED | MPUSIZE_1K |
    RASR_SCB | RASR_USER_RW;
    MPU_CTRL = 0;
    DMB();
    mpu_set_region(3, (uint32_t)start, attr);
    MPU_CTRL = 1;
}
```

These further restrictions have limited the possibility for the currently implemented tasks to access any resources directly. In order to maintain the same functionalities as before, the example system must now export a new safe API for the tasks to request system operations.

System calls

The latest evolution of the example operating system implemented in this chapter no longer allows our tasks to control system resources, such as input and output peripherals, and does not even allow the tasks to block voluntarily, as the `sleep_ms` function would not be allowed to set the pending flag to initiate a context switch.

The operating system exports an API that is accessible by the tasks through a system-call mechanism using the SVCall exception, handled by the `isr_svc` service routine, and triggered at any time from tasks through the instruction `svc`.

In this simple example, we use the `svc 0` assembly instruction to switch to handler mode, by defining a shortcut macro, `SVC()`:

```
#define SVC() asm volatile ("svc 0")
```

We wrap this instruction within a C function, to allow us to pass arguments to it. The ABI for the platform provides the first four arguments of the call across the mode switch inside the R0-R3 registers. Our example API does not allow us to pass any arguments to the system calls, but uses the first argument in R0 to identify the request passed from the application to the kernel:

```
static int syscall(int arg0)
{
```

```
        SVC();
    }
```

This way, we implement the entire system-call interface for this operating system, consisting of the following system calls with no arguments. Each system call has an associated identification number, passed as `arg0`. The list of the system calls is the contract for the interface between the tasks and the kernel, and the only way for the tasks to use the protected resources in the system:

```
#define SYS_SCHEDULE 0
#define SYS_BUTTON_READ 1
#define SYS_BLUELED_ON 2
#define SYS_BLUELED_OFF 3
#define SYS_BLUELED_TOGGLE 4
#define SYS_REDLED_ON 5
#define SYS_REDLED_OFF 6
#define SYS_REDLED_TOGGLE 7
#define SYS_GREENLED_ON 8
#define SYS_GREENLED_OFF 9
#define SYS_GREENLED_TOGGLE 10
```

Each of these system calls must be handled in `isr_svc`. Controlling peripherals and system block registers is allowed by calling the driver functions in the handler context, even if here this is done just for brevity. In a proper design, operations taking more than a few instructions to complete should be instead deferred to be run by the kernel task the next time it is scheduled. The following code is used just to show a possible implementation of `isr_svc` that reacts to user requests allowed by the system API, to control the LED and the button on the board, while also providing a mechanism that can be expanded to implement blocking system calls.

The `svc` service routine executes the requested command, passed as an argument to the handler itself. If the system call is blocking, such as the `SYS_SCHEDULE` system call, a new task is selected to complete a task switch within the handler.

The PendSV routine can now handle internal commands, such as:

```
void __attribute__((naked)) isr_svc(int arg)
{
    store_user_context();
    asm volatile("mrs %0, psp" : "=r"(t_cur->sp));
    if (t_cur->state == TASK_RUNNING) {
        t_cur->state - TASK_READY;
    }
    switch(arg) {
        case SYS_BUTTON_READ:
```

```
                button_start_read();
                /* fall through */
            case SYS_SCHEDULE:
                t_cur = tasklist_next_ready(t_cur);
                t_cur->state = TASK_RUNNING;
                break;
            case SYS_BLUELED_ON:
                blue_led_on();
                break;
            /* case ... */
        }
```

And so on, for the other LED-related system calls. The context is resumed at the end of the routine, in the same way as within PendSV. Though it is optional, a task switch might have occurred if the call must block:

```
    if (t_cur->id == 0) {
        asm volatile("msr msp, %0" ::"r"(t_cur->sp));
        restore_kernel_context();
        asm volatile("mov lr, %0" ::"r"(0xFFFFFFF9));
        asm volatile("msr CONTROL, %0" ::"r"(0x00));
    } else {
        asm volatile("msr psp, %0" ::"r"(t_cur->sp));
        restore_user_context();
        mpu_task_stack_permit(((uint8_t *)((&stack_space)) +
        (t_cur->id << 10)));
        asm volatile("mov lr, %0" ::"r"(0xFFFFFFFD));
        asm volatile("msr CONTROL, %0" ::"r"(0x01));
    }
    asm volatile("bx lr");
}
```

While limited in its functionalities, the new system exports all the API needed for our application threads to run again, once all the prohibited privileged calls have been removed from the task code, and the newly created system calls are invoked instead:

```
void task_test0(void *arg)
{
    while(1) {
        syscall(SYS_BLUELED_ON);
        mutex_lock(&m);
        sleep_ms(500);
        syscall(SYS_BLUELED_OFF);
        mutex_unlock(&m);
        sleep_ms(1000);
    }
```

```
    }

    void task_test1(void *arg)
    {
        syscall(SYS_REDLED_ON);
        while(1) {
            sleep_ms(50);
            mutex_lock(&m);
            syscall(SYS_REDLED_TOGGLE);
            mutex_unlock(&m);
        }
    }

    void task_test2(void *arg)
    {
        uint32_t toggle_time = 0;
        syscall(SYS_GREENLED_OFF);
        while(1) {
            button_read();
            if ((jiffies - toggle_time) > 120) {
                syscall(SYS_GREENLED_TOGGLE);
                toggle_time = jiffies;
            }
        }
    }
```

The code size of a safe operating system may grow quickly if it implements all the operations in kernel space and has to provide the implementation of all the system calls allowed. On the other hand, it has the advantage of physical memory separation among tasks, and it protects system resources and other memory areas from accidental errors in the application code.

Summary

In this chapter, we explored the components of an embedded operating system, by implementing one from scratch, with the only purpose of studying the internals of the system, how the various mechanisms can be integrated in the scheduler, and how blocking calls, driver APIs, and synchronization mechanisms can be provided to tasks.

There are, however, a number of open source and free software embedded operating systems available to run on similar platforms. In the next chapter, we'll see a few of them, and we'll evaluate their characteristics and key features to find out more about their implementation and design choices.

Embedded Operating Systems

11

While the bare-metal, single-thread approach is still the most popular when designing embedded solutions, many systems can benefit from multitasking scheduling, centralized resource management, and a safer environment; several existing implementations are available to select an operating system that works well with the specific design.

Building a scheduler tailored to a custom solution from scratch is not impossible and, if done properly, would provide the closest approximation of the desired architecture, while focusing on the specific characteristics offered by the target hardware. In a real-life scenario, however, it is advisable to consider one of the many open source embedded operating systems available and ready to be integrated in the architecture, among those supporting the selected hardware platform. Some of the available kernels are in a healthy development state, deserving their well-established role in the embedded market, and sufficiently tested to provide a foundation to build reliable embedded multitasking applications.

On many 32-bit microcontrollers, hardware features are provided to facilitate the design of multithreaded systems. As we saw `Chapter 10`, *Parallel Tasks and Scheduling*, carefully selecting which optional feature to implement is a critical aspect that might impact the safety of the system and its performance figures. The design choice depends on the compromises that the OS developers may decide to implement, such as latency versus performance, and code size versus safety. For this reason, no system is the same as another, and each one has peculiar characteristics that make it usable for a specific purpose rather than others, depending most of the time on the platform and the use cases the system had been originally designed for.

The API offered to applications is often customized to reflect the characteristics of the system. In some cases, this means that applications must be written using the provided API in order to run on a specific system. Operating systems in personal computers and mobile devices follow interface standards, such as POSIX, which can be implemented in embedded systems, taking into account the restriction on resources and physical memory mapping.

Selecting the operating system that best fits the purpose and the platform under development is a delicate task that impacts the overall architecture, may have consequences on the whole development model, and may introduce API lock-ins in the application code base. The criteria for selection vary according to the hardware characteristics, the integration with the other components, such as third-party libraries, the facilities offered to interact with peripherals and interfaces, and, most importantly, the range of use cases that the system is designed to cover.

With a few exceptions, operating systems include, alongside the scheduler and the memory management, a set of integrated libraries, modules, and tools. Depending on the purpose, an embedded system may provide:

- Platform-specific hardware abstraction layers
- Device drivers for common peripherals
- TCP/IP stack integration for connectivity
- Filesystems and file abstractions
- Integrated power-management systems

Depending on the implementation of the thread model in the scheduler, some systems are expected to run with a fixed amount of predefined tasks, configured at compile time, while others opt for more complex processes and thread hierarchies that allow us to create new threads at runtime, and terminate them at any point in the execution.

More complex systems introduce some overhead due to the additional logic in the system exceptions code, and are less fit for critical real-time operations, which is the reason why most successful RTOSes nowadays maintain their simple architecture, providing the bare minimum to run multiple threads with a flat-memory mode that is easy to manage and does not require additional context switches to manage the privilege of the operations, keeping the latency low for real-time tasks.

While these solutions are designed to provide support to build devices with a specific purpose, such as integrated signal processing systems, the increasing popularity of connected and low-power devices has encouraged the development of new operating systems that integrate connectivity features, low-power management APIs, device drivers, and specific system support for their reference platforms.

High-end microcontrollers also offer the means to build complete development platforms, flexible and reusable for different purposes, often just by loading new application software to improve and extend their functionalities with little or no downtime. In the recent history of microcontrollers, high-end platforms available in the market have become more powerful than the average personal computer of just 20 years ago, and have started to offer more and more support to run operating systems. A 32-bit microcontroller has enough features to run an operating system in kernel mode, thanks to privilege separation, multiple stack pointers, memory protection, and supervisor calls, despite the restricted amount of resources and the lack of an MMU.

Following the direction of general-purpose systems, some research has been conducted to develop operating systems implemented according to the POSIX standards, to encourage the development of portable application software, which also shares many similarities with modern UNIX-like systems. Adopting POSIX standards introduces a number of benefits on many levels.

In other scenarios, it is important to detect and counter the effects of defects in the application software, which may impact the integrity or the stability of the system.

Running systems with a flat-memory model and without any privilege separation or memory segmentation may increase the risk of critical issues in the system that are also difficult to identify on those systems running a higher number of applications. A safe system provides the mechanisms needed to isolate the processes and supervise all the operations involving any critical part of the system, denying direct access to resources and reserved memory areas. New software technologies are available to build safe operating systems, providing more effective strategies for process isolation.

In this chapter, we'll analyze some of the most popular open source operating systems through their features and design choices, and we'll discuss the approach taken by different communities on features such as power management, connectivity, communication security, and system safety.

We have put a few open source systems in groups, based on the similarities of their design choices and their field of application. The sections covered in this chapter are:

- Real-time application platforms
- Low-power IoT systems
- POSIX-compliant systems
- The future of safe embedded systems

Real-time application platforms

One of the most desired characteristics of embedded operating systems, especially in life-critical and high-reliability systems, is the presence of a hard real-time scheduler. As mentioned in Chapter 10, *Parallel Tasks and Scheduling*, a real-time scheduler provides deterministic and short reaction times for real-time tasks, given that the load of the system does not exceed the resources available. For this reason, system developers often have based their design on real-time schedulers with static priorities.

A solid and well-designed scheduler implementation is the most fundamental part of preemptive real-time systems, and it is the base for building all the other features.

Embedded operating systems designed to run a fixed set of tasks with static priorities do not implement standard interfaces for the applications, and tend to be small in code size and memory usage, by keeping a small code base with a restricted set of functionalities. Libraries for hardware abstractions and advanced functionalities may be developed and maintained separately from the kernel.

Safety is not one of the goals of these systems; however, some implementations provide basic support for MPU regions and task memory segmentation, and use mostly, or exclusively, static memory allocations in the kernel.

Real-time schedulers that are designed to be integrated in tailored embedded solutions are often based on a very simple, flat model with no real separation between kernel and userland. They are the ideal solution for stepping up from bare-metal applications to a multithreading environment, with a fixed, constant amount of tasks and deterministic deadlines.

FreeRTOS

Possibly the most popular among the open source operating systems for embedded devices, FreeRTOS is a well-established project with more than 15 years of development history, and it is extremely portable across many embedded platforms, with more than 30 hardware-specific ports.

Designed with small-code footprint, simple interfaces in mind, this system does not offer a complete driver's platform or advanced CPU-specific features, but rather focuses on two things: real-time scheduling of the threads and heap memory management. The simplicity of its design facilitates the port to a large number of platforms, and keeps the development focus on a restricted amount of well-tested and reliable operations.

Nevertheless, third-party libraries and example code provided by hardware manufacturers often integrate FreeRTOS, which facilitates building more complex systems based on its scheduler. Third-party code that is not integrated in FreeRTOS promotes competition among different solutions, as, for example, it is possible to integrate it with many TCP/IP stack implementations to provide networking support, even though none of them is part of the core system or tightly integrated with the kernel. Device drivers are not included in the kernel, but there are several demos of complete systems based on the integration of FreeRTOS with board-support packages distributed by the manufacturers.

The scheduler is preemptive, with fixed priority levels and priority inheritance through shared mutexes. One of the most interesting features offered by FreeRTOS, though, is the heap memory management, available in five flavors optimized for different designs:

- **Heap 1**: Allows only one-time, static allocation in the heap, with no possibility of freeing up the memory. This is useful if the applications are able to allocate all the space needed at the beginning, as the memory will never become available to the system again.

- **Heap 2**: Allows freeing memory, but does not reassemble the freed blocks. This mechanism is suitable for implementations with a limited number of heap allocations, especially if they keep the same size of previously freed objects. If used improperly, this model may result in a heavily fragmented stack, with the risk of running out of heap in the long run even if the total size of the allocated object does not increase, due to the lack of memory reorganization.

- **Heap 3**: This method is a wrapper for a `malloc`/`free` implementation provided by a third-party library that ensures that the wrapped memory operations become thread-safe when used within the FreeRTOS multithreading context. This model allows us to define a custom memory management method, by defining the `malloc`/`free` function in a separate model, or by using the library implementation and attaching the `sbrk()` system call, as seen in Chapter 5, *Memory Management*.

- **Heap 4**: A more advanced memory manager, with support for memory coalescence. Contiguous `free` blocks are merged and some housekeeping is done to optimize the use of the heap across heterogeneous allocations from different threads. This method limits the fragmentation of the heap and improves memory usage in the long run.

- **Heap 5**: Using the same mechanism as heap 4, but allowing us to define multiple non-contiguous memory regions to be part of the same stack space. This method is a ready-to-use solution to physical fragmentation, provided that the regions are defined during the initialization and provided to the system through the available API.

Support for MPU and thread mode is available, and threads can be run in restricted mode, where the only memory accessible is the one assigned to the specific thread. When running threads in restricted mode, the system API is still available, as the system functions are mapped in a specific area in memory. The main safety strategy consists of voluntarily placing tasks in the restricted mode and defining memory access boundaries, by allowing the task to access only its own stack and up to three configurable regions in the mapped memory.

Low-power management is limited to sleep mode, and no deep-sleep mechanism is implemented by default. The system, however, allows us to redefine the scheduler callback functions to enter custom low-power modes, which may be used as starting points to implement tailored power saving strategies.

Recent versions of FreeRTOS include specific distributions with third-party code as a starting point for building secure connected platform for IoT systems. The same authors have created a TCP/IP stack that is designed for FreeRTOS, and it is distributed in a FreeRTOS Plus bundle package alongside the kernel and wolfSSL library to support secure socket communication.

Despite being designed for simplicity of use, the application API is not standard, but rather unique and tailored to the specific implementation of the system, making applications written for FreeRTOS very hard to port to other platforms.

The project has recently abandoned its historical GNU-modified free software license to adopt a more permissive, open source license, so, despite the name, the project is no longer free software.

ChibiOS

Designed for context-switch performance, the real-time kernel of ChibiOS has a well-established history, with more than 10 years of active development and a community of enthusiastic contributors and maintainers. The concept behind the scheduler is a fixed-priority preemption, with priority inheritance mechanisms for priority inversion avoidance. The scheduler is the core component of the ChibiOS architecture, which also includes a complete hardware abstraction layer, containing a high-level abstraction of multiple devices, and peripherals that are common across different platforms.

The design is based on multiple levels of abstractions, each designed to be as independent as possible from the others. The core of the operating system interfaces with the HAL using a lightweight interface, the OS abstraction layer, which can be implemented by different kernels, making the architecture of the entire system independent by the choice of the real-time scheduler.

The HAL is accessed directly by the threads, which always run in flat mode, with no support for privilege separation through protected system calls. Each task is relegated to its assigned address space, and its boundaries are checked through the MPU, when available on the system, but the MPU is set using global flags in the task switch, not differentiating between privileged and user code to access system control registers or peripheral regions.

Core memory safety is one of ChibiOS's major points of strength, mostly due to the completely static design of the kernel. The kernel code does not rely on any single dynamic allocation, and uses specific data structures to assign memory for objects at compile time.

Even if the use of dynamic memory is discouraged, due to the implications on safety, a heap allocator is provided as a separate optional module, and can still be used by application code. The allocator supports pool separation, with a fallback to a default pool of shared system memory if none is provided.

No specific low-power modes are implemented in the HAL, even though the layered design may help to fine-tune single device drivers using API functions to implement platform-specific low-power modes in the application logic.

ChibiOS is free software, as its kernel implementation is distributed under the GNU general public license, even if the HAL and its interfaces are distributed with other more permissive open source licenses. A limited set of third-party libraries is distributed as plugins that interacts with the kernel through specific OSAL extensions. The choice of third-party libraries includes a FatFs open source implementation, **lightweight IP (lwIP)** for TCP/IP connectivity, and wolfSSL to provide transport layer security support for IoT projects.

Low-power IoT systems

Mostly built on top of constrained microcontrollers, such as the Cortex-M0, low-power embedded systems are often little, battery-powered or energy-harvesting devices, sporadically connecting to remote services using wireless technologies. These small, inexpensive systems are often used in install-and-forget scenarios, where they can operate for years on a single integrated power source with nearly no maintenance costs.

Bare-metal architectures are still very popular in these scenarios, however, a few very lightweight operating systems have been designed to organize and synchronize tasks using as few resources as possible, while still keeping a specific focus on power saving and connectivity. The challenge for the development of this kind of operating system is to find a way to fit complex networking protocols into a few kilobytes of memory. Future-proof systems designed for the IoT services offer native IPv6 networking, often through 6LoWPAN, and fully equipped yet minimalist TCP/IP stacks, designed to sacrifice throughput in favor of smaller memory footprints.

Due to their small code size, these systems may lack some advanced features. For example, they do not provide any specific safety strategies, as they are based on a flat model where applications are allowed to access all the resources mapped in memory.

Contiki OS

Contiki OS is an open source real-time operating system designed for low-power, connected devices, and focuses on providing a simple platform to develop IoT applications, mostly oriented to 6LoWPAN and 802.15.4 technologies. The focus of Contiki development is clearly on IPv6 connectivity, being one of the first embedded systems to support IPv6 and 6LoWPAN. In fact, other than the relatively simple scheduler, all the libraries, modules, components, and development tools distributed with Contiki make this system particularly interesting.

The TCP/IP support is provided by uIP, which is a very small custom implementation of the protocol stack, designed to process one buffer at a time. This particular design choice lowers the amount of memory required by the stack to the bare minimum, and thus provides full TCP/IP socket-based networking using only a few kilobytes of RAM. On top of the stack, a few IoT message protocols are implemented, such as CoAP and MQTT, for end-to-end communication with remote services using standard protocols.

Another interesting feature provided by Contiki is the possibility to dynamically load and execute code from modules at runtime. The system includes an ELF loader that can load position-independent code into memory and make it available for the application to execute, in a similar fashion to the `dlopen()` and `dlsym()` POSIX calls. This facilitates the execution of remote updates over the air on running systems to correct the behavior on the field or introduce new features to a system while it is running.

The Coffee module is a small filesystem designed for read/write operations on the flash, hiding the underlying complexity introduced by the flash-access mechanisms. The filesystem creates a temporary copy of each block upon write operations, alters the content of the file being written, erases the physical block if necessary, and restores the content from memory. Offering filesystem support on the built-in flash provides long-term storage even on these constrained devices where the storage space is limited to the capacity of the integrated flash and improves the range of use cases that can be implemented on top of Contiki.

Support for low power is provided as a system service, with the possibility for the application to activate stop mode and standby to provide the infrastructure for battery-powered and energy-harvesting modes.

An important missing feature is the support for secure socket communication. Despite the not able effort to bring compliant TCP and UDP socket connectivity over IPv6, no extensions are available on the system to secure the application protocols, even though the technologies supported, such as MQTT and CoAP, could benefit from transport layer security. Implementing secure solutions on top of Contiki is still possible, but requires the manual integration of a third-party TLS library. The lack of end-to-end transport security mechanisms may impact the security model of the entire distribution system, especially considering how easy it is to capture unencrypted information traveling over a wireless link.

Riot OS

Riot OS has perhaps the fastest-growing community of enthusiasts and system developers among embedded systems nowadays. The goal of the project is to provide a system designed for low power consumption, taking into account the requirements to integrate the device in larger distributed systems. The core system is very scalable, as single components can be excluded at compile time.

Riot offers wireless drivers and network connectivity, making it IoT-friendly, but takes a different approach on the system API provided by the other systems seen so far. The Riot community is attempting to standardize the API toward a POSIX-like interface, which facilitates the application development for these programmers coming from different backgrounds, and used to writing code using the standards offered by the C language to access the resources on the system. The system, however, still runs on a flat model. Privilege separation is not implemented at system level, and user space applications are still supposed to access system resources by referencing the system memory directly.

As an additional safety measure, the MPU can be used to detect stack overflows in the single threads, by placing a small read-only area at the bottom of the stack, which triggers an exception if threads are attempting to write past the limit of their assigned stack space.

Riot implements its own TCP/IP stack, called **GNRC**, but offers an interface to include other networking components as replacements or integration of the features supported. GNRC is an IPv6-only implementation tailored to the features of the underlying 802.15.4 network and providing a socket implementation to write IoT applications. An lwIP compatibility layer is provided as an alternative to the default TCP/IP stack when the system needs to implement IPv4 communication. A port of a picoTCP module has also been considered for inclusion.

Even if no SSL or TLS library is integrated by default in Riot OS, the possibility to swap the TCP/IP stack using wrappers for the same device drivers and the POSIX-compliant socket API facilitate the integration of existing solutions for secure socket communications for IoT applications.

One of the interesting features offered by Riot is access to the configuration of low-power modes, which is integrated in the system through the power management module. This module provides the abstraction for managing platform-specific features, such as the stop and the standby modes on Cortex-M platforms. Low-power modes can be activated at runtime from the application code, to facilitate the integration of low-power strategies in the architecture, using the real-time clock, the watchdog timer, or other external signals to return to normal running mode.

Riot OS is free software, distributed with the **Lesser General Public License (LGPL)**, which does not require a redistribute application code using the same license, as long as derivatives are not changing the code of the API provided at platform level. Its mission is to be an active part of the development of the IoT market, by promoting community development, open source software, and the adoption of open standards and protocols.

POSIX-compliant systems

All the embedded systems analyzed so far represent the ideal solutions for classic embedded systems designed with a single set of tasks in mind, where features such as memory protection and task separation are not interesting enough to invest system resources in. Riot OS provides a subset of POSIX API calls, mostly to access the TCP/IP features, with the purpose of smoothing the learning curve experienced by developers when taking their first steps in developing software for embedded platforms.

Due to the remarkable progress in the last decade of microcontroller-based embedded systems, we have seen that it is not impossible to develop general-purpose, universal, software development platforms, offering standard APIs to run standalone, self-contained applications. Models for this kind of approach to multithreading systems exist in other worlds, and are applied to build operating systems for types of devices other than microcontroller-based embedded systems. Despite the amount of resources being still very far from those of mobile phones or personal computers, and the absence of memory virtualization, it is still possible to implement kernels that provide memory segmentation, privilege separation, and proper kernel-user space communication based exclusively on supervisor calls. As we saw in Chapter 10, *Parallel Tasks and Scheduling*, 32-bit microcontrollers are capable of providing techniques implemented in hardware for privilege separation, context switches and, in some cases, memory segmentation.

The POSIX standard provides the guidelines to integrate these kinds of tools into universal operating systems, offering a standard API for the application to interact with the kernel and request specific operations that require supervision according to the planned safety strategy of the system.

Implementing the POSIX interface has several advantages for the system. The first one is the benefit for developers who can recognize the similarities of the standard C library interface to access the resources available to other environments they might be familiar with, such as GNU/Linux or other popular UNIX-like systems. When writing an operating system, this can be achieved by providing the same signatures for the API calls as those available on a mobile device or a desktop system to build user applications. However, writing a POSIX-compliant system means including many other features related to process and thread management, interactions with the filesystem, and some kind of separation among the processes, and between each process and the kernel.

A POSIX system must be able to create both processes and threads, with standard interfaces to organize and manage them in precise hierarchical parent-child structures. POSIX indicates the implementation strategy of instruments for thread synchronization and inter-process communication, through standard calls implemented in kernel space. The full POSIX specification is often too big to fit the needs of a generic, yet small, operating system that still has to cope with the limited resources and the lack of virtual memory pages. Some subsets of the features recommended by POSIX regulating user accounts and permissions would be overkill for a system that is not designed for multiple users, while other things are impossible to implement due to the lack of features.

An example of the limitations of embedded platforms, when it comes to POSIX implementation, is the fork system call, which is described as the default mechanism to create a new process on the system. Due to its intrinsic characteristic, the implementation of the fork in the kernel requires virtual memory mapping, in order to coordinate the parent and child process from the moment of creation to the separation of the address spaces. According to POSIX, the `fork` system call can be replaced by `vfork`, which has the same purpose, but does not allow the scheduler to return the control to the parent task, until the child has called `exec`, which resets all the local references in the child task and allows us to complete the separation of the address spaces.

One of the interfaces that is likely to change the approach to designing multitask applications is `poll`. A system implementing `poll`, and providing all the resources as file descriptors as recommended by POSIX, can provide a blocking system call, supervising multiple heterogeneous resources at the same time. In a UNIX-like system, every I/O resource can be accessed from a process using the file abstraction, which means that all share the same handle, the file descriptor, used as a reference in input and output operations. A single `poll` call is often used as the central blocking point of applications, because it is capable of managing TCP/IP sockets, input sensor devices, inter-process communication mechanisms, serial ports, and other resources, at the same time. While a process or a thread is suspended, polling multiple file descriptors, any related event, among those enabled with `poll`, would wake up the calling process, which is otherwise not being scheduled while there is no activity on any of them. For an embedded application managing multiple interfaces at the same time, a single `poll` can often replace multiple threads that a classic RTOS design would require, due to the lack of mechanisms for efficiently multiplexing the management of input and output operations.

The flexibility of a POSIX system allows us to integrate software that is written for other platforms in the easiest way possible, even though it requires an intermediate layer of standard C libraries, distributed along with the system to compile portable applications to run on the system. POSIX-compliant embedded systems are able to run software that is designed for UNIX-like platforms, given it is not using excessive resources or any subset of system calls not implemented by the target platform. This feature in particular allows us to directly integrate a wide range of software, including small daemons and libraries, facilitating the integration of existing software, including application protocols and transport security for IoT applications.

Besides supporting standard C applications, compilers, and interpreters, high-level languages other than C can be integrated, as long as they are built against a standard **libc**, shorthand for the **C library**. Supporting multiple languages and paradigms at system level expands even further the possibilities of creating general-purpose platforms.

Probably the most important benefit of adopting the POSIX specifications in embedded systems comes from the isolations of the tasks and the definition of the interface between kernel and user space as a set of system calls, with a standardized contract. The kernel can be designed to supervise all the operations that may have any impact on the integrity of the systems or the other tasks running, and react to any misbehavior before any consequence.

NuttX

NuttX is another open source, real-time operating system for embedded devices, portable across a number of different platforms and architectures. Its first goal is the compliance to the POSIX and ANSI standards, and it provides quite an extensive set of interfaces, libraries, and command-line tools to offer a broad compatibility with existing software originally written for other platforms, and supports effective system management through standard tools.

Each feature, including the scheduler internals, can be enabled and tuned separately at compile time. This means that the same code base can produce small, static, and flat RTOS as well as feature-rich POSIX systems for high-end microprocessors with actual process separation through virtual memory management. NuttX integrates a TCP/IP stack in kernel space that is based on Contiki's uIP, and it has a well-designed power management, supporting stop and standby modes, which makes it a competitor in the low-power IoT systems category.

The user space includes a basic set of command-line tools integrated in the shell, which allows users to interact with the system. The APIs devices, peripherals, process management, and network communication are as close as possible to those defined by POSIX, and an interface is provided for standard C library calls from the applications.

On Cortex-M, by default, NuttX is built in flat mode, with no memory separation among tasks, and between applications and the kernel. The system calls are invoked directly by the applications and executed in place, and there is no switch between kernel and thread mode.

The separation between kernel and userland is activated by building the system in *protected mode*. The system calls are invoked by the applications by using an SVCall interrupt to directly request a context switch. The system provides two types of execution units: threads, using the default `pthread` interface, and tasks, an approximation of the POSIX process, adapted to fit the implementation. If the system is compiled to run in protected mode, user applications are not supposed to access any functionality present in the drivers or other components of the system other than requesting the operation to be performed by the kernel through the system call interface. That guarantees the separation of the stack spaces, and allows the kernel to supervise and coordinate the access to all the important system resources. Some of the task management operations, such as task termination and signal handling, are simplified and slightly diverge from the standards, to still be able to guarantee acceptable and measurable deadlines for real-time operations on microcontrollers.

The NuttX kernel is distributed with a wide selection of drivers, a set of embedded-tailored filesystems, and a complete userspace, with a command-line shell, **NuttX Shell (NSH)**, integrating some of the default built-in tools expected in a UNIX-like system, but developed considering the right compromises to produce a system that is still usable in real-time contexts.

Frosted

Frosted is a free and open source operating system, currently only running on Cortex-M microcontrollers, focused on exploring the possibility of a complete user/kernel space separation through the mechanism that can be implemented on a device with physical memory mapping. The POSIX interface is uniquely exposed through the system calls, and with exactly the same signatures as mandated by the standards.

Unlike NuttX, Frosted can only run in privilege separation mode, and processes have strict parent-child relationships. The kernel memory and the stack spaces of the other processes and threads cannot be accessed by the running task, and this is enforced through the MPU, by sending a fatal signal to the offending process, which is immediately terminated. System call arguments that contain pointers to user memory areas are thoughtfully checked by the kernel before executing any requested operation in supervisor mode.

Frosted offers an in-kernel TCP/IP implementation through picoTCP, exposing a BSD socket interface through standard POSIX system calls. The kernel is designed around the hierarchy of processes and `pthread`, signal distribution, terminal control, and management of the resources in use. Applications are compiled as standalone binaries, by using the `arm-frosted-eabi` toolchain, based on GCC and integrating a modified `newlib`, which has been extended to implement most of the standard C library and link the POSIX function calls to the relative kernel system calls through SVCall events. System tool binaries, including a shell and other default tools, are distributed in a separate repository, compiled apart and assembled into a filesystem that is flashed on a separate partition than the one in use by kernel code.

User space code and kernel code never mix up in the same binary, or share any symbols. All applications are position-independent, linked into the GCC binary flat format and can be executed in place from the filesystem, or loaded in RAM.

The most common system calls are implemented in Frosted, offering a platform to run applications written for standard, UNIX-like systems with little or no changes to the original code. One of the subsets that are not included is the user account and permission mechanism, which does not add any useful features for the target platform and would result in a much bigger implementation. System-specific interfaces, such as power modes management, are implemented as nonstandard extensions, but still accessed through system calls.

The Frosted license model is inspired by Linux. The kernel is distributed with a GNU GPL license, but due to the separation of the kernel space with no symbol shared, and the more permissive licenses of `newlib`, user space code is never considered a derivative, thus applications with any license can run in user space while all the kernel code is guaranteed to be GPL only, without the need for special linking exceptions.

The future of safe embedded systems

Progress in microelectronics pulls the technology market toward lower prices, higher performance, less power consumption, and smaller sizes. New microcontrollers on the market will be capable of more complex execution models, to keep up with the increasing complexity of the services running on a single device. When embedded devices become multi-functional, connected, and reprogrammable, the same paradigms adopted in other domains, such as servers and personal computers, must be applied and scaled down on microcontrollers.

The new generation of ARM Cortex-M microprocessors, which has recently been announced, will provide a broader range of configurable memory regions in the MCU, to extend the granularity of memory protection mechanisms, and an additional layer of execution isolation through the introduction of new execution modes within the trusted execution state. Introducing another level of trust in the execution chain of the embedded systems will facilitate the definition of even stronger safety mechanisms where untrusted applications can run in a confined environment and all the related operations can be accurately supervised.

On the currently available hardware, improvements in process isolation and running mutually mistrusted software tasks on the same system are being researched by one community in particular, developing an embedded system called Tock.

Process isolation – Tock

Tock is an open source operating system for embedded devices, based on a cooperative scheduler and aimed at exploring the characteristics of the Rust programming language, to take advantage of the intrinsic safety characteristics of the language to write an embedded operating system.

Rust is a recently developed programming language, different from all other languages because it provides memory safety through checks at compile time, without the need to track the lifetime of the objects allocated manually, but also without the use of a garbage collector or any runtime component.

The language itself is oriented to the development of the next generation of secure web browser engines, but the lack of runtime components, the possibility to write inline assembly code, and the strong typing put Rust in a comfortable position within the category of system programming languages. The generated binaries are almost as fast as C, and can be almost as small. The little overhead of the safety checks introduced by the compiler does not impact the performance significantly, and it enables all the safety-related paradigms that are built into the language.

Researchers have been looking for new type-safe languages to build safe operating systems, but none of the proposed models have met the requirements because of the characteristics of the language used. Before Rust, no other language could provide a safe memory-management model without the use of a garbage collector or another kind of runtime feature built into the language to resolve memory references. This feature does not fit well with the strict time requirements of embedded systems, because it introduces non-interruptible and non-deterministic pauses in the execution, to allow the runtime to arrange its allocations. Rust memory management is safe because the syntax of the language forces it to create memory references that are resolved at compile time, thus pre-determining the lifetime of each object using an explicit ownership technique, thus eliminating the need for a garbage collector in the language logic.

The development of Tock is aimed at researching the best strategy to implement an inherently safe system by using the language characteristics of Rust. This is achieved by limiting the amount of trusted code needed for a few critical operations, such as context switches, to a restricted number of instructions allowed to run in unsafe mode. One of the goals of the project is to minimize and clearly identify all the trusted code needed to run the kernel core and the language functionality, implemented in Rust within the language-core library. This kind of approach is beneficial for multipurpose embedded platforms running untrusted application code.

Summary

Open source operating systems are designed for different purposes and use cases. In this chapter, we have analyzed a few of the available implementations and research projects, in search of the ideal solution to better fit the design of embedded systems, from lightweight RTOS purely designed for performance, through more advanced strategies for process separation and standard interfaces, to the effort in redefining security through process isolation using new programming paradigms. For most embedded systems, a tailored solution with the smallest overhead introduced by the thread management mechanisms is still the preferred option, while high-end multipurpose systems might benefit from the increased level of safety of more complex designs. Increased safety, however, increases the real-time process latency and may slightly impact performance. In conclusion, while more complex architectures may benefit from the added security and compatibility of more advanced operating systems, many projects still benefit from the small footprint and simple flat-memory model schedulers, which guarantee the best real-time performance.

Other Books You May Enjoy

If you enjoyed this book, you may be interested in these other books by Packt:

Embedded Linux Development Using Yocto Project Cookbook - Second Edition
Alex González

ISBN: 978-1-78839-921-0

- Optimize your Yocto Project setup to speed up development and debug build issues
- Use Docker containers to build Yocto Project-based systems
- Take advantage of the user-friendly Toaster web interface to the Yocto Project build system
- Build and debug the Linux kernel and its device trees
- Customize your root filesystem with already-supported and new Yocto packages
- Optimize your production systems by reducing the size of both the Linux kernel and root filesystems
- Explore the mechanisms to increase the root filesystem security
- Understand the open source licensing requirements and how to comply with them when cohabiting with proprietary programs
- Create recipes, and build and run applications in C, C++, Python, Node.js, and Java

Mastering Embedded Linux Programming - Second Edition
Chris Simmonds

ISBN: 978-1-78728-328-2

- Evaluate the Board Support Packages offered by most manufacturers of a system on chip or embedded module
- Use Buildroot and the Yocto Project to create embedded Linux systems quickly and efficiently
- Update IoT devices in the field without compromising security
- Reduce the power budget of devices to make batteries last longer
- Interact with the hardware without having to write kernel device drivers
- Debug devices remotely using GDB, and see how to measure the performance of the systems using powerful tools such as perk, ftrace, and valgrind
- Find out how to configure Linux as a real-time operating system

Leave a review - let other readers know what you think

Please share your thoughts on this book with others by leaving a review on the site that you bought it from. If you purchased the book from Amazon, please leave us an honest review on this book's Amazon page. This is vital so that other potential readers can see and use your unbiased opinion to make purchasing decisions, we can understand what our customers think about our products, and our authors can see your feedback on the title that they have worked with Packt to create. It will only take a few minutes of your time, but is valuable to other potential customers, our authors, and Packt. Thank you!

Index

Made in the USA
Monee, IL
22 July 2024

62489261R00181